Critical Studies in Education Series

Critical Pedagogy and Cultural Power
David Livingstone and Contributors

Education and the American Dream: Conservatives, Liberals and Radicals Debate the Future of Education
Harvey Holtz and Associates

Education and the Welfare State: A Crisis in Capitalism and Democracy
H. Svi Shapiro

Education under Seige: The Conservative, Liberal and Radical Debate over Schooling
Stanley Aronowitz and Henry A. Giroux

Literacy: Reading the Word and the World
Paulo Freire and Donaldo Macedo

The Moral and Spiritual Crisis in Education: A Curriculum for Justice and Compassion
David Purpel

The Politics of Education: Culture, Power and Liberation
Paulo Freire

Popular Culture, Schooling and the Language of Everyday Life
Henry A. Giroux and Roger I. Simon

Teachers As Intellectuals: Toward a Critical Pedagogy of Learning
Henry A. Giroux

Women Teaching for Change: Gender, Class and Power
Kathleen Weiler Between Capitalism and Democracy: Educational Policy and the Crisis of the Welfare State
Svi Shapiro

Critical Psychology and Pedagogy: Interpretation of the Personal World
Edmund Sullivan

PEDAGOGY AND THE STRUGGLE FOR VOICE

PEDAGOGY AND THE STRUGGLE FOR VOICE

Issues of Language, Power, and Schooling for Puerto Ricans

Catherine E. Walsh

CRITICAL STUDIES IN EDUCATION
Edited by
HENRY A. GIROUX AND PAULO FREIRE

BERGIN & GARVEY
New York • Westport, Connecticut • London

Copyright Acknowledgement

The author and publisher are grateful for permission to reprint from the following:
Laviera, Tato. *La Carreta Made a U-Turn*. Houston, Tex: Arte Publico Press, 1981.
Used by permission.

Library of Congress Cataloging-in-Publication Data

Walsh, Catherine E.
    Pedagogy and the struggle for voice : issues of language, power,
and schooling for Puerto Ricans / Catherine E. Walsh.
       p.   cm—(Critical studies in education)
      Includes bibliographical references (p.   ) and index.
    ISBN 0-89789-234-8 (alk. paper).—ISBN 0-89789-235-6 (pbk. :
alk. paper)
    1. Puerto Rican children—Education—United States. 2. Puerto
Rico—Languages—Political aspects. 3. Education, Bilingual—United
States. 4. Puerto Ricans—United States—Social conditions.
I. Title. II. Series: Critical studies in education series.
LC2693.W35   1991
370. 19'34—dc20   90-719

British Library Cataloguing-in-Publication Data is available.

Library of Congress Catalog Card Number: 90-719
ISBN: 0-89789-234-8 (hb.)
       0-89789-235-6 (pbk.)

First published in 1991

Bergin & Garvey, One Madison Avenue, New York, NY 10010
An imprint of Greenwood Publishing Group, Inc.

Printed in the United States of America

The paper used in this book complies with
the Permanent Paper Standard issued by the National
Information Standards Organization (Z39.48–1984).

10 9 8 7 6 5 4 3 2 1

Contents

Preface

About sixteen years ago I first became interested in the significance of language, the nature of cultural difference, and the processes and conditions through which children come to know, that is, come to be aware of, the social world, themselves, and the meanings that inscribe their experiences and relations. This interest was sparked by a five-year-old Puerto Rican child in my kindergarten class. As I vividly recall, she spoke to me one day about language, describing in a metalinguistic sense, how language functioned to help frame her understanding and expression of the world. "Sometimes I two-times think," she said. "I think like in my family and in my house. And then I think like in school and other places. Then I talk. They aren't the same, you know."

Buffy was bilingual. Her languages, however, were not contextually separate. Since her mother was English-dominant and her father Spanish-dominant, both languages were used in the home. Yet, even at the age of five, Buffy was aware that her ways of speaking and interacting at home were divergent from those of others in the school and in Anglo-dominanted society. She also knew that the ways of "others" were by far the more acceptable. As she told me on numerous occasions: "It makes me feel funny, all alone . . . different."

By listening to and observing Buffy, I began to become more cognizant about the complex interaction of language, culture, and experience and the ways this interaction informed my own as well as students' relations. While it was not until quite a few years later that I began to formally study and more fully understand this interaction, these early revelations served to impart a sensitivity and excite an interest that has personal as well as professional consequences. My own bilingual/bicultural development is one such result.

Buffy is certainly not the only child who is mindful of lived experience or of "minority" status. Nor is she the only child whose identity and perspectives are informed by divergent cultural, historical, and political realities, and social as well as semantic contradictions. Yet how often are these children's perspectives recognized, listened to, and taken into account pedagogically? How often do we educators open our ears to students' "voices"—to the words, narratives, discourses, and stories that help express the dynamics of social experience and help shape and position the subjective understanding of this experience within consciousness?

It seems incredible that young children can be so aware of the ways that language and culture position them in society while adults—their teachers—can so easily discount, disregard, and displace the relations and practices in which differences are constituted and voices fashioned. It is even more incredible to think that many of these teachers are themselves bilingual, racial or ethnic "minorities," have working-class roots, are women, and/or have had other experiences that distinguish them from the middle-class, Anglo and male-oriented "mainstream." This putting aside of difference in schools reflects not so much the individual or collective desire of teachers as it does the political, social, and ideological conditions and the relations of power at work within the educational institution.

Language is one of the principal sites where power is realized, for it is through language—its a range of linguistic forms and discursive practices—that values, meanings, identities, and subjectivities are shaped and positioned. It is through language that people construct a sense of who they are and where they fit in particular contexts or settings. Since language plays a major part in the formulation of pedagogies and the presentation and legitimation of particular ideas and perspectives within schools and classrooms, the relation of language and power is also integral to much of what goes on in education. Part of this power is made evident in the objective ways language is presented. By offering some meanings, interpretations, and experiences as universal and by belittling or leaving out others, schools—as does society in general—impart a language which teachers as well as students are expected to internalize and assume as exigent and indisputable. While multiple conflicts and struggles are waged within, through, and over language, this discordance is typically ignored, excluded, or disregarded. What is recognized and encouraged instead is a reified, unitary, and hegemonic treatment and understanding of language that, if singularly accepted, would only serve to sustain the social structure.

Language has long been considered a cohesive force in society, providing a shared medium of syntax, words, and meanings through which individuals can communicate with one another. In so doing, language suggests, although in an illusory fashion, a coalescense or unification. It is the English language, for example, that is often described in the United States as the common thread that unites us as an immigrant nation. Yet this belief in the unitary nature of language is not naively conceived, nor is it without political implication. Proponents of official language policies and legislation argue, for instance, that English affords unity to diversity, that English somehow ensures a shared system of cultural values and, as a result, should be the only language taught in our public schools and permitted in other social institutions. Such efforts toward linguistic cohesion resonate with a kind of colonial domination, a hegemony that threatens to silence the less powerful. Moreover, this focus on the unitary function of language attempts to render invisible the complex, abstract, socio-ideological nature of language. It shrouds what the Soviet literary thinker Mikhail Bakhtin (1981) referred to as "heteroglossia"—the centrifugal, stratifying forces of language—by maintaining that access to and relations within language are equal. Difference is thus viewed as both a deference to and a deviance from the established linguistic (and cultural) norm.

In the United States, the English language clearly serves a societal function. But while English can bring people together, it does not and cannot unify the multiple and diverse reflections and experiencing of experiences that occur across race, ethnicity, class, and gender. Language's unitary function is counteracted by its polyphonous and disjunctive nature. Bakhtin addressed this uncomfortable balancing of cohesiveness and diversity. He posited a dialectic, an ongoing struggle between the societal need for a unitary language and the social and linguistic heterogeneity of society's members, and situated this dialectic socially, culturally, and politically. As he detailed:

> A unitary language gives expression to forces working toward concrete verbal and ideological unification and centralization, which develop in vital connection with the processes of sociopolitical and cultural centralization.... [Yet] at any given moment of its evaluation, language is stratified not only into linguistic dialects ... but also into languages that are socio-ideological: languages of social groups, "professional" and "generic" languages, languages of generations and so forth.... Alongside the centripetal forces, the centrifugal forces of language carry on their uninterrupted work; alongside verbal-ideological centralization and unification, the uninterrupted processes of decentralization and disunification go forward. (Bakhtin 1981:271-272)

Bakhtin's writings make clear that the relations of power in language do not merely represent the unidirectional, hierarchical control exercised by individuals and groups involved in verbal and ideological unification. More important, they represent a shifting balance of force and resistance that develop, as Foucault (1980) has pointed out, through interaction in a multiplicity of relationships. Power, in this sense, is tied to the ongoing conflicts and struggles of lived lives, to the discourses through which these lives are ordered, mediated, and legitimated, and to the silent and spoken voices that emerge within and because of them. An awareness of the presence of this power and of the dialectic at work in language is important to an understanding of the domination and subordination proffered in schools and the agency, voices, and resistance of students.

As active participants in the shifting balances of power, in the dialectic of language, and in the battle over whose knowledge, experience, and voice are recognized and accepted, minority students are uniquely aware of the relation between language and power. While they may not be able to specifically talk about the relation, it remains ever-present in consciousness, framing their conceptions, perspectives, and understandings of and action in the world around them. This book demonstrates the essence, significance, and complexity of this relation by examining how children understand and how education can help them grasp how this process occurs. In so doing, it situates understanding historically, investigating the ways in which language and culture come together with history, ideology, and experience in the construction of meanings and the composition of voices. And it also looks at the tensions and struggles of Puerto Rican students trying to make sense out of and fashion a voice from the multiple and often contradictory realities that comprise their daily existence.

My decision to undertake this project stemmed from both an intrigue with the cognitive and sociocultural intricacies of bilingualism and a concern with the academic difficulties of language minority students, particularly Puerto Ricans. Through my work with teachers in schools, I had observed students learning English; yet, when given English texts and tests, these same children demonstrated understandings that were divergent from native English speakers. Seldom were these divergencies recognized, addressed, or discussed in instruction. I had also witnessed a differential treatment of students: Puerto Ricans tended to be chastised for disinterest, disruptive behavior, poor motivation, and high mobility and publicly contrasted with other ethnic, cultural, and linguistic minorities. While my experience within the Puerto Rican community, and directly with parents, had taught me about the values they instilled in their children, their respect for education, and their desire for their children to learn English and succeed in the United States, I kept hearing a good number of teachers and school officials comment about just the opposite. Complaints regarding Puerto Rican families' movement back and forth from the Island were rampant as was commentary regarding unemployment, matriarchal households, and dependence on welfare. Administrators, teachers, and the textbooks of bilingual education or English as a second language did not seem to consider the unique circumstances that differentiate Puerto Ricans from immigrants and/or refugees. The colonial status of Puerto Rico and the historic effect this status has had on the political, socioeconomic, and psychological reality of the people is rarely discussed, nor its effect on children's identity, language development and use, and on their semantic understandings.

My purpose in this text is to shed light on the importance of this history, to illustrate how the past and present intersect in people's voices, inform pedagogy, and shape both the conditions under and the struggles through which students come to know. This is accomplished less by my written words than through the incorporation of the spoken words—the voices—of those people who made the history and those who bear its burden in the present. It is these individuals' words that ground the text, reveal the complexity and salience of the category of "voice," and give this project life and significance.

There are four general themes that frame the text's organization. The first is specifically concerned with history—with the lived effect of colonialism, linguistic and cultural imposition, and struggle as revealed by the voices of both Puerto Ricans and the U.S. colonizers. The second theme focuses directly on language—how an understanding of language, of agency, and of the oppositions posed in its theory and lived practice can help explain the emergence of voice and account for its dialectical possibilities. The third theme makes language, representation, and meaning problematic; it addresses the contradictory significance of Puerto Rican children's words and the substance and tensions of their voices. Finally, the fourth theme speaks to pedagogy—to the contradictory nature of schooling as perceived by adolescents and to the ways an understanding and recognition of voice, and of students' lived realities, can edify pedagogy and direct instructional practice.

Acknowledgments

Writing a book is never a simple or an ephemeral task. It consumes one's waking moments as well as one's dreams. The development of this book was initiated by discussions about my doctoral dissertation with Paulo Freire and Henry Giroux at the 1986 First Working Conference on Critical Pedagogy at the University of Massachusetts at Amherst, which I helped organize. In the years following, I have revised my theoretical and pedagogical perspectives, have done new research, have been actively involved in Latino community struggles, and have come to better understand some of the tensions of U.S. schooling for Puerto Ricans. This manuscript is a reflection of this ongoing and still incomplete process.

A number of individuals have been instrumental throughout the writing of the text. The person whom I wish to thank most is my dear friend Deborah Britzman. The endless hours of dialogue that we have shared, coupled with her thoughtful readings of and comments on the manuscript, challenged me to more deeply theorize my own understandings and to speak with a clearer voice. Her comradery remains significant in my life, her friendship and humor essential. Marie E. Torres-Guzman was particularly helpful in helping me fine tune my own voice within the first chapter.

Paulo Freire has been an important influence as an author, a colleague, and a friend. I wish to thank Henry Giroux who, because of his belief in me and my work, helped bring this text to fruition. Meyer Weinberg's comments and support over the years will also not be forgotten. The community-based ethnographic and popular educational work of colleagues from El Centro de Estudios Puertorriqueños, particularly Pedro Pedraza, has served as an invaluable resource. I also owe my gratitude to numerous Puerto Rican/Latino students, parents, and community members in Massachusetts. Finally, appreciation goes to my *compañero*, Juan Aulestia. It is he who helped keep me sane throughout this project.

Series Introduction:
Rethinking the Pedagogy of Voice, Difference, and Cultural Struggle

The struggle over public schools cannot be separated from the social problems currently facing this society. These problems are not only political in nature but are pedagogical as well. That is, whenever power and knowledge come together, politics not only functions to position people differently with respect to the access of wealth and power, it also provides the conditions for the production and acquisition of learning. Put another way, it offers people opportunities to take up and to reflect on the conditions that shape themselves and their relationships with others. The pedagogical in this sense is about the production of meaning and the primacy of the ethical and the political as a fundamental part of this process. This means that any discussion of public schooling has to address the political, economic, and social realities that construct the contexts that shape it as an institution and the conditions that provide its diverse populations of students. This perspective suggests making visible the social problems and conditions that affect those students who are at risk in our society while recognizing that such problems need to be addressed in pedagogical and political terms, both inside and outside of the schools. The problems that are emerging do not auger well for either the fate of public schooling or the credibility of the discourse of democracy itself as it is currently practiced in the United States. For example, it has been estimated that nearly 20 percent of all children under the age of eighteen live below the poverty line. In fact, the United States ranks first among the industrialized nations in child poverty; similarly, besides South Africa, the United States is the only industrialized country that does not provide universal health care for children and pregnant women. Moreover, the division of wealth is getting worse, with a growing polarization between the rich and poor. In fact, the division of wealth was wider in 1988 than at any other time since 1947. As Sally Reed and Craig Sautter have recently pointed out; "The poorest 20 percent of families received less than five percent of the national income, while the wealthiest 20 percent received 44 percent. . . . [Moreover,] 1 percent of families own 42 percent of the net wealth of all U.S. families."[1] At the same time, it is important to note that the neo-conservative attempt to dismantle public schooling in this country during the last decade has manifested itself not only in the call for vouchers and the development of school policy based on the market logic of choice, but also in the ruthless cutbacks that have affected those most dependent on the public schools: the poor, people of color, minorities, the working class, and other subordinate groups. The Reagan "commitment" to education and the underprivileged manifested itself shamefully in policies noted for slashing federal funds to important programs such as Aid to Families with Dependent Children, drastically reducing federal funding for low income housing and, in general, cutting over 10 million dollars from programs designed to aid the poor, the homeless, and the hungry. At the same time the Reagan government pushed the cost of military spending up to $1.9 trillion dollars.

Within this perspective, the discourse of democracy was reduced to conflating patriotism with the cold war ideology of military preparedness, and the notion of the public good was abstracted from the principles of justice and equality in favor of an infatuation with individual achievement. Greed became respectable in the 1980s while notions of community and democratic struggle were either ignored or seen as subversive. Absent from the neo-conservative public philosophy of the 1980s was any notion of democracy that took seriously the importance of developing a citizenry that could think critically, struggle against social injustices, and develop relations of community based on the principles of equality, freedom, and justice.

Although *Pedagogy and the Struggle for Voice* does not take up directly the relationship between schools and democracy, I believe that its analysis of public education with regard to its treatment of Puerto Rican students provides a set of categories that theoretically advances a radical politics of democracy of schooling while enriching a discourse of critical pedagogy. I am particularly concerned with Catherine Walsh's attempt not only to develop a broader understanding of how language and voice intersect with power and knowledge to delimit and constrain particular groups of students but also to take up these issues as part of a politics of difference that extends its implications beyond the specifics of her own pedagogical encounters. In what follows, I want to situate her work within a broader debate on language, difference, voice, and pedagogy, exploring how it both

criticizes and advances various theoretical tendencies currently being analyzed by a variety of educators.

SCHOOLING AND THE POLITICS OF LANGUAGE

> Education may well be, as of right, the instrument whereby every individual,
> in a society like our own, can gain access to any kind of discourse. But we all
> know that in its distribution, in what it permits and prevents, it follows the
> well-trodden battle lines of social conflict. Every educational system is a
> political means of maintaining or modifying the appropriation of discourse
> with the knowledge and powers it carries with it.[2]

There is a long tradition in the United States of viewing schools as
relatively neutral institutions whose language and social relations mirror
the principles of equal opportunity. For example, liberal theories of education are grounded upon the belief that students have open access to the
language and knowledge that schools provide as part of their public responsibility to educate. Catherine Walsh draws on a number of theoretical
traditions that link language and power to disprove this assumption. Not
only does she expose the naiveté of such views by revealing the social and
political constraints that operate upon language, she provides an intricate
reading of how school language functions through a web of hierarchies,
prohibitions, and denials to reward some students and deny others access to
what can be learned and spoken within the confines of dominant schooling.
For Walsh, schools are sites where knowledge and power enter into relations articulating conflicts being fought out in the wider society. Central to
her thesis is the assumption that the language of schooling is implicated in
forms of racism that attempt to silence the voices of Latino students whose
primary language is not English. There are three important elements in
Walsh's view of language that need to be reiterated. First, language has a
social foundation and must be viewed as a site of struggle implicating the
production of knowledge, values, and identities.

Second, as a social phenomenon, language cannot be abstracted from the
forces and conflicts of social history. In other words, the historicity of the
relationship between dominant and subordinate forms of language offer
insights into countering the assumption that the dominant language at any
given time is simply the result of a naturally given process rather than the
result of specific historical struggles and conflicts. This is especially evident
in Walsh's analysis of the ways in which the United States attempted to
control Puerto Rico after 1898 through the imposition and legitimation of
English as the official language. In effect, Walsh provides an important
lesson in refusing to analyze the language/power relationship in simply
synchronic and structural terms. While she is acutely concerned with taking
up the ideologies that structure dominant language paradigms and the ways

of life they legitimate, she does not abstract this type of inquiry from particular forms of historical and social analyses. That is, rather than developing an analysis that is simple concerned with the codes, classifications, orderings, and distribution of discourse, she is also attentive to the historical contexts and conflicts that are central to its purpose and meaning. In effect, Walsh builds upon Mikhail Bakhtin's insight that specific languages cannot be uprooted from the historical struggles and conflicts that make them "heteroglossic" rather than unitary. Bakhtin is clear on this issue and argues that

> at any given moment of its historical existence, language is heteroglot from top to bottom: it represents the co-existence of socio-ideological contradictions between the present and the past, between differing epochs of the past, between different socio-ideological groups in the present, between tendencies, schools, circles and so forth, all given a bodily form. These "languages" of heteroglossia intersect each other in a variety of ways, forming new socially typifying "languages."[3]

In her analysis, Walsh makes clear that any claim to a totalizing and unitary language is the result of forms of social, moral, and political regulation that attempt to erase their own histories. At stake here is the need to make clear that language is always implicated in power relationships expressed, in part, through particular historical struggles over how established institutions such as education, law, medicine, social welfare, and the mass media produce, support, and legitimate particular ways of life that characterize a society at a given time in history. Language makes possible both the subject positions that people use to negotiate their sense of self and the ideologies and social practices that give meaning and legitimacy to institutions forming the basis of a given society.

Third, Walsh is not content to simply situate her analysis of language in the discourse of domination and subjugation. She is also concerned with a "language of possibility." In this case, she is concerned with perceiving language as both an oppositional and affirmative force. She lays claim to discursive practices deconstructing and reclaiming new forms of knowledge, as well as providing new ways of reading history through the reconstruction of suppressed memories whose identities challenge and contest the very conditions through which history, desire, voice, and place are experienced and lived. It is within this context that Walsh offers educators a critical approach to pedagogy forged in the discourse of difference and voice.

DISCOURSES OF VOICE AND DIFFERENCE

Defined in opposition to hegemonic codes of culture, subjectivity, and history, a number of social theorists have begun recently to use a discourse of difference to challenge some of the most fundamental dominant assertions that characterize mainstream social science. For example, theorists writing in anthropology, feminism, liberation theology, critical education, literary theory, and a multitude of other areas firmly reject mainstream assumptions regarding culture as a field of shared experiences defined in Western ethnocentric terms. In addition, critical theorists have rejected the mainstream humanist assumption that the individual is both the source of all human action and the most important unit of social analysis. Moreover, many critical theorists reject the view that objectivity and consensus are the privileged and innocent concerns of dominant social science research. Reading in opposition to these assumptions, the notion of difference has played an important role in making visible how power is inscribed differently in and between zones of culture, how cultural borderlands raise important questions regarding relations of inequality, struggle, and history, and how differences are expressed in multiple and contradictory ways within individuals and between different groups.

While theories of difference have made important contributions to a discourse of progressive politics and pedagogy, they have also exhibited tendencies that have been theoretically flawed and politically regressive. In the first instance, the most important insights have emerged primarily from feminist women of color. These include: "the recognition of a self that is multiplicious, not unitary; the recognition that differences are always relational rather than inherent; and the recognition that wholeness and commonality are acts of will and creativity, rather than passive discovery."[4] In the second instance, the discourse of difference has contributed to paralyzing forms of essentialism, ahistoricism, and a politics of separatism. In what follows, I first want to explore the dialectical nature of the relationship between difference and voice that informs Walsh's view of critical pedagogy. I conclude by pointing to some of the broader implications that a discourse of difference and voice has for what I call a "liberatory border pedagogy."

It is important to note that Walsh views culture as a vital source for developing a politics of identity, community, and pedagogy. In this perspective, culture is not seen as monolithic or unchanging, but as a site of multiple and heterogeneous borders where different histories, languages, experiences, and voices intermingle amidst diverse relations of power and privilege. Within this pedagogical culture borderland known as school, subordinate cultures push against and permeate the alleged unproblematic and homogeneous borders of dominant cultural forms and practices. It is in this context, that Walsh is not content to merely map how ideologies are inscribed in the various relations of schooling, whether they be the curriculum, forms of school organization, or in teacher-student relations. Of course, Walsh recognizes that these are important concerns for critical educators but she goes beyond them by analyzing how ideologies are actually taken up in the voices and lived experiences of her students as they give meaning to the dreams, desires, and subject positions that they inhabit. In this sense, Walsh lets her students speak so that she can both affirm their lives and engage the consistencies and contradictions that characterize their voices.

As Bell Hooks points out, "coming to voice" means

> moving from silence into speech as a revolutionary gesture ... the idea of finding one's voice or having a voice assumes a primacy in talk discourse, writing, and action. ... Only as subjects can we speak. As objects, we remain voiceless—our beings defined and interpreted by others. ... Awareness of the need to speak, to give voice to the varied dimensions of our lives, is one way [to begin] the process of education for critical consciousness.[5]

This suggests that educators need to approach learning not merely as the acquisition of knowledge but as the production of cultural practices that offer students a sense of identity, place, and hope. To speak of voice is to address the wider issue of how people become either agents in the process of making history or how they function as subjects under the weight of oppression and exploitation within the various linguistic and institutional boundaries producing dominant and subordinate cultures in any given society. In this case, "voice" provides a critical referent for analyzing how students are made "voiceless" in particular settings by not being allowed to speak, or how students silence themselves out of either fear or ignorance regarding the strength and possibilities in taking up the multiple languages and experience that connect them to a sense of agency and self-formation. At the same time, voices forged in opposition and struggle provide the crucial conditions by which subordinate individuals and groups can reclaim their own memories, stories, and histories as part of an ongoing collective struggle to challenge those power structures attempting to silence them.

Walsh's book both embodies and extends these theoretical insights. By listening to the voices of her students, she becomes a "border crosser" in her ability to not only make different narratives available to herself and other students but also by legitimating difference as a basic condition for understanding the limits of one's own voice. It is in this context that Walsh brings the concept of culture, voice, and difference together to create a borderland where multiple subjectivities and identities exist as part of a politics of difference providing the potential to expand the politics of democratic community and solidarity. Walsh's pedagogy serves to make visible those marginal cultures that have been traditionally suppressed in American schooling. Moreover, she makes available to her students the range of identities and human possibilities that emerge among, within, and between different zones of culture. But she approaches this task by not merely giving equal weight to all zones of cultural difference; on the contrary, Walsh links the creation, sustenance, and formation of cultural difference as a fundamental part of the discourse of inequality, power, struggle, and possibility. Difference in this sense is not about merely registering or asserting spatial, racial, ethnic, or cultural differences but about historical differences that manifest themselves in public and pedagogical struggles. The strengths of Walsh's position on difference and voice can be further elaborated by a number of concerns that are integral to a politics of "border pedagogy."

RESISTING DIFFERENCE AND THE DISCOURSE OF BORDER PEDAGOGY

To take up the issue of difference is to recognize that the concept cannot be analyzed unproblematically. In effect, the concept has to be used to resist those aspects of its ideological legacy used in the service of exploitation and subordination as well as to develop a critical reference for engaging the limits and strengths of difference as a central aspect of a critical theory of education. In what follows, I want to look briefly at how the concept of difference has been used by conservatives, liberals, and radicals in ways which either produce relations of subordination or undermine its possibility for developing and deepening a radical politics of democracy.

Conservatives have often used the term in a variety of ways to justify relations of racism, patriarchy, and class exploitation by associating difference with the notion of deviance while simultaneously justifying such assumptions through an appeal to science, biology, nature, or culture. In all of these cases, difference functions as a marker of power to name, label, and exclude particular groups while simultaneously being legitimated within a reactionary politics of public life couched in the discourse of nationalism, patriotism, religious fundamentalism, or a specious appeal to democracy. What needs to be noted here is that there is more at stake than negative definitions of identity. Difference, when defined and used in the interests of inequality and repression, is "enacted in violence against its own citizens as much as it is against foreigners."[6]

Liberals generally take up a dual approach to the issue of difference. This can be illuminated around the issue of race. On the one hand, liberals embrace the issue of difference through a notion of cultural diversity in which it is argued that race is simply one more form of cultural difference among many that make up the population of a country like the United States. The problem with this approach is that "by denying both the centrality and uniqueness of race as a principal of socio-economic organization, it redefines difference in a way that denies the history of racism in the

United States and thus denies white responsibility for the present and past oppression and exploitation of people of color."[7] In this view, the systems of inequalities, subordination, and terror that inform the dominant culture's structuring of difference around issues of race, gender, and class are simply mapped out of existence. On the other hand, liberals often attempt to both appropriate and dissolve cultural differences into the melting pot theory of culture. In this position, the history, language, experiences, and narratives of the Other are relegated to invisible zones of culture, borderlands where the dominant culture refuses to hear the voice of the Other while celebrating a "white, male, middle-class, European, heterosexuality [as] the standard of and the criteria for rationality and morality."[8] Under the rubric of equality and freedom, the liberal version of assimilation wages "war" against particularity, lived differences, and imagined futures that challenge culture as unitary, sacred, and unchanging and the identity as unified, static, and natural.

On the other hand, radical theorists have taken up the issue of difference around two basic considerations. First, difference has been elaborated as part of an attempt to understand subjectivity as fractured and multiple rather than unified and static. Central to this approach is the notion that subjectivities and identities are constructed in multilayered and contradictory ways. Identity in this sense is seen not only as a historical and social construction, but is also viewed as part of a continual process of transformation and change. This position is of enormous significance for undermining the humanist notion of the subject as both unified and as the determinate source of human will and action. As significant as this position is, it is fraught with some theoretical problems.

By arguing that human subjectivities are constructed in language through the production and availability of diverse subject positions, many radical theorists have developed a theory of subjectivity that erases any viable notion of human agency. In effect, subjectivity becomes an effect of language and human agency disappears into the discredited terrain of humanist will. Lost here is any understanding of how agency works within the interface of subject positions made available by a society and the weight of choices constructed out of specific desires, forms of self-reflection, and concrete social practices. In this case, there is little sense of how people actually take up particular subject positions, what individuals and groups are privileged in having access to particular positions, and what the conditions are that make it impossible for some groups to take up, live, and speak particular discourses.[9]

The second approach to difference that radical social theorists have taken up centers around the differences between groups. In this sense, a number of theorists, particularly feminists, have developed what can be called a discourse of identity politics. In the most general sense, identity politics refers to "the tendency to base one's politics on a sense of personal identity—as gay, as Jewish, as Black, as female."[10] This is a politics of identity that celebrates differences as they are constructed around the categories of race, class, gender, and sexual preference. Again, I will first point to the limitations that have emerged around this position only to later highlight the importance of identity politics within a broader notion of difference, politics, and culture.

Initially, identity politics offered a powerful challenge to the hegemonic notion that Eurocentric culture is superior to other cultures and traditions by offering to subordinate groups political and cultural vocabularies through which they could reconstruct their own histories and give voice to their individual and collective identities. This was especially true for the early stages of the feminist movement when the slogan "the personal is the political" gave rise to the assumption that lived experience offered women the opportunity to insert themselves back into history and everyday life by naming the injustices they had suffered within a society constructed in patriarchal social relations. A number of problems emerged from the conception of difference that informed this view of identity politics. A number of theorists argued that there was a direct correlation between one's social location and one's political position. At stake here was the assumption that one's identity was rooted in a particular set of experiences that led rather unproblematically to a particular form of politics. This position is questionable on a number of grounds. First, there is no guarantee that a particular social experience or location will give rise to a specific political position. To accept the authority of experience unproblematically is to forget that identity itself is complex, contradictory, and shifting and does not unproblematically reveal itself in a specific politics. Second, the emphasis on the personal as a fundamental aspect of the political often results in highlighting the personal through a form of confessional politics that all but forgets how the political is constituted in social and cultural forms outside of one's own experiences. Jenny Bourne puts the issue well in her comment that

> The struggle for social change and the transformation of society . . . has been obscured by a feminism which is separatist, individualistic and inward-looking. The organic relationship we tried to forge between the personal and the political has been so degraded that now the only area of politics deemed to be legitimate is the personal.[11]

Another problem with the radical notion of difference is that it sometimes produces a politics of assertion that is both essentialist and separatist. As a form of essentialism, identity politics ignores the notion that "the politics of any social position is not guaranteed in advance."[12] The essentialism at work in particular constructions of feminism has been made clear by Audre Lorde, Angela Harris, and others who have criticized white women for not only privileging patriarchy over issues of race, class, sexual preference, and

other forms of oppression, but also for defining patriarchy and the construction of women's experiences in terms that excluded the particular
narratives and stories of women of color.[13] In this case, racial and class
differences among women are ignored in favor of an essentializing notion of
voice that romanticizes and valorizes the unitary experience of White,
middle-class women, who assumed the position of being able to speak for
all women. Moreover, forms of identity politics that forgo the potential for
creating alliances among different subordinate groups run the risk of repro-
ducing a series of hierarchies of identities and experiences which serves to
privilege their own form of oppression and struggle. All too often this
position results in totalizing narratives that fail to recognize the limits of
their own discourse in explaining the complexity of social life and the
power such a discourse wields in silencing those who are not considered
part of the insider group. June Jordan captures this sentiment well in her
comment that "Traditional calls to 'unity' on the base of only one of these
factors—race or class or gender—will fail, finally, and again and again, I
believe, because no simple one of these components provides for a valid
fathoming of the complete individual."[14]

Far from suggesting that critical educators should dispense with either the
notion of difference or an identity politics, I believe that we need to learn
from the theoretical shortcomings analyzed above and begin to rethink the
relationship among difference, voice, and politics. What does this suggest
for a liberatory theory of Border Pedagogy? I want to end by pointing to a
number of suggestions, all of which are either taken up explicitly or implic-
itly in Catherine Walsh's book.

First, the notion of difference must be seen in relational terms that link it
to a broader politics, one which deepens the possibility for reconstructing
democracy and schools as democratic public spheres. This means organizing schools and pedagogy around a sense of purpose and meaning that
makes difference central to a critical notion of citizenship and democratic
public life. Rather than celebrating specific forms of difference, a politics of
difference must provide the basis for extending the struggle for equality and
justice to broader spheres of everyday life. This suggests that the discourse
of difference and voice be elaborated within rather than against a politics of
solidarity. By refusing to create a hierarchy of struggles, it becomes possible
for critical educators to take up notions of political community in which
particularity, voice, and difference provide the foundation for democracy.
Chantal Mouffe argues that this represents a postmodern notion of citizenship.

> An adequate conception of citizenship today should be "postmodern" if we
> understand by that the need to acknowledge the particular, the heterogeneous
> and the multiple. . . . Only a pluralistic conception of citizenship can accom-
> modate the specificity and multiplicity of democratic demands and provide a

pole of identification for a wide range of democratic forces. The political community has to be viewed, then, as a diverse collection of communities, as a forum for creating unity without denying specificity."[15]

Second, critical educators must provide the conditions for students to engage in cultural remapping as a form of resistance. That is, they should be given the opportunity to engage in systematic analyses of the ways in which the dominant culture creates borders saturated in terror, inequality, and forced exclusions. At the same time, students should be allowed to rewrite difference through the process of crossing over into cultural borders that offer narratives, languages, and experiences that provide a resource for rethinking the relationship between the center and margins of power as well as between themselves and others. In part, this means giving voice to those who have been normally excluded and silenced. It means creating a politics of memory in which different stories and narratives are heard and taken up as lived experiences. Most importantly, it means constructing new pedagogical borders where difference becomes the intersection of new forms of culture and identity.

Third, the concept of border pedagogy suggests not simply opening diverse cultural histories and spaces to students, it also means understanding how fragile identity is as it moves into borderlands crisscrossed with a variety of languages, experiences, and voices. There are no unified subjects here, only students whose voices and experiences intermingle with the weight of particular histories that will not fit into the master narrative of a monolithic culture. Such borderlands should be seen as sites for both critical analysis and as a potential source of experimentation, creativity, and possibility. This is not a call to romanticize such voices. It is instead to suggest that educators construct pedagogical practices in which the ideologies that inform student experiences be both heard and interrogated.[16] Moreover, these pedagogical borderlands, where Blacks, Whites, Latinos, and others meet, demonstrate the importance of a multicentric perspective that allows students to not only recognize the multilayered and contradictory ideologies that construct their own identities but also to analyze how the differences within and between various groups can expand the potential of human life and democratic possibilities.

Finally, the notion of border pedagogy needs to highlight the issue of power in a dual sense. Not only does power have to be made central to understanding the discourse of difference from the perspective of historically and socially constructed forms of domination, but also from the perspective of how teachers can use power through a politics of authority that provides them with basis for reading differences critically. Difference cannot be merely experienced or asserted by students. It must also be read critically by teachers who can speak for those not available to speak; moreover, teacher authority can be used to provide the conditions for students to engage their own views through critical dialogue. At stake here is constructing pedagogical practices that neither position students defensively nor allow them to speak by simply asserting their voices and experiences, simultaneously refusing to interrogate the claims or consequences such assertions have for the social relationships they legitimate. Larry Grossberg is correct in arguing that teachers who refuse to assert their authority or take up the issue of political responsibility as social critics and committed intellectuals often end up "erasing themselves in favor of the uncritical reproduction of the audience [students]."[17]

What Catherine Walsh demonstrates in this book is that voice, difference, and culture need to be refashioned through pedagogical practices that both affirm and transform their articulation with categories central to public life: citizenship, justice, and democracy. This is an important book that will redefine the interplay of culture, power, and schooling.

Henry A. Giroux
Miami University

Notes

1. Sally Reed and R. Craig Sautter, "Children of Poverty: The Status of 12 Million Young Americans," *Phi Delta Kappan* (June 1990), p. K5.

2. Michel Foucault, "The Discourse on Language," *The Archaeology of Knowledge* (London: Tavistock, 1972), p. 227.

3. Mikhail M. Bakhtin, *The Dialogic Imagination*, ed. by Caryl Emerson and Michael Holquist, trans. by Michael Holquist (Austin, University of Texas, 1981), p. 291.

4. Angela P. Harris, "Race and Essentialism in Feminist Legal Theory," *Stanford Law Review* 42 (February 1990), p. 581. For an analysis of women of color who have contributed significantly to a theory of difference, see Henry A. Giroux, "Postmodernism as Border Pedagogy: Redefining the Boundaries of Race and Ethnicity," in Henry A. Giroux, ed., *Postmodernism, Feminism, and Cultural Politics: Redrawing the Boundaries of Educational Discourse* (Albany, SUNY Press, in press). Not included in the latter article are important contributions by feminist women of color in critical legal studies. A very partial list would include: Kimberle Crenshaw, "Demarginalizing the Intersection of Race and Sex: A Black Feminist Critique of Antidiscrimination Doctrine, Feminist Theory and Antiracist Politics," *The University of Chicago Legal Forum* (1989), pp. 139-167; Regina Austin, "Sapphire Bound!" *Wisconsin Law Review* (Fall, 1989), pp. 539-578. I am deeply indebted to Linda Brodkey for bringing this literature to my attention. Also see her excellent piece, "Toward a Feminist Rhetoric of Difference," unpublished paper, University of Texas at Austin, 1990, 24 pp.

5. Bell Hooks, *Talking Back* (Boston: South End Press, 1989), p. 12.

6. Sean Cubbit, "Introduction: Over the Borderlines," *Screen* 30:4 (Autumn 1989), p. 5.

7. Paula Rothenberg, "The Construction, Deconstruction, and Reconstruction of Difference," *Hypatia* 5:1 (Spring 1990), p. 47.

8. Paula Rothenberg, "The Construction, Deconstruction, and Reconstruction of Difference," *Hypatia* 5:1 (Spring 1990), p. 43.

9. Larry Grossberg, "The Context of Audiences and the Politics of Difference," *Australian Journal of Communication* 16 (December 1989), p. 29.

10. Diana Fuss, "Lesbian and Gay Theory: The Question of Identity Politics," in D. Fuss, *Essentially Speaking: Feminism, Nature, and Difference* (New York: Routledge, 1989), p. 97.

11. Jenny Bourne, "Homelands of the Mind: Jewish Feminism and Identity Politics," *Race and Class* XXIX (1987), p. 2.

12. Lawrence Grossberg, "The Context of Audience and the Politics of Difference," *Australian Journal of Communication* 16 (December 1989), p. 28.

13. The literature on this issue is much too extensive to list here, but three excellent examples can be found in Angela Harris, "Race and Essentialism"; Audre Lorde, *Sister Outsider* (Freedom, CA: The Crossing Press, 1984); and Bell Hooks, *Talking Back*.

14. June Jordan, "Waiting for a Taxi," *The Progressive* (June 1989), p. 16.

15. Chantal Mouffe, "The Civics Lesson," *The New Statesman and Society* (October 7, 1988), p. 30.

16. Renato Rosaldo, *Culture and Truth* (Boston: Beacon Press, 1989).

17. Larry Grossberg, "The Context of Audiences," p. 30.

1

The Tension of Voices Past and Present: Colonization, Schooling, and Linguistic Imposition

A S COLLECTIVE BEINGS, our lives are imbricated with social and cultural meaning and imbued with the history of previous generations. Yet, in the electronic, technologically oriented world of today, history, community, and social relations are often treated as obsolete or unimportant. We thus seldom think about the community-based saliency of our existence or reflect upon the ways the past impacts our present reality. Such rumination, however, could contribute to a more critical understanding of who we are and how we came to be.[1]

This same inattention carries over to the classroom. As teachers, how frequently do we explore the diverse and multiple realities of our students? That is, do we endeavor to understand the histories they bring with them and all the tensions these histories may imply? And, what about the sociocultural perspectives, semantic understandings, and intentional actions that are partially fashioned from history and from present lived relations? Do we interpret them only in light of our own? In the rush of daily school life, such considerations are probably also uncommon, despite the fact that they could help us better comprehend our students, guide instruction, and offer insight into how it is that students come to know.

Language is one of the principal ways people define themselves; through language we establish alliances with a community, undertake interactions with others, and communicate and receive information. Volosinov (1973) maintains that language both reflects and refracts the sociohistorical circumstances of its speakers. While these circumstances may not be heard in the surface of words, they are infused in consciousness and spoken in what Bakhtin (1981) refers to as the "voice" of the individual. Voice, in this sense, both represents and resonates with the collective memories, experiences, subjectivities, and meanings of individuals that develop and accrue through activity in a social world. But how does history actually come to affect voice? In other words, how do the experiences lived by others in the past come to impact those living in the present? Similarly, what are the conditions through which history is made? And, what are the lived tensions and struggles that define this process? Karl Marx's well-used words from *The Eighteenth Brumaire of Louis Bonaparte* afford a base for discussion:

> Men [sic] make their own history, but they do not make it just as they please; they do not make it under circumstances chosen by themselves, but under circumstances directly encountered, given and transmitted from the past. The tradition of all the dead generations weigh like a nightmare on the brain of the living. (1963:15)

Marx illuminates an understanding of history as action. People, not texts, create history, a creation governed by the ideological past and present. Thus while all humans have an equal chance to make history, the unequal relations of power that exist between groups (and classes) place limits on the conditions of this making. Conflicts of a social, economic, cultural, linguistic, racial, sexual, and political character are made and fought in history; they are also internalized in language and in consciousness and reconstructed from generation to generation.

This chapter draws from both Marx's and Bakhtin's perceptions of the importance of history in people's activities, language, and consciousness by analyzing the sociohistorical context underlying the voices of Puerto Rican students. Through a recount of the spoken and written words of North Americans and Puerto Ricans on or associated with the Island from 1898 to the early 1960s, the chapter presents a portion of the "unofficial" story of colonization, schooling, and linguistic imposition, a disconcerting history of which most U.S. educators are totally unaware. In so doing, it illuminates the lived attitudes, actions, tensions, and struggles of the not so distant past and foregrounds the significance of colonialism—that with which their ancestors and relatives in Puerto Rico were confronted and the existence of which lives on in both the minds and bodies of Puerto Ricans residing in the emigrant colony—the continental United States—today. "Colonialism" or "colonization" can be understood as the aggregate of policies used by dominant countries to extend control over and establish occupation of sovereign nations. The design of colonization is to penetrate the consciousness of the masses and, in so doing, to render them powerless. As such, the maintenance of dominant and subordinate relations is thought to be ensured.

Language has always served as a primary force in colonization because it touches both the cultural and psychological being of a people. Imperialist powers presume that by doing away with a nation's language, or by greatly limiting its public use, they will be able to capture the souls of the masses; that by imposing their language they might exploit the intimate connection between language, consciousness, and activity (Marx 1971). Language thus becomes the symbolic force for the implantation of an inferior status and for the installation of submission and colonial control. As Antonio Gramsci notes,

> Each time that in one way or another the question of language comes to the fore, that signifies that a series of other problems is about to emerge, the formation and enlarging of the ruling class, the necessity to establish more "intimate" and sure relations between the ruling groups and the national popular masses, that is, the reorganization of cultural hegemony. (Translated by and cited in Salamini 1981:35)

Key in the development of this hegemony is the establishment of a linguistic dualism and the internalization of a subordinate identity. The use of the language of the colonizer in government, in the public sphere, and in social institutions (like schools) relegates the indigenous tongue to a private, substandard existence. The populace is thus forced to publicly participate in the psychological and cultural realms of the colonizer through the utilization of his language.[2] The "colonial bilingualism" which results entails not the possession of two tools of communication but the embrace of two tongues and subsequently two worlds in tension and conflict—those of the colonizer and the colonized (Memmi 1965). Emerging from this linguistic duality can be the possible gradual negation of self and of nationality, history, and culture. This is partially accomplished through a repositioning of the identity that existed prior to colonization. In its place, a pseudo-identification with the colonizer is shaped, an identification that is superficial at best since full inclusion by the colonizer (which would entail a doing away with the colonial relationship) must be forever denied. The result can be a sort of "thingification" (Césaire 1972) that forces the people to ask themselves the question: In reality who am I? (Fanon 1963). Frantz Fanon describes this duality well:

> The setting up of a colonial system does not of itself bring about the death of the native culture. Historical observation reveals, on the contrary, that the aim sought is rather a continued agony than a total disappearance of the pre-existing culture. This culture, once living and open to the future, becomes closed, fixed in the colonial status, caught in the yoke of oppression. Both present and mummified, it testifies against its members. It defines them in fact without appeal. The cultural mummification leads to a mummification of individual thinking. The apathy so universally noted among colonial peoples is but the logical consequence of this operation. The reproach of inertia

constantly directed at "the native" is utterly dishonest. As though it were possible for a man [*sic*] to evolve otherwise than within the framework of a culture that recognizes him and that he decides to assume. (1967:34)

Education has served as a principal site for colonization throughout the world. Because the colonizers control the government and its institutions, they can determine how the content, medium, format, and uses of schooling can best meet their (the colonizers) needs rather than the needs of the colonized (Altbach and Kelly 1978). Schools thus most often become the location for socializing individuals into compliance and for perpetuating class divisions and the status quo. Children are alienated from meaningful symbolic interaction within their culture in order to diffuse group solidarity and dissipate collective identity; they are acculturated into a mold that favors those in power. Through the control of discourse and of school practices, the colonizer seeks to implant his ideas and policies and, in so doing, to reproduce cultural hegemony. Language is one of the major forces that institutes this subjugation.

While colonialism has exercised the power of language to suppress cultural (and national) unity, language, as a dynamic and dialectic force, has also stimulated antagonism and opposition. In order to understand the dialectics of linguistic imposition and linguistic resistance, it is important to situate language in history, in experience, and in the relations of power and struggle that determine, legitimize, and/or constrain particular ways of being. Thus while language is generally viewed as the common denominator of a people—a sociocultural unifier or composite force that brings together individuals for the purpose of meaningful interaction—language does not preclude a commonality of experience, equal relations of power, or a sharing of purpose. It is rather through language that individuals fashion a "voice," a "speaking consciousness" as Bakhtin (1981) has called it, that is rooted in their collective history, struggles, and lived experience, and in their relation to one another, to society, and to the ideological and material forces that surround them. "Voice" is never singular or unitary but reflects a connection of individuals to realities that are sometimes multiple and often contradictory. As such, the voice or voices of individuals frequently reveal much about the conditions and relations that position and surround them.

In colonial nations, the voice of the colonizer is heard above all others. The colonized masses, however, seldom accept this domination without opposition. What ensues throughout the process of colonization (and later through imperialism) then is a clash of voices, the various talking groups whose objective discourses legitimate, confront, and negate colonial policy. The project of colonization is to penetrate the psyche of the masses, yet, somehow, the people find ways to speak of oppression; their collective actions and words struggle to overcome it. In response to this counter activity, the political, economic, and social practices of the colonizer are directed at silencing the voice of the people, destroying their collective unity, which is seen as a threat to the colonizer's dominion. Thus it is partially through the battle for voice that the war of colonization is waged; it is through language imposition and practices in schools that colonization is, in part, effectuated.

Within the context of the United States, the realization of this battle is probably nowhere as blatantly visible as in the case of Puerto Rico. In 1898, the United States "peacefully" invaded the island, its winnings from the Spanish-American War. After nearly four centuries of Spanish rule, the Puerto Rican people were said to welcome the representatives of their neighboring democracy believing that with them came the prospects for national respect and for freedom and prosperity. Instead, the United States came armed with the gift of "civilization," a well-planned policy of political, economic, social, cultural, and linguistic subjugation that attempted to break the spirit of the Puerto Rican people and make them amenable to and dependent on U. S. colonial rule. The site for the implementation of (and the resistance to) this policy was, and continues to be, in the public schools.

Together, it is the past and present history of colonial domination in Puerto Rico and its contemporary extenuation in the United States that helps shape the voices of Puerto Rican students, setting them off from Anglos and from other racial and ethnic minorities. Embedded in these voices are realities lived on the streets, in the workplace, barrios, homes, and schools. They are realities riddled with social, political, and economic contradictions—paradoxes imbued with clashing voices and defined by the social forms, meanings, cultural practices, and subjectivities that have emerged through struggle within the relations of colonial power and domination that have existed for Puerto Ricans for nearly half a millenium.

Through the social and linguistic policies of English imposition, deculturation, and the implantation of American values, schools have attempted to refashion the voices of the Puerto Rican masses, debilitating their history and national identity and promoting a dependence on and an alliance with imperialist rule. While the violence of colonialism perpetuated through education has penetrated people's lives, it has not been without confrontation. Schools have served as sites not only of pacification but also for antagonistic relations. It is here that the voices of colonizer and colonized, imperialist and worker, bourgeois elite, nationalist, and *independista*, teacher and student speak to the lived experience of colonialism, of domination and of resistance. It is by listening to these voices, to the "speaking consciousness" of groups and of individuals, that we can begin to construct and dissect the texts of history, the texts that chronicle the linguistic, social, psychological, political, and economic subordination of Puerto Ricans and that reveal the reconstitution of culture and identity, the texts from which both the external and the internal psychological and linguistic reality of

Puerto Ricans is forged, shaped, and positioned. It is to this task that this chapter is directed.

THE EXPERIENCE OF PUERTO RICO: U.S. COLONIZATION AND PUERTO RICAN RESISTANCE

> Colonization carried forward by the armies of war is vastly more costly than that carried forward by the armies of peace, whose outposts and garrisons are the public schools of the advancing nation.
>
> U.S. Bureau of Education, 1902:257

The above Commissioner's annual report articulates the initial focus of the United States' involvement in Puerto Rico. Education was to serve as the heart of colonization, the site from which imposition, domination, and control would flow. It was to be a policy both developed and implemented without understanding of the people, their culture, or lived realities. As Fernández García, a Puerto Rican, wrote in 1918:

> Who has seen the Commissioners put themselves in direct contact with our people, study the customs of our peasants, their habits, psychology, cultural state, beliefs as well as superstitions, and afterwards proceed with the developement of a public instructional plan that is in consonance with the conditions of the people for whom it is to apply? (1975:1098, translation mine)

In a report to the Governor in 1898, Victor S. Clark, U.S. citizen and president of the Island's Board of Education, formulated the underlying social and political transformationist policy of Puerto Rico's new school system:

> If the schools are made American and pupils are inspired with the American spirit ... the island will become in its sympathies, views, and attitude toward government essentially American. The great mass of Puerto Ricans are as yet passive and plastic. ... Their ideals are in our hands to create and mold. We shall be responsible for the work when it is done, and it is our solemn duty to consider carefully and thoughtfully today the character we wish to give the finished product of our influence and effort. (Davis 1899:180)

The U.S. War Department reiterated Clark's position, defining the discourse of schooling that was to follow:

> We believe that the public school system which now prevails in the United States should be provided for Porto Rico and that the same system of education and the same character of books now regarded most favorably in this

country should be given to them. . . . The teachers in these schools should, in a great part, be Americans who are familiar with the methods, system, and books of the American schools, and they should instruct the children in the English language . . . Porto Rico is now and is henceforth to be a part of the American possessions and its people are to be Americans. . . . At present only one out of every ten persons on the island can read and write. . . . Why, therefore, should we attempt to teach the other nine Spanish instead of English. The question of good citizenship and education can be more easily settled through the public schools than by any other method. (U.S. Department of War 1899:53)

The influence and effort that the United States was to assert was not aimed, however, at converting Puerto Ricans into North Americans; rather, its goal was to colonize the people, socializing them into compliant subjects in order that they might passively accept U.S. domination. Entailed in this process was the supposed creation of a new consciousness that defined itself according to North American norms. The year 1898 was to be seen as the birth of "Porto Rico" (an anglicized version of the Spanish name); documents and books making any reference to the history and literature before this time were shipped to the National Library in Washington (Beauchamp 1980). Although some of these materials were given back to the Institute of Culture a little over a year later, they were not returned to the schools.

Aware that language, as history, is also intimately tied to a peoples' consciousness, the United States instituted English as the language of government, of education, and of public life. Its effect, however, was most pronounced in the schools. There, curricular practices attempted to shape young children into colonial pawns. This policy appeared planned from the time of the invasion, as evident in a 1899 *New York Sun* article by Fensler:

One of the most powerful means of social and political transformation which we can employ in our new Spanish possessions will be the introduction of the English language in them through our public school system. (Epica Task Force 1976:68)

In order to legalize its governance over the Island, the U.S. Congress passed the Foraker Act in 1900, making Puerto Rico an "unincorporated territory" subject to the absolute will of Congress. Yet, Puerto Rico's people were denied American citizenship and claim to the U.S. Constitution. As one Democrat remarked, Puerto Ricans became a people without a country. "Can any man conceive of a more tyrannical form of government?" (cited in Carr 1984). With the passage of the Foraker Act, the structural format for enforcing colonization through education was ensured. The Act created an 11-member executive council appointed by the president of the United States. Included in this council was a commissioner of education who was to oversee all aspects of insular schooling.[3]

At the time of the U.S. takeover in 1898, 92 percent of the Island's children aged five to seventeen were not enrolled in school (Allen 1901); Spain had considered education a threat to its dominion. The few schools that did exist were either private or religious and primarily served offspring of the upper classes.[4] In contrast, the major project of the first U.S. Education Commissioner, Martin Brumbaugh, was to organize a highly centralized islandwide system of public schooling—to provide education to a larger percentage of the population and to establish a curriculum which would inculcate American ideals. In his first report to the Governor in 1900, Commissioner Brumbaugh reiterated the metropolis' plan for colonial control:

> The spirit of American institutions and the ideals of the American people, strange as they seem to some in Puerto Rico, must be the only ideals incorporated in the school system. (U.S. Bureau of Education, 1900)

Although English language instruction was viewed as the way to implant this spirit and instill these ideals. Brumbaugh realized the opposition this would draw and so opted for an initial transitional bilingual policy where Spanish would eventually be phased out to English instruction. The Commissioner assured the Governor in this same report that there would be little resistance:

> A majority of the people . . . do not speak pure Spanish. Their language is a patois almost unintelligible to the natives of Barcelona and Madrid. It possesses no literature and little value as an intellectual medium. There is a bare possibility that it will be nearly as easy to educate these people out of their patois into English as it will be to educate them into the elegant tongue of Castile. Only from the very small intellectual minority in Puerto Rico, trained in Europe and imbued with European ideals of education and government, have we to anticipate any active resistance to the introduction of the American system and the English language.

From the outset, the colonizers' plan to use education as the way to win over the masses appeared to be working. By June 1901, the percentage of children in school had increased to 19 percent; 33,802 students were enrolled in 733 primary schools throughout the Island (Epstein 1970). However, according to the *Puerto Rico Herald*'s July 27, 1901, edition, the conditions in these schools were abominable. In one school, fifty-four pupils were crowded into a 12-by-16-foot room. Some schools were without roofs and many had unfit out building facilities. The paper quoted the Commisioner as saying, "The schools are full, but let us get more pupils!"

Massive efforts continued during the first part of the twentieth century with over one-third of the Island's budget going toward education and the building of schools. U.S. Protestant churches played a major role in this effort.[5] Calculations in 1928 showed illiteracy (i.e., the inability to read and write in any language) to have decreased from 80 to less than 50 percent while the number of schools had increased from 560 in 1898 to 2,238 with an enrollment totalling more than 230,000 (Wagenheim 1973).[6] By this same year, only 19 percent of the populace were able to speak English (United States-Puerto Rico Commission 1966).

The extension of the educational system included not only the building of schools and the recruitment of students; one of its primary functions, as the Education Commissioner had stated, was Americanization through the teaching of English. In order that this might be accomplished, a law was established requiring one native English-speaking teacher be employed in each city or town with a public school (U.S. Bureau of Education 1899–1900, vol. 2). At the outset, most of these teachers were young men who had come to the Island with the U.S. Army, militarizing the schools and advancing little in the area of pedagogy. But with the appearance of more schools, these male teachers were insufficient. It was thus, beginning in 1901, that hundreds of North American women teachers were brought to the Island. Most had previously taught on U.S. Indian reservations. As Commissioner Brumbaugh described in his report to the Governor that same year, these were the "true patriots" and the "solemn and sacred sacrifice for the Americanization of the people of Puerto Rico." Imported with them were U.S. textbooks, materials, and methods. The cost of these materials, as well as the expenses and salaries of the teachers, was assumed not by the mainland but by the insular economy. There, the military governor imposed a mandatory one dollar school tax on property owners, professionals, and artisans (U.S. Senate, 1900). In fact, the U.S. takeover of education and demand for English instruction was never backed by American dollars.

The charge of the newly installed foreign work force was to impart English, inculcate North American values, and promote an obedient student populace; patriotic exercises became the mandated norm.[7] The scarcity of teachers could not be met, however, merely with the introduction of North American women.[8] In order to sustain the United States' educational policy of colonization, it was crucial to gain the support of native teachers and to teach them English. Summer normal institutes were thus established in 1901, providing ten weeks of intensive English instruction; permission to teach was granted after passing an exam. But, it soon became evident that the teachers' halting English and lack of familiarity with North American values were obstacles in the acculturation process. In response, the colonial government organized in 1903 what was called the "Porto Rican Teachers Summer Study Trip to the United States." Teachers were enticed by the commissioner's propaganda that alleged the trip would broaden knowledge and "refine the faculty of perception and stimulate intelligence" and that suggested that "attendance at a summer course in a good college will not only improve your knowledge of English, it will also improve your work at school . . . a motive to progress in your profession" (Commissioner Samuel Maccune Lindsay, cited in Meyn 1983:97). While teachers showed an interest in the courses, it was not necessarily intellectually motivated. Commissioner Lindsay (1902–1904) had instituted a policy of yearly renewal of teaching licenses with criteria for renewal solely based on substantial individual progress in a more indepth exam on the English language.

Lindsay's successor, Roland Faulkner, further extended the Americanization of Puerto Rican teachers by organizing weekly compulsory English classes taught by the U.S. teachers. His efforts led to the passage of a law making mandatory the annual English examination. Those who failed were faced with the loss of their teaching license.

With the training of teachers now under their control, the United States had created a situation in which Puerto Ricans could begin to assume the work their colonizers had designed. Their jobs were to mold passive Americans, their tools, U.S. texts, and their work sites named after the Spanish "explorers," Columbus and Ponce de León, or American "statesmen"—Washington, Lafayette, Franklin, Jefferson, Jackson, Adams, Lincoln, Grant, McKinley, Longfellow, Prescott, Webster, Hamilton, Garfield, Horace Mann, and Peabody (Negrón de Montilla 1971). Their pay was nearly half that of their American counterparts and, like their compatriots in the plantations, they had no job security or benefits.

Education had truly become the voice of colonization, striving to destroy national solidarity and to create what Memmi (1965) referred to as the patriotism of the colonized. From the outset, school curriculum, policy, and practices had been clearly directed toward this objective. Words from Brumbaugh's report to the Governor in 1901 serve as illustration:

> In almost every city of the island, and at many rural schools, the children meet and salute the flag as it is flung to the breeze. The raising of the flag is the signal that the school has commenced and the flag floats during the entire session. The pupils then sing America, Hail Columbia, Star Spangled Banner, and other patriotic songs. The marvel is that they sing these in English. The first English many of them know is the English of our national songs. The influence is far reaching. . . . Washington's birthday exercises were proposed and outlined by this department in a circular letter to the supervisors. . . . The exercises were a fitting occasion to display their patriotism and their school training. In each case the exercises consisted of patriotic songs and speeches on Washington and on patriotism by the people. . . . At least 25,000 children participated in these exercises and perhaps 5,000 citizens joined in the patriotic demonstration. These exercises have done much to Americanize the island, much more than any other single agency. The young minds are being molded to follow the example of Washington. It is one of the gratifying results so far achieved in our work. (Allen 1901:361-362)

Even though English was the compulsory language of instruction in the schools, Spanish teaching was permitted during the first ten years of U.S. colonial rule in order to "ease" the acculturation process. Metropolitan authorities assumed that by increasing students' exposure to English and to the dominant values this instruction promoted, Puerto Rican children would quickly take on an "American" identity, would feel tied to the "mainland," and would develop a dependency that would legitimate colonial policy. In fact, the colonizers saw the significant increases in school enrollment in the early 1900s to be reflective of parental support for their assimilationist-like actions. Oliver S. Kern, director of San Juan High School, in 1902 described what he perceived to be parents' desire for English instruction:

> It is painful to see parents struggling to be first in line; they are so anxious to enroll their children in the school where they will learn English. At times, this line is converted into a mob, each parent defending himself in a voice louder than that of their neighbor and repeating the special reasons why they should be next attended to. (U.S. Bureau of Education 1899–1900, vol. 1:1221-1222)

Kern's perception of wide-ranging support for English language instruction was not shared by all educators on the Island. In 1900 teachers publicly spoke against the use of English in *La Educación Moderna*, the journal of Puerto Rican teachers. Even Assistant Director of Public Instruction Victor Clark, who just one year before had helped formulate the colonial school policy, questioned the effectiveness of forced English instruction as it was being implemented and the class character it was promoting:

> It could suggest a strong class sentiment in some of the towns and villages where the vast majority of the people are illiterate. These people may consider that that the introduction of English, unless accompanied by an increase in the availability of educational facilities and the instruction of English to all children, is an attempt to establish a class regime. It was indicated to me that there could exist a tendency on the part of the rich to monopolize English, using it both to maintain political and commercial control and to further oppress the lower classes. (Letter to General John Eaton, March 14, 1899, translation mine)

Clark was correct in describing the class character of early colonial schooling and English imposition. In the countryside, education was, until 1909, primarily in Spanish; the design was to transform the peasant children into a rural proletariat, the future workers for the sugar plantations controlled by U.S. capital (Meyn 1983; Picó de Hernández 1971). Education for the urban and middle class sectors (predominantly in English) was geared to the preparation of the professionals so essential to colonialism's success. Antonio Santiago addresses this link between schooling and labor force development:

> The intrinsic rationale of the public instruction system was not the mere "creation of docile minds" that felt "at home with the North American colonial enterprise," but mainly the forging of a labor force that would correspond to the technical and socio-economic needs of the sugar plantations and mills, the tobacco factories, the domestic needle products manufacture and the new state within the context of the extraction of colonial surplus value. The docile minds and the pro-American sentiment were the natural consequence that resulted from this forging and from these needs. (Translated by and cited in Jiménez-Muñoz 1989:17)

It is interesting to note here how language was differentially used to marginalize the population, to silence, and to create class formations. In order to maintain a rural working class to serve the economic needs of the United States, children were educated in the language of their class and were taught respect and obedience to U.S. authority. Schooling was limited to the early primary years so as to ensure subservience. Children of the middle and upper classes, however, were schooled so as to assume the language and, eventually, the position and voice of the colonizer. It would be they who would control the rural working class and who would promote a new form of cultural hegemony.

But, after a decade of U.S. control, the rural masses (an increasing number of whom were unemployed) were less than servile; even the middle classes had not fully acquired English or adapted to the "North American way." Dismayed at the people's efforts to maintain unity through language, mainland authorities abolished all Spanish instruction in 1909, relegating the people's language in all schools to a special subject.

Primary school children were the first to rebel, staging a strike and refusing to attend classes unless they were instructed in the language of their fathers and their country (Coll y Cuchi 1922). The colonial power tried to quell the rebellion by exerting its authority. Children refusing to attend English classes were expelled from school. Island politicians and educators opposing the English only policy joined forces and, shortly thereafter, founded a Spanish school, the José de Diego Institute.

The outspokeness of the students disturbed U.S. officials who presumed their linguistic policies would not meet such active resistance. In order to further instill subordination and discipline in the students, they instituted military drill as an organized part of the curriculum. By 1910, 1,089 boys had "enlisted." Money was provided by the Legislative Assembly for their encampment at Fort Henry and U.S. Army equipment was loaned by the University of Puerto Rico. According to Commissioner Dexter, the militarization of education had positive effects on school discipline, inculcating "a prompt and cheerful obedience to orders" (U.S. Bureau of Education 1912).

While colonial authorities acted to further control the students, adults did not stand silent. Politicians joined the struggle, introducing numerous bills in the Puerto Rican legislature just to have them vetoed by the governor. Teachers, unionized in 1911 into an association, and parents continued to protest the language policy on the grounds that the excessive attention given to English impeded the school's primary function—that of educating children. At their annual meeting in 1912, the Teachers' Association of Puerto Rico passed the first of many resolutions on the language question. Included were three major recommendations: (1) that urban schools begin instruction in first grade in Spanish and, that in the upper-elementary grades, instruction be divided between Spanish and English; (2) that rural schools utilize Spanish as the sole medium of instruction; and (3) that high schools instruct in English. The recommendations were modified a year later to include Spanish as the medium of instruction in urban schools throughout the first four grades (Rodríguez Pacheco 1976). Other Puerto Ricans vehemently spoke out against the unwritten agenda of the language policy and of the need for collective resistance. Such was the case with a resident of Caguas who identified himself in 1913 only as Rocinante:

> We are witnessing the brutalizing of the faculties of the spirit, which has begun by compelling our own children to speak in an exotic language which estranges them from the pure sentiments of their home, where that language is not used. . . . The government of our hated conquerors has understood it in this way and for that reason has composed the system of instruction, the system of nullifying and barbarizing all that pertains to the ideals of the fatherland. . . . To secure their liberty and to show their decency people do not need to go to school, and much less to Yankee schools in a colony of slaves. (Rodríguez Pacheco 1976:117)

While their demands for a return to the vernacular were not initially met, the people's voices had brought to the forefront what U.S. authorities referred to as the "language problem" or "language question" (which they feared was a stimulus for the increase on the Island of nationalistic sentiment). According to then Commissioner Barlow, the language question had become "the football of certain political agitators who would have people believe that the scheme of education now in force is an insidious attempt to eliminate Spanish, the thin entering wedge to destroy the personality of the people of Porto Rico" (U.S. Bureau of Education 1915:343). In order to quiet the growing resistance, the colonial government offered a concession, the reinstatment of Spanish as the medium of instruction in the first four grades. While Island politicians saw this liberalizing of the "English only" policy as a small victory, it in fact served to demonstrate the continued class character of colonial schooling, because—as officials pointed out—most poor, rural children terminated their education at grade four anyway (Fisher 1971).

Although U.S. authorities still argued its benefits, Puerto Rican educators began to document the detrimental effects of "English only" instruction on students' academic achievement. José Padín, who later became Education Commissioner, in 1917 illustrated in a pioneer study that the English medium encouraged memorization on the part of the pupils (Cebollero 1945) and inhibited the learning of other subjects (Fisher 1971). Other studies conducted in the 1920s demonstrated academic retardation in reading and comprehension, and maintained that the sole use of English as the language of instruction was a disadvantage to the learning of English itself.[9] Cebollero, in his recount of school language policy explains:

> To take the time necessary to correct all the mistakes in language made by pupils in the course of lessons in other subjects would amount to converting every class into a class in English conversation. Consequently, oral use of the foreign medium frequently defeats the very purpose for which it is recommended. Moreover, the use of English as medium of instruction makes it necessary to devote more time than otherwise would be required to the teaching of the several subjects of the elementary school curriculum. The use of the vernacular medium would make it possible to reduce the time needed by the subjects other than English, and the time thus saved could be devoted profitably to the teaching of English as a subject. (1945:172-173)

While educators decried the sole use of English on pedagogical grounds, their voices went unheard by those in authority. In fact, it appeared the U.S. colonial plan was to effectively destroy any semblance of Puerto Rican discourse by negating the populace's identity, both their language and historical roots, by allying them more closely with the colonizer. With the passage of the Jones Act in 1917, Puerto Ricans were involuntarily made U.S. citizens, subject to the responsibilities of this citizenship including military duty, but denied many of its inalienable privileges, including the right to vote in U.S. national elections. Those who refused the bestowing of this "gift" could remain citizens of Puerto Rico but with limited civil participation, prohibited from voting or holding public office (Wagenheim 1973).

The imposition of alien citizenship was not passively accepted. José de Diego, a well-known poet and leader of the Insular House of Representatives, decried the action:

> Never before in the realm of international law has such a thing been seen in the democratic nations of the world: 1,200,000 human beings, who by the law of the Congress of a Republic . . . are stripped of their national citizenship but under the menace and coercion of losing their right to vote or be eligible

for public office, in the country where they are obliged to respect all the laws of the State, and pay military tribute to the dominant nation; in the country of their birth and life, where they aspire to be buried, Puerto Ricans who for some heretofore known crime—the love of their own citizenship—are reduced to the condition of being foreigners in their homeland; they are exiled from their land and thus, out of fear, and due to the harshness of the punishment, only a tiny number of Puerto Ricans renounce the citizenship imposed on them; almost all of them accept, and thus present before the world—this unusual fact, the false demonstration that the Puerto Ricans did voluntarily and joyfully accept the citizenship of the U. S., and with it abandoned the ideals of joining their country with the other free and sovereign nations of America. (Wagenheim 1973:174)

It is not out of coincidence that the passage of the Jones Act occurred as the United States was preparing to enter World War I. The increasing population growth on the Island coupled with a decrease in agricultural production (due to the U.S. takeover of plantations) had created what colonial officials referred to as a "surplus population," mainly poor and unemployed. According to then Governor Arthur Yager, the only real remedy to this problem was the "transfer of large numbers of Puerto Ricans to some other region" (History Task Force 1982:100). Plans were made for the permanent displacement of several hundred thousand Puerto Ricans to Santo Domingo, a neighboring island where the United States had also assumed dominion. However, as the inevitability of World War I became more apparent, the colonizers shifted their strategy, capitalizing on the potential draft force that, with the passage of one law, they could easily muster.

The granting of citizenship thus provided political as well as social grounds for forced assimilation, denationalization, and the continued imposition of English. Men were sent overseas with English-speaking American troops to defend the values of "their nation," others were sent to work in the United States to aid in the war effort. In the schools, children learned the U.S. history of the times and about those Americans (including their fathers) who were dedicating their lives to defend it. Education majors at the university were told that if their views in any way contradicted the "Americanization" policies of the education authorities, they would not receive teacher appointments (Negrón de Montilla 1971).

The decade of the 1920s under the direction of Education Commissioner Juan B. Huyke was probably one of the strongest in terms of colonial domination in the schools and English language imposition. Huyke, who as a Puerto Rican led the fight against legislative attempts to eliminate English as the medium of instruction, had an explicit goal of Americanization. For him, this signified a merging of Puerto Ricans "in the national life, to enjoy the pleasures of our victories, to study the national problems as if they were our own" (1921:9).

> For me, Americanization is a state of mind, a desire to live associated with Americans by ties of deep fraternity and absolute loyalty. . . . It is not only an idea. It is a plan that must be carried out. (Huyke 1929:5)

The educational policy of the time reflected Huyke's obsession. Ranking among schools was determined according to performance on English tests, high school diplomas became dependent on the passing of oral English examinations, the printing of school newspapers in Spanish was prohibited, and the required language of all official school documents and at meetings of teachers was English. A School Society for the Promotion of the Study of English was organized in the eighth through tenth grades in all schools; members were required to wear small American flags in their buttonholes and to speak English everywhere to one another (Negrón de Montilla 1971).

Student protests and Teachers' Association demands mounted in protest. Yet these actions did not occur in isolation. In the broader sociopolitical context, overall support and tolerance for direct U.S. control over the Island was diminishing.

As the economy on the mainland worsened during the 1920s, the contradictions on the Island became more apparent. Coffee, tobacco, and sugar cultivation and processing, the economic mainstay of the Island, fell off and thousands more were left without work. In 1929, Luis Muñoz Marín, Economic Commissioner of the Legislature of Puerto Rico in the United States, described the socioeconomic climate as an outgrowth of thirty years of U.S. colonial dominion:

> By now the development of large absentee-owned sugar estates, the rapid curtailment in the planting of coffee—the natural crop of the independent farmer—the concentration of cigar manufacture into the hands of the American trust have combined to make Porto Rico a land of beggars and millionaires, of flattening statistics and distressing realities. More and more it becomes a factory worked by peons, fought over by lawyers, bossed by absentee industrialists, and clerked by politicians. It is now Uncle Sam's second largest sweat shop. It is a sweat shop that has a company store—the United States. American dollars paid to the peons are so many tokens, redeemable in the American market exclusively, at tariff-inflated prices. The same tariff that protects the prices of sugar and tobacco, controlled by the few, skyrockets the prices of all commodities that must be consumed by all. . . . So far as the bulk of the population is concerned, only an 80 cent wage paid during six months of the year to each family and redeemable only in the world's highest market, separates them from the angels. (Muñoz Marín 1929)

Years of American ineptitude promoted by the constant turnover of government officials had brought about the crisis situation that Muñoz Marín described. The people were no longer able to silently accept the colonizer's rule; disenchantment and unrest became more outwardly visible and nationalism was on the rise. Even the landholders, who had once collaborated with the colonizers, assumed a posture of resistance including the defense of the vernacular (Meyn 1983).

It was the Nationalist Party (founded by intellectuals in 1922) who directly confronted the colonial system and its politics of cultural assimilation and English language imposition. As its leader, Pedro Albizu Campos declared in one of his addresses:

> The gravest aggression that has been perpetrated against the Puerto Rican nationality has been the creation of this systematic tyranny about the native intellect. . . . No place on the globe has there been constructed a judge of the knowledge and culture of a people as in Puerto Rico. . . . To the educational system certain fundamental questions must be asked: Why are we citizens? Why do we educate the Puerto Rican children? . . . Education cannot be an instrument of domination; education should mold informed men of a patriotic standard and not slaves to an imperial regime. (1975:179, translation mine)

With the excuse of teaching English, the public education system of Puerto Rico was passing on the language of the invader at a cost of $4 million a year. Albizu Campos and his party believed the time had come to end this foreign intervention.

Governor Theodore Roosevelt, aware of the rising discontent with Island schooling and the increasingly vehement voice of the Nationalists, made a conciliatory gesture by appointing José Padín, a well-respected Puerto Rican educator, as Education Commissioner in 1930. But, Roosevelt's successor, Robert Gore (1933–1934) cared little about appeasing the people and was more intent on creating a Democratic party through the judicious handout of jobs (Carr 1984). Padín, who spoke Spanish, approved of teaching the vernacular, and reportedly had no interest in politics or in allowing politicians to meddle in his schools (Wagenheim 1973), was seen by Gore as un-American. This probably could not have been further from the truth.

Educated in the United States under a scholarship program initiated by Commissioner Brumbaugh, Padín referred to himself as more American than Puerto Rican. In fact, during his reign as Assistant Commissioner from 1916–1930, Padín actively supported the assimilationist language policies of his predecessor (Meyn, 1983). Padín's perspectives were decidedly more liberal than previous commissioners, however. This, coupled with his outspokenness on maintaining Spanish while teaching English, won him widespread popular support. Although Gore's efforts to replace Padín with a staunch Democratic supporter of President Franklin Roosevelt received backing from Washington, Puerto Rican educators along with educators from the United States publicly decried the action of "paying party debts with the schools of Puerto Rican children" (Herring 1933:618).[10] For a time, the voice of the people actually won out and Padín remained. But, as changes in instructional methodology began to actually take place, the U.S. government's concern mounted: they feared a loss of colonial authority over schools and a diminishing of English imposition and Americanization. Padín's efforts, in reality, threatened neither.

Based on his earlier research, Padín proposed teaching "less bad English and more good English" through appropriate English as a second language instruction. His proposal was accepted by Gore's successor.[11] With the Padín Reform of 1934, English language instruction was restricted to high schools; in the upper elementary grades, content instruction was provided in Spanish (although textbooks were in English). Twice as much time was devoted to the teaching of English as a subject. Both the people of Puerto Rico as well as the colonial authorities saw the reform as a reinstatement of native language instruction, neither understanding the full implications of increased but separate English instruction. Indeed, Padín's efforts were not to resurrect Spanish to equal status but to temporarily silence the anti-colonial movement. To use June Jordan's (1972) metaphor, this was a "dry victory."

The specifics of pedagogy, however, continued to be of little concern to the U.S. government, which, in the midst of an ailing economy in Puerto Rico and the Great Depression at home, saw any support for Spanish as indicative of an increased nationalism and a disregard for colonial rule. The school-related actions of Padín and the then governor, coupled with a growing militant labor movement (which held major strikes in 1934) and mounting social unrest, prompted the United States to take punitive actions. President Franklin Roosevelt moved quickly, appointing Blanton Winship, a veteran of Cuba in 1898 and of World War I and the Philippines, as the new governor. Through the use of troops, wage concessions, and New Deal investments,[12] control was temporarily established. In the schools, Americanization was reaffirmed as the voice of the colonizer reigned loud: English once again became the language of instruction in all grades. To lift one's voice against it was equivalent to sedition. Padín was forced to resign.

By the late 1930s, it had become clear to most that the significance of the English language mandate extended far beyond school policy. Not only did the colonial authorities want to make Puerto Ricans American-like, they wanted to pacify the people, to take away their voice (i.e., their language, history, and consciousness) so that they might better serve the economic and political needs of the colonizer. By the end of the decade, over 6,000 men had been sent to combat in World War II and U.S. forces had transgressed the Island, constructing massive naval and air bases in order to shield the Panama Canal. But, as the U.S. government flexed its muscles, opposition did not dissolve. Through the Nationalist Party, protest became more radical. Albizu Campos pronounced in a speech in the early 1930s that it was time for Puerto Rico to create a grave crisis in the colonial administration in order that its demands be heard. . . . A nation like the United States with enormous national and international problems has no time to pay attention to submissive, servile men. What is needed is a rebel organization . . . to make a clean break with the colonial regime, and to request recognition of our independence from the free nations of the world. (Reprinted and translated by Wagenheim 1978:270)

The Nationalist Party became the voice for the masses, many of whom had long been silent, publicly decrying colonialism and U.S. intervention.[13] In the above speech, Albizu Campos articulated the promises and reality this *yanqui* discourse had engendered:

The *yanqui* invasion of 1898 . . . meant the coming of a regime of liberty, equality, fraternity, and material prosperity to judge by *yanqui* propaganda. . . . They imposed a regime with absolute powers, to control all taxes and privileges, and to determine the displacement of all native wealth into the hand of the invaders. Thus agriculture, industry, commerce, and the communications media all practically became theirs . . . but *yanqui* propaganda again benumbed the Boricuan conscience . . . workers came to believe that good salaries depended upon the *yanqui* government . . . farmworkers were warned against the possible demagoguery of the working class . . . businessmen became convinced that they ought to deposit their money in the banks of the invaders because *yanqui* propaganda subtly accused everyone of lack of honesty; teachers were convinced that they should teach everything in English; in sum, the nation assented to its moral and material dismemberment anesthetized by so-called good intentions.

The Nationalist Party's actions helped draw the contradictions of Puerto Rico's political and social status to the forefront. Independence became a viable issue worth struggling for; the Island government saw the party as a threat to the stability of the colony. After an American insular police chief was killed by two young nationalists, Albizu Campos and other leaders were charged with conspiracy to overthrow the American government and the rights of free speech and assemblage (guaranteed in the Organic Act) were disbanded.[14] Angry at the conviction of Albizu Campos, people from diverse sectors of the population chose to march in peaceful protest. Police fired into the crowd, killing and wounding men, women, and children. The "Massacre of Ponce," as it is known, demonstrated that the U.S. government would go to any length to maintain its grip on the small Caribbean island. Local support for its actions, however, was weakening.

In order to ensure its dominion over the political, economic, and geographic spheres of the Island, the United States clearly had to seek ways to maintain social supremacy. President Roosevelt, like his predecessors, saw the base of this control in the continued imposition of the English language.

In a letter to his new Commissioner, José Gallardo, Roosevelt argued for what he referred to as "forced bilingualism":

> Puerto Rico came under the American flag 38 years ago. Nearly 20 years ago Congress extended American citizenship to Puerto Ricans. It is regrettable that today hundreds of thousands of Puerto Ricans have little and often virtually no knowledge of the English language. . . . It is an indispensable part of the American policy that the coming generation of American citizens in Puerto Rico grow up with complete facility in the English tongue. It is the language of our nation. . . . Clearly there is no desire or purpose to diminish the enjoyment or the usefulness of the rich Spanish cultural legacy. . . . What is necessary, however, is that the American citizens of Puerto Rico should profit from their unique geographical situation . . . by becoming bilingual. But bilingualism will be achieved . . . only if the teaching of English . . . is entered into at once with vigor, purposefulness, and devotion, and with the understanding that English is the official language of our country. (cited in Osuna 1949:376-77)[15]

Gallardo attempted to implement Roosevelt's policy under the harsh criticism of both educators and politicians. But, by 1941, he realized the "vigor, purposefulness, and devotion" were just not there and subsequently restricted English instruction to secondary schools. The University followed with a categorical requirement that all lectures be given in Spanish (Rodríguez Pacheco 1976). Gallardo's realization of the pedagogical implications of English only instruction was not shared by his colonial superiors who publicly reprimanded him for not having followed the President's instructions (Epstein 1970). Secretary of the Interior Harold Ickes wrote to Gallardo in 1943, reminding him that in accepting his appointment as Commissioner of Education, he accepted the moral as well as political obligation to enforce English. As Ickes noted,

> Naturally, American citizens should be able to speak English. Each succeeding generation of the island's residents should have the opportunity of sharing in the cultural, social, and economic progress of the nation as a whole. Puerto Rico is attacking its problems on all fronts; language is not the exclusive factor in question. However, the lack of facilities to learn English, or any policy tending to decrease these facilities, would constitute an obstacle with which I do not believe Puerto Ricans should have to contend. (1970:27)

However, as Ickes and his colonial brethren attempted to mask the political power of language and negate the resistance of the Puerto Rican people, the opposition was again assuming momentum. Under pressure from the Teachers' Association as well as from the general populace, a bill to make Spanish the language of instruction was passed by the Puerto Rican legislature over the veto of the governor in 1946. Then President Truman immediately replied with his own veto, asserting the will of the colonial authority over the explicit will of the people who wished to preserve their cultural heritage and educate their children in the vehicle best able to impart knowledge (Epstein 1970).

In many ways, the issue of language helped clarify the contradictions inherent in the Island's colonial status, uniting the people across class and urban/rural boundaries in their struggle for voice, national identity, and political autonomy. As an article in *El Mundo* in 1946 illuminated, there was an irony in the fact that a so-called "democratic" nation like the United States was unable to tolerate any deviation from established norms—a nation, whose efforts toward Americanization and the imposition of English, whose limited political vision of the power of language and of a people, assumed that the roots of a citizenry could be torn from the ground like that of a weak plant. Rather than to continue to give the citizenry the perception that they had some measure of control over the Island and their lives, the article suggested the United States showed its true face:

> The President's veto places in sad evidence the government of the United States before history and before the rest of civilized peoples. To go along with this veto, Mister President should name a continental North American (even if its a cowboy from the west) to the vacant position of Commissioner of Education of Puerto Rico, and then, immediately after, he should send a shipment of continental North Americans to take the place of the Puerto Rican teachers. Then the picture would be complete. (Muñoz Morales 1946:30, translation mine)

While the United States probably would have liked to follow Muñoz Morales' advice, the political climate would not tolerate such overt actions as those utilized in earlier colonial years. By the late 1940s, the economy was in ruins and unrest on the rise. From the colonizer's perspective, it was time to seek ways to both encourage and promote the investment of private U.S. capital and contain the Island's increasingly militant labor movement. Two key legislative measures—the Industrial Incentives Act, which brought in U.S. investors, and the Taft-Hartley Act, which assured the investors of "industrial peace"—were enacted satisfying both these goals (Rivera 1986).

Steps were taken to increase local autonomy, changing, at least superficially, the political character of the colonial relationship. Puerto Rico was allowed to elect its own governor and name the directors of executive departments, including the secretary of education.[16] In 1948, elections were held and the popular party candidate, Luis Muñoz Marín became the first governor elected by the Puerto Rican people. Shortly thereafter, a constitution was drafted and the "Commonwealth" status established. Ultimate authority over matters affecting the relationship between the United States and Puerto Rico, however, still rested unilaterally in the hands of the U.S. Congress.

THE DISCOURSE OF AUTONOMY AND THE PARTITION OF VOICES

It seemed as if the voice of the people had finally triumphed when, immediately after the election, Muñoz Marín used his authority to abolish mandatory English language instruction. The reinstatement of Spanish instruction, however, had contradictory consequences: on the one hand, promoting a false sense of autonomy and, on the other, giving the people the illusion they had regained their history, subjectivities, and identities.

From the outset, the new Commonwealth government (under the watchful eye of the United States) used Spanish nationalism to promote its own aims. The reinstatement of Spanish instruction coincided with the adoption of Operation Bootstrap, or *Manos a la Obra* as it was known in Puerto Rico, an economic development plan designed to attract U.S. industry to the Island. The populace was led to believe the Island's new autonomy meant Puerto Ricans would now govern Puerto Rico; modernization (i.e., Operation Bootstrap) was viewed as a process of "national" economic development (Campos and Bonilla 1976). The Island's image of one of slums, straw shacks, disease, indolence, and poverty was transformed to that of "a small community resolutely set on an approved course of self-improvement" (Carr 1984:334). But incentives, including government subsidies, corporate tax exemptions and writeoffs, and cheap labor, were highlighted to lure private foreign investment. U.S. companies moved to the Island in great numbers and the insular colonial government welcomed them with open arms.

Industrialization brought profound changes in the economic and social structures of the Island including improvements in health, housing, and education. By the end of the decade, the literacy rate had risen to about 78 percent, and 63 percent of school-aged children were enrolled in school as compared to 50 percent in 1940 (Dietz 1986).[17] But improvements were not without cost. The change from an agrarian-based economy to one of light industry resulted in the creation of even more of a "surplus population" for whom there were no jobs.[18] Close to half a million Puerto Ricans (and nearly half of the working class) were forced to migrate to the United States in the late 1940s and the 1950s (Flores 1988; History Task Force 1979).[19] As the U.S. government had planned, this massive migration, the "escape valve" as it was called, stabilized the colonial economy, helped consolidate and expand the colonial bureaucracy, and helped to attract more U.S. capital. According to metropolitan economists, the impressive economic growth on the Island was attributable to "migration and the low cost, skill, resilience, responsiveness, and general docility of the Puerto Rican worker under popular leadership" (History Task Force 1979:129). The Island was developing an even deeper dependency on the mainland as U.S. corporations took over the economy and their interests began to permeate the social institutions, including schools.

In theory, commonwealth status gave Puerto Rico autonomy in matters of education, shifting direct responsibility from U.S. appointed officials to the colonial bureaucracy. Secretary of Education Candido Oliveras provided the definition of the philosophy of this "autonomy" in the Preamble of the Free Associated State Constitution: "It was to consider U.S. citizenship as a determining factor in our life as a people" (cited in Silen, 1971:95). As Silen goes on to note:

> Along with this went "loyalty to the postulates" of the U.S. Constitution and coexistence of the two great cultures, Puerto Rico and North America. Government employees [including teachers] were required to sign a loyalty oath denouncing their involvement with or support of any internal or external enemy.

With the change in status and the abandonment of forced English instruction, it was now the insular government itself which was promoting a colonized mentality. A return to Spanish had not meant a return to the identities, subjectivities, or relations held before the U.S. invasion. In fact, insular autonomy had only worked to diffuse the collective sense of Puerto Ricaness—dispersing large numbers of the populace to the continent, improving access on the Island to housing, employment, and education (particularly for the middle classes), and allying both the upper and middle classes more closely with the colonizer. Colonial education had moved to a new phase; overt Americanization was transformed into a more subtle process of deculturation that involved the psychological implantation of U.S. values under the guise of capitalist expansion and economic advancement. Negrón de Montilla details the effect of this new system of control in the schools:

> The "careful" selection of reading material . . . the methodology used in the classroom . . . the primary level children's songs . . . the promotion of secondary level student organizations—Civil Air Patrol, Boy Scouts, Camp Fire Girls, Junior Achievement, English Clubs, and the rest of the alienating instruments—all the curricular content has been designed to create in Puerto Ricans a sense of total identification with the metropolis and a desire to integrate into it in order to achieve security and prosperity. (1972:8)

Although Spanish was the language of instruction, the unique history, values, beliefs, and social vision that informs its use among Puerto Ricans was effectively eliminated from the contents of formal schooling. Through the curriculum, discourse practices, school activities, and texts, the United

States's power over developing Puerto Rican minds continued to be circulated. English as a second language remained as a requirement in all grades with U.S. cultural activities and holidays, for example Independence Day, Halloween, Valentine's Day, Lincoln's and Washington's birthdays, Thanksgiving, and Christmas (rather than Three King's Day), an integral part of instruction. While these additions to the curriculum were perceived by authorities as essential to a shaping of "belonging" to the "mainland," it was in the actual organization, presentation, and representation of knowledge that their true efforts were directed. History books about Puerto Rico, for example, did not begin documentation until 1898; Spanish colonialism was wiped out as was the Island's indigenous and African heritage. References to Puerto Rican heroes and patriots were omitted in these texts and only the powerful and affluent American protector and its heroes portrayed. Moreover, "America" was depicted through images of success (including modernization, industrialization, and democratic opportunity), and described as the savior of Puerto Rico. This selective representation of the past has served, in part, to shape students' perceptions and understandings of themselves and their people. Furthermore, the deterministic view of politics, geography, and economics perpetuated by texts (which even in the sixties were still in use) aimed to create, as one Puerto Rican nationalist described, individuals who "think and act in terms of 'permanent union' " (Silen 1971:100). By design, it was intended to render invisible both individual and collective struggle.

This attempted pacification of the student populace by the colonial bureaucracy was not without its moments of resistance. This resistance was no longer directed at the colonizer per se but at the colonizer's agents, their fellow Puerto Ricans. In fact, such reaction was integral to the maintenance of power relations. As Bonilla (1980) notes, part of the success of the colonizer was that it pitted Puerto Ricans against Puerto Ricans.

In the early 1960s, strikes, uprisings, and actions against property were prevalent; with the formation of the *Federación Estudiantes Pro Independencia* (FEPI)—the Student Federation for Independence—in 1964 there was direct confrontation with the police. School authorities and the government responded with suspensions, expulsions and economic threats. Repression also began to take new forms. Under pro statehood Governor Luis Ferre, teachers advocating independence were listed as subversive with many actually dismissed from their jobs. Names of students with independence tendencies were sent to the Selective Service. As a result, both national and class consciousness were awakened; upper class families used their power to keep their children out of the army and working class youth turned toward more violent resistance (Silen 1971).

Under the Commonwealth status, the class divisions among the population were also widened and promoted.[20] Public schools were overwhelmingly composed of students of the working and underemployed classes, many of whom, not coincidently, were of darker complexion. In counter-distinction, private schools took on the task of training a middle-class (primarily white) colonial cadre, creating an indigenous managerial and bureaucratic class who, eventually, could assume positions of authority within the industrial and governmental sectors.[21] The number of private schools, mostly Catholic, greatly expanded in the years 1950–1970. There, English language instruction and American texts most often reigned; enrollment skyrocketed. The middle classes appeared to have moved to a new stage of colonialism—now, they themselves were "voluntarily" seeking Americanization. This search was grounded in a socioeconomic, imperialist reality in which "command of the English language was the essential tool of social mobility in a business world dominated by stateside firms" (Carr 1984:289).

Not all of the middle class accepted the private schools' imposition of English. Candido Oliveras, the secretary of education who had helped draft the Constitution's Preamble ten years before, even threatened to withdraw accreditation from the Catholic schools in 1962, charging that the Puerto Rican Church was systematically depriving Island children of an important aspect of their cultural heritage. Several U.S. congressmen threatened to cut federal support to the public schools—in the form of subsidized lunches—if the secretary went through with his threat (Seda Bonilla 1972). But denial of food was not necessary. Governor Ferre accused Oliveras of using the educational system for his own political ends and of subverting the natural right of parents to decide the content of education for their children (Epstein 1970). Oliveras' voice was silenced as had been his predecesor, José Padín, thirty years before. Private Catholic education was thus preserved with its "English only" assimilationist policy intact. The overt colonialism through English submersion that took fifty years of struggle to end, was now sanctioned by the Puerto Rican government.[22]

As a corporation with significant financial backing, the Church brought teachers and textbooks from the United States and sought the best trained teachers on the Island. The quality of education offered in the state schools was not able to compete with these privately financed educational institutions and, as a result, a dual system of education was once again (as with the rural/urban distinctions of the early 1900s) created. Rafael Cintron Ortiz (1972) describes this duality as the uniting of external and internal forces of domination in order to sustain two societies: separate and unequal that continue to function to this day. Whereby private schools pave the way for university training and economic opportunity, public schools (particularly at the secondary level) have become temporary holding institutions for the poor, surplus population. With less than one half of sixteen- to eighteen-year-olds attending school (Silen 1971) and drop-out rates exceedingly high, the alternatives for young people are the street, drugs, the neighborhood gang, and a tragic existence.[23] The Island's poor are "schooled in a sense of inferiority toward the better schooled," a social illusion which, Cintron Ortiz maintains, results in an "increasing allocation of public funds for the education of the colony's elite and an increasing acceptance of social inferiority by the majority of the population" (1972:106). Anibal Ponce details:

> Not only do the ruling classes cultivate their own . . . but they see to it that the working class accepts educational inequality . . . as something imposed by the nature of things against which it would be madness to rebel. (1961:35)

The fact that English language instruction and quality education continue to go hand in hand on the Island does not mean, however, that the masses aspire to learn English or attend private schools. In reality, resistance to forced linguistic imposition remains strong. Puerto Ricans returning from the United States are criticized and chastised for their lack of fluency in Spanish. And opposition to bilingual education programs that help English speaking students with the transition to Spanish remains fierce. However, while signaling a rejection of forced Americanization by linguistic imposition, this resistance has also problematized the question of national and ethnic identity. The class and cultural struggles and relations of Puerto Ricans residing in the United States are negated, including their resistance to internal colonialism and forced assimilation as well as anti-colonial resistance (Flores, Attinasi, and Pedraza 1981). In fact, English proficiency alone does not ensure cultural integration although schools and governments both on the Island and on the mainland would encourage us to believe so. For them, English has served as an instrument of positioning and control, a way to shape personal and collective consciousness by manipulating subjectivities, identities, and meanings for economic gain.

Through its use of the English language, its imposition of U.S. values, and its emphasis on and maintenance of a dominant/subordinate ideology, schooling in Puerto Rico has contributed to what might be termed a sort of psychological domestication; hindered have been individuals' creativity, self-confidence, and self-determination. From early childhood, students are taught that Puerto Rico is small and the United States is big, that Puerto Rico is poor and the United States rich, and that Puerto Rico is weak and the United States strong. Outside of the United States, Puerto Rico has no history, no heroes or heroines; Puerto Rico has never been able to stand alone. This hegemonic positioning, according to some, has perpetuated a sort of national inferiority complex, a population that is torn between their own cultural roots and histories and those of the colonizer.[24] Others contend that the dynamic at work is much more complex and multilayered and that it must also consider the psychological, sociocultural, and ideological struggles and the acts of resistance, cultural work, and solidarity that have been forged and waged by Puerto Ricans in the United States as well as on the Island.[25]

The study of Puerto Rican reality must clearly maintain as present the significance of a century of colonialism, the push and pull of contradictions, and the tensions that have defined this history. But while years of colonialism have undoubtedly had their toll and modern-day imperialism its consequences, the results can be neither simply explained nor deterministically characterized. Instead, the impact and import of history—both that lived by those in the past and that reconfronted by those in the present—interacts with a polyphony of meanings and experiences that underlie a broader social and cultural formation. It is this interaction that shapes the voices of Puerto Rican students in U.S. schools today and that mediates our understanding of these voices as well as of the various voices heard in this chapter.

My intent in this chapter was to provide a glimpse into the lived cultural, linguistic, and political struggles of Puerto Ricans in Puerto Rico, primarily during the first half of this century. It was to show that, because of the uncomfortable relationship between Puerto Rico and the United States, past and present struggles that occur both on the Island and the continent are neither separate nor simple but are complex and intricately interwoven. My desire was to offer a historical lens through which to view the present, a lens that, as the chapters that follow will demonstrate, requires that we focus not on images (or on superficial words) per se, but on our own perceptions as well as those of others that position the subject or subjects of attention. To begin to understand the current struggles for voice of Puerto Rican students within the pedagogy of U.S. schools and the significance of voice as a conceptual category for analysis, we must be aware of the struggles and experiences of the past and of the ways language, culture, class, and ideology are always dialectically connected. The next chapter is devoted to this concern.

NOTES

1. While we may not maintain as present how history, culture, and language shape our thought and position social relations, there is a whole tradition of literature from John Dewey to Paulo Freire that reminds us this is so.

2. The male pronoun is purposefully utilized here since, historically, colonizers have always been men.

3. As Section 23 of the School Law of 1901 details,

> The Commissioner of Education, being required by act of Congress of April 12, 1900, to supervise education in Puerto Rico, he shall ... appoint ... supervisors or superintendents of schools who shall be subject to the Commissioner in all respects; he shall prepare and promulgate all courses of study; conduct all examinations, prepare and issue all licenses or certificates to

teachers; select and purchase all school books, supplies and equipments . . . approve of all plans for public school buildings to be erected . . . and formulate such rules and regulations that he may from time to time find necessary for the effective administration of his office. (Osuna 1949:140)

These dispositions can still be found in the Annotated Laws of the Island (Torres-Gonzales 1983).

4. Roame Torres-Gonzales (1983) provides a detailed account of education under Spanish rule as well as during the first thirty years of U.S. dominion.

5. See Ramos (1985) for a detailed analysis of the Protestant and the Catholic churches' role in the domination of Puerto Rico.

6. Conditions, particularly in rural areas, continued to be deplorable. According to Osuna (1949), one school in the countryside had 250 pupils assigned to an eighteen-year-old teacher. As a result, attendance on any one day averaged less than 30 percent.

7. At the same time the United States was establishing colonial control through education in Puerto Rico, North American agents were establishing a parallel policy of passification in the Philippines, another Spanish bounty. The economic, political, and linguistic conquest mirrored step by step that of its Caribbean counterpart. It seems the United States had taken on the business of diluting nationalism through the capturing of minds. As in Puerto Rico, schools were built, texts imported, English imposed and enlisted army men initially assigned as teachers. Soon it was necessary to deluge the archipelago with more "solemn patriots":

> The immediate adoption of English in the Philippine schools subjected America to the charge of forcing the language of the conquerors upon a defenseless people. Of course such a system of education as the army contemplated could be sucessful only under the direction of American teachers. . . . Arrangements were promptly made for enlisting a small army of teachers in the U. S. At first they came in companies, but soon in battalions. The transport Thomas was fitted up for their accommodations and in July 1901, it sailed from San Francisco with 600 teachers—a second army of occupation—surely the most remarkable cargo ever carried to an oriental colony. (Charles Burke Elliot cited in Constantino 1982:3)

8. Indeed, while the job of these U.S. teachers was to promote the voice of colonization in the schools, they themselves were also the victims of a different variety of colonial oppression, that which affected them as women. As Michael Apple (1987) documents, the feminization of teaching in the United States in the late 1800s and early 1900s supported the economic interests of the nation: "Class and gender interacted within limits set by economic formations" (1987:60). Until 1850, a majority of elementary teachers were men. However, as it was discovered that women could do the same job for one-half to one-third of the salary, men moved on to better paid positions and early schooling became dominated by women. By 1920, 89 percent of the teaching force in the United States was female.

9. Such has been the contemporary argument for bilingual education programs in the United States. See, for example, Cummins (1981; 1984).

10. Gore's efforts to support U.S. interests were also evident at the University of Puerto Rico, considered a haven of anti-American activity. There his attempt to

appoint a politician to the board met with widespread anger on the part of students, faculty, and alumni. Numerous marches and demonstrations ensued (one to Gore's house with a coffin labeled *cultura* (culture) and a strike followed until Gore's candidate submitted his resignation (Herring 1933).

11. Gore had been forced to retire due to a major student strike at the University where he had also attempted to place his appointee.

12. This included more than $47 million, over half of which went to relief wages and personal services (Mathews 1960).

13. While Albizu Campos was considered the Party's leader, women were also actively involved in the leadership, Lolita Lebron being probably the most well known for her actions against *yanqui* imperialism.

14. The political assassination had repercussions in Washington as well. Legislation was proposed in Congress to grant independence to the Island but with terms of separation that would have destroyed the Island's already weak economic structure. It is clear that this action was to destroy the independence movement since, as a May 2, 1936, *Business Week* article noted, "The best informed sources in this country feel confident that Puerto Rico can't afford to sever its connections with the country under the terms of this proposal." The insular government and the Island bourgeoisie thus opposed the measure and it never left Congress.

15. Roosevelt's words seem to have strong parallels with the current situation in the United States. The present push to do away with transitional bilingual education programs (whose goal is clearly to teach English) in favor of intensive English as a second language instruction closely resembles the policy of "forced bilingualism" in Puerto Rico. The intent of both is forced assimilation and imperialist dominion. While English was not then nor has it ever been the official language of the United States, efforts to make it so have occurred in different periods of history when racism and xenophobia have been particularly evident. The implications of "forced bilingualism" thus extend beyond the mandatory learning of English. There are social, political, and economic incentives as well as psychological and linguistic repercussions that accompany such a policy (whether it be in the first half of this century in Puerto Rico or in the current situation in the United States). These implications are discussed in depth in the following chapters.

16. The establishment of local autonomy on the Island was part of a well-organized colonial plan already implemented several years before in the Philippines. There, through the provisions of the Jones Act, a U.S. groomed Filipino governor-general was appointed. As Renato Constantino points out, a new generation of Filipino-Americans had been produced. "There was no longer any need for American overseers in this field because a captive generation had already come of age, thinking and acting like little Americans" (1982:4). A U.S. appointed vice-governor worked by his side, also serving as the head of education.

17. The literacy rate was calculated on individuals ten years of age and over and included the ability to read and write in either language.

18. From 1920 to 1948, agricultural input declined from 60 percent to 17 percent (U.S. Department of Commerce 1979). By 1976, the contribution of the agricultural sector had been reduced to less than 3 percent (History Task Force 1979).

19. While this was by far the largest migration, Puerto Ricans had been actually living in the United States (primarily in New York City) since before the turn of the

century. For lucid accounts of this early migration see the memoirs of Bernardo Vega (1984), Jesus Colon's *A Puerto Rican in New York* (1961), and Juan Flores, (editor) *Divided Arrival* (1988).

20. The maintenance of class distinctions and the perpetuation of a colonized mentality in Puerto Rican schools has its parallels in the United States. Upper- and middle-class families migrating from the Island frequently enroll their children in Catholic schools or move to the more affluent suburbs. Working class children, on the other hand, are overwhelming located in urban public schools where over-crowded classrooms, lack of materials, untrained teachers, and poor physical condi-tions contribute to a form of internal colonialism. Language also plays a role in this duality. The economically privileged are able to fall back on their English training from the Island while the less privileged are placed in what are perceived by the general public as "compensatory" programs of transitional bilingual education. It is this situation that has contributed, in part, to the class character of bilingual programs.

21. For a discussion on the racial and ethnic contrasts and historical relations to power within Puerto Rico, see González (1980). Flores (1984) offers an interesting critique of this work, pointing out the dialectical interrelation between race and class.

22. Although the U.S. Congress had passed a motion in 1959 designating English as a modern foreign language in Puerto Rico, thus making it possible under the National Defense Education Act to funnel more money into English instruction, both Congress and the insular bureaucracy preferred submersion. The Church's efforts were therefore wholeheartedly supported. In fact, the Church, in many ways, appeared to be speaking in concert with the imperialist authority.

23. There are clear parallels between this situation of Puerto Rican youth on the Island and urban youth living in the United States The dropout rates of Puerto Rican students in the United States, for example, range from 50 to 80 percent.

24. See, for example, René Marqués (1977) and Eduardo Seda Bonilla (1972).

25. See, for example, Flores, Attinasi, and Pedraza (1981), and *Centro de Estu-dios Puertorriqueños* (1988).

2

The Rudiments of Voice: Toward an Understanding of Dialogic Opposition

S OME OF US have struggled long and hard to have a voice we call our own, to speak with an authority that reveals the self-assured person we presume to be. Yet, in the course of a day, a year, an epoch, there are voices too numerous to count that engage our thoughts, challenge our conceptions, and provoke new and different understandings. There are voices that, when spoken, work to limit, to constrain, to asymmetrically position, and to silence those who listen. There are voices that arouse emotion and there are those that call for response; some hang on unnoticed, while others quickly pass with hither a recollection.

As with language itself, the voices we fashion are never fixed or stable but are in a constant state of shift as a result of our interrelations. Both the degree and substance of this shift, however, has much to do with our place within the social order and to the conflicts and tensions that circumscribe it. Such was made clear in the linguistic, social, economic, and political struggles around U.S. colonialism described in the previous chapter. Consider the collective intentions and competing tensions that were resonated; it is these elements which generate the history of language to communities, living on in the memories of elders, in the sociocultural baggage they pass to their children, and in the current relations, practices, and policies that are engendered by the intersection of voices past and present.

The philosopher Ludwig Wittgenstein (1972) maintained that to know a language is to be able to participate in the forms of life within which it is expressed and which it expresses. This notion of participation is important because it grounds language as an activity that is social both in purpose and in constitution. When people speak they do so not as individuals per se, but as socially and historically inscribed beings whose voices bear, as Morson points out, "the imprint of a collection of values and a distillation of experiences" (1968:5).

Language is more than a mode of communication or a system composed of rules, vocabulary, and meanings; it is an active medium of social practice through which people construct, define, and struggle over meaning in dialogue with and in relation to others. And because language exists within a larger structural context, this practice is, in part, positioned and shaped by the ongoing relations of power that exist between and among individuals. As such, language affects as well as reflects the individual reality of its speakers, and the sociohistorical and ideological environment in which these speakers reside.

Knowing a language may thus permit one to participate in communicative expression, but, as was illustrated in Chapter 1, knowing a language does not ensure full or equal participation in the social setting. Bakhtin explains:

> Language is not a neutral medium that passes freely and easily into the private property of the speaker's intentions; it is populated—overpopulated—with the intentions of others. Expropriating it, forcing it to submit to one's own intentions and accents is a difficult and complicated process. (1981:249)

Chapter 1 illuminated the non-neutrality of language and the ways in which language can serve as a battleground for different epistemological and ideological interests. In the antagonisms and oppositions presented through and within language in Puerto Rico, historically specific voices can be seen to emerge, shift, and clash. Embedded in these competing voices are differentially lived and understood experiences and meanings; experiences and meanings which, in part, were produced, mediated, and legitimated by and through the relations, discourses, and practices of domination and subordination. While language served as a site of struggles, conflicts were not merely over language per se, but over a much larger goal, that of cultural and political hegemony.

The concept of hegemony is key to understanding the rudiments of voice and the struggles (linguistic and otherwise) from which voices are somehow able to surface. Its theoretical and conceptual underpinnings derive principally from the work of the Italian Communist Antonio Gramsci. Gramsci defined hegemony as the power of one class "to articulate the interest of other social groups to its own" (Mouffe 1979:183). This power was thought of not just in terms of brute force, but also in terms of the ideological control dominant groups use to subordinate other groups. Put differently, Gramsci believed that the domination of one class over another in advanced capitalistic societies is exercised by popular "consensus" as well as through physical coercion. He understood the state as not merely imposing domination but transforming beliefs, values, cultural traditions, and social practices in order to mask the "real" and to perpetuate the existing order (Gramsci 1971; Boggs 1976). In this sense, hegemony occurs not just in the political domain but also in complex ways in other domains. As Stuart Hall (1985) points out, these domains are outside of the direct sphere of the state itself but are nevertheless articulated by it. Such domains might include familial relations, civil society, the Church, schools, gender, race, and economic relations, as well as relations in and around language. Hegemony can thus be conceived as representative of a complex reproductive process by which people come to assume that certain ideas, practices, and discursive positions are natural, permanent, and universal (Hall 1985; Giroux 1980). Yet, as Hall asserts, how this reproduction actually occurs is not easily explained or documented nor is it readily observable. Raymond Williams maintains that hegemony acts as a sort of culture because it constitutes reality for most people in a society, "a culture which has also to be seen as the lived dominance and subordination of particular classes" (1977: 110). It is a culture that permeates subjective as well as collective consciousness and shapes and positions the discourses and systems of meaning that inform and construct them.

In the case of Puerto Rico, hegemony took on different forms at various moments in history and for divergent groups of individuals. While colonialism served as the overriding political project, colonialism as such did not always direct practices, discourses, relationships, or even institutions. What did direct them were the wider cultural and ideological categories of the society that were informed by and representative of ongoing colonial and power relations. Furthermore, as the struggles, tensions, and the polyphony of voices that emerged from this lived reality illustrated, the implementation and existence of hegemony is neither passive, static, or deterministic. It is continually renewed and recreated, defended and modified, resisted and challenged. Thus while the presence of hegemony in Puerto Rico has remained constant from the U.S. invasion of the Island to today, this dominance is not exclusive; from it has surfaced a counter-hegemony, evident in those antagonistic voices of worker, teacher, and student, among others, that have sounded in opposition.

Hegemony/counter-hegemony arises because of human agency—because people are capable of action. And it is in this process of acting in and on their environment that people's voices are fashioned. But while voice is tied to subjectivity and identity, its ongoing shaping and formulation are part of a broader social and cultural formation. As such, voice is not an expression of individual consciousness but a reflection of and a coming to terms with the multiple and complex social relations and realities that inform consciousness and position the individual with respect to an "other." It is in this positioning that the tensions in both voice and hegemony are frequently realized. Manifestation is at two levels: (1) at the direct level of conflict where opposing interests are in contradiction, and (2) at the more intimate level of consciousness where individuals struggle with the competing tensions and dualities of meanings that arise from their own individual and group conditions.[1]

The oppositions that can arise in voice (and that are posed by hegemony) are not oppositions in the traditional sense of antitheses or static dualisms. Rather, they suggest possibility. Because the voices are those of real, dynamic people who act and reflect on their situations and realities and, as a result, constantly create new meaning, the oppositions themselves are in constant flux (as are the voices), shifting as individuals regroup and as alliances are shed and formed.[2] Viewed in this way, opposition thus suggests a kind of dialogic action in that the opposing tendencies (e.g., voices, meanings, classes) are in dynamic strain. Embedded in this interaction are relations of resistance and of struggle that are grounded in the hope of victory; if this did not exist, the more subordinate group would just give up its opposition.

The concept of opposition has been utilized by theorists in such diverse fields as economics, sociology, women's studies, education, psychology, and philosophy. It has informed the dialectical method of Marx, the cultural pedagogy of Freire, the hegemony theories of Gramsci as well as recent resistance perspectives and poststructuralist analyses. All contribute to a more complex understanding of the relationships any opposition articulates and the possibilities opposition can envision.

Use of the notion of opposition has also been prevalent in the study of language. However, it has often taken a problematic and non-dialogic form. Bakhtin is one of the few who speaks of the dynamic tension of language—that we own language but it is not ours—which suggests a dialogic relation between individual and society. Numerous linguists and language theorists argue, on the other hand, that the conventions of language (i.e., the social component) and speech (i.e., the individual element) are dualistic; in other words, that they constitute a traditional opposition.

The dichotomy of traditional versus dialogic opposition derives from a wider debate on structure and agency (for example, see Giddens 1979). Its essence centers on divergent views of human agency, that is of action. Simply described, dialogic oppositions are dynamic in the sense that they are ongoing and continuous, are recognized as socially, historically, and temporally situated, and can be impacted by people's actions. As such, dialogic oppositions help assert visions of what is possible. In contrast, traditional oppositions sever people from their capacity to act. They are posed as essential, static, inevitable, and outside human control. Traditional oppositions negate the possibility of voice; dialogic oppositions enable voice and allow it to be spoken.

Mainstream theories of language have often assumed a stance that negates human agency and supports a dualist understanding. Reflected in these theories is not only an explanation of the system of language, but a particular view of people. For example, when language is conceptualized as an imitative function, as the utilization of systematic conventions passed genetically from one generation to another (as Bloomfield and Chomsky suggest), humanity is thought of as essentially passive, as unable to act on and shape the experiences, both linguistic and otherwise, that comprise people's daily lives. Similarly, by describing language as the expression of individuals (as does the structuralist school), one assumes an anti-dialogic stance, suggesting that both language and activity are the product of individuals and not generated through the dynamic interactions that emerge from within social groups.

In counterdistinction, views that emphasize the social and historical character of language (as do Gramsci, Freire, and Bakhtin) illuminate rather than negate the dialectical connection between language and a people's existence. This dialectical connection is highlighted by Giddens (1979:4) when he describes language as "intrinsically involved with that which has to be done: the constitution of language as 'meaningful' is inseparable from the constitution of forms of social life as continuing practices." In these authors' works, individuals are seen as actively creating the society in which their discourse occurs.

Every theory of language suggests a view of social practice. That is, in seeking to explain a particular conception of language, theorists (knowingly or not) shape practice as well as understanding. The evidence of this influence is most apparent in public schools. There, the use of language, the discourses, meanings (and voices) that are supported and given significance, the instructional approaches, and the linguistic attitudes all give credence to specific views of language (and hence people) and of language's relation in the wider social sphere.

The purpose of this chapter is to present the multiple oppositions, static and dynamic, divisive and dialogic as they are perceived and experienced in the study of language, in the ways language and languages have been both thought about and discussed, and in the language-related practices and policies that schools proffer. The dualisms of individual and society, of class as it relates to language, and of bilingualism in the United States are examined. It is by analyzing the contradictions and possibilities posed by each of these oppositions that we can begin to unearth the rudiments of voice for Puerto Rican students, and better explain the significance of its tension within the educational setting.

THE DIALECTICS OF THE INDIVIDUAL AND SOCIETY

> The individual is related to a language as "his [sic] own" only as a natural member of a human community. Language as the product of an individual is nonsense. . . . Language itself is just as much the product of a community, as in another aspect, the existence of the community—it is, as it were, the communal speaking for itself. (Marx 1971:390)

As Marx's words illustrate, language is a sociocultural, collective phenomenon. It lives in the history of the relations among groups and in the words, meanings, and modes of thinking that are negotiated between adult and child and which are acted upon and recreated with each successive generation.

It is through family and community socialization that children first construct perceptions and conceptions of the world, of themselves, and of themselves in relation to those around them. This construction is ongoing, interactive, and historical, shaped by the lived experiences and social relations and influenced by past perceptions, relations, and interactions both at the level of the individual as well as that of her/his community. Thus while the child develops a personal viewpoint that is reflected in thought and in the use of and meanings behind language, this perspective exists only because of the social environment within which it is constructed and given significance. The development of these viewpoints and meanings occurs throughout life, shifting and adjusting to the subjective circumstances and social conditions. What this suggests is that the way we come to know language is directly related to how we come to know reality and to the conditions of this knowing. This relation can be understood as a dialectical interplay between sociality and subjectivity, language and consciousness, and the individual and these institutions and relations.

In his work on the social construction of reality, Peter Berger (1967) describes the relation between the individual and society in terms of people's ability to act and to be acted upon. He identifies three simultaneous moments that constitute this relation as it occurs in consciousness. The first, "externalization," refers to individuals' activity in structuring society. The second moment is "objectivation," concerning society's coercive power and capacity to direct behavior and impose sanctions. The third moment is "internalization": by internalizing the objectivated world such that "the structures of this world come to determine the subjective structures of consciousness itself" (Berger 1967:15), the individual not only comes to understand the sociocultural world but comes to identify with and be socialized by it (Wuthnow et al. 1984). As Berger (1967:4) explains,

> It is through externalization that society is a human product. It is through

objectivation that society becomes a reality sui generis. It is through internalization that man [*sic*] is a product of society.

Berger's identification of the moments of externalization, objectivation, and internalization is helpful in that it both underscores the dialectical relation between the individual and society and details, albeit in simplistic terms, the elements that position this relation. It also provides a framework through which one can come to recognize the dialogic opposition that could be posited by this relation. Emerging from these moments and shaped by these oppositions is voice—the speaking of consciousness and the speaking to reality.

As with language, voice cannot be considered an individual phenomenon but must be seen as the product and process of society, identity, and reality. This perspective, however, goes counter to much of the theoretical literature in linguistics that espouses a clear subjective/objective separation.[3] In this literature, the individual is divorced from social reality; the society and the person are in traditional opposition. In order to unearth the full significance a dialogic opposition suggests, it is important to analyze its adverse—traditional opposition—and to examine in more detail both the ways language has been thought about and portrayed, and to reveal how this perspective both negates the possibility of voice and works to limit collective action.

Traditional Oppositions: Their Substance and Contradictions

The study of language has been of interest to social scientists for generations. Approaches to this study, however, have varied as have their influence on practice. Anthropologists and sociologists interested in linguistics have mostly assumed a subjectivist position, investigating the individual, creative act of speech and its function in human activities and in the organization of social behavior. This position is called subjectivist because it focuses on the individual as an acting subject; language is viewed as the activity of this subject for, as Edwards (1976:3) notes, "It can be patterned in ways which reveal or define who the speakers are, what their relationship is, and how they perceive the situation in which they speak." The theoretical emphasis is thus on language use as distinct from language structure.[4]

For a majority of social scientists within the subjectivist school, the study of language has been perceived as part of the study of the general science of culture. People's historical and immediate sociocultural circumstances are thought to affect speech; individual, cultural, social and, as a result, linguistic differences are thus the major focus of study. Among other areas, research has shaped educational practice, language, and social policies in and out of schools, legislation, as well as practices of public welfare.

The opposing position reflected in the study of language is that of the objectivist school. Here language is conceived of as an abstract, normative system, independent of individual intention. Antecedents can be traced back to the seventeenth and eighteeneeth centuries to Cartesian rationalism and to Leibniz's conception of a universal grammar (Bakhtin 1973). In this century, the objectivist tendency can be identified in the work of Leonard Bloomfield (1926; 1933), who advocated investigation into the mechanics of language, formulating the field that is now known as formal linguistics. For Bloomfield, culture and experience were thought to be minor. Language was conceived of as a scientific system, as an abstract objective, grammatical form extracted from history and from day-to-day use. It is in this divorce of human agency from language that a traditional opposition is formed; its realization is most visible in the work of Bloomfield's contemporary, Noam Chomsky, who divides language into competence and performance.

The distinction of competence, the tacit understanding of the rule system of language equally possessed by all, and performance, the use of this rule system in social communication, severs the objective and subjective, separating people from their modes of thinking and expression. In maintaining that the competence that underlies performance is, for the most part, "independent of intelligence and the wide variations in individual experience" (1972:64), Chomsky both suggests that a person's sociocultural reality has little or no impact on language and that a person's actions have little or no effect on changing his/her (linguistic) reality. In other words, the individual as subject is divorced from the objective ready-made, fixed system of language which she/he somehow acquired. The roots of this dualism lie within another widely recognized and accepted opposition, that put forth by the philosopher, Ferdinand de Saussure.

Saussure envisaged linguistics as part of a larger discipline that he called semiology: "the science of the life of signs within society." It was within this study of language as a system of signs that Saussure distinguished language (*langue*) from speech (*parole*):

> But what is language? It is not to be confused with human speech, of which it is only a definite part, though certainly an essential one. It is both a social product of the faculty of speech and a collection of necessary conventions that have been adopted by a social body to permit individuals to exercise that faculty. Taken as a whole, speech is many-sided and heterogeneous; straddling several areas simultaneously—physical, physiological, and psychological—it belongs both to the individual and to society.... Language, on the contrary, is a self-contained whole and a principle of classification (1959:9)

At first glance, Saussure's *langue/parole* (as well as Chomsky's competence/performance) distinction may appear to promote a synthesis of the objectivist and subjectivist schools since both include a systematic and an individual component. However, upon further examination it becomes clear that this duality is an objective one; the subjectivist school differs from Saussure in two important ways. First, the subjectivist school equates language and speech, conceptualizing language as the creative ability of individuals. Second, it situates language within a social and cultural milieu. Studies examine the ways this milieu has impacted individual speech. In contrast, Saussure's dichotomy of *langue/parole* isolates the individual from society. The individual act of communicating a message is perceived as distinct from the social, collective institution of language from which the code derives (Emerson 1986).

The separation of the conventions of language from the exercising of these conventions in a message has also had the effect of formally dividing the field of linguistics into objective, synchronic versus subjective, diachronic analyses. *Langue* thus became the more formal study of linguistics as an independent, autonomous system (the precursor of Chomsky and of generative grammar) while *parole* assumed the secondary position of a sort of sociolinguistics, an investigation into the social context in which individual speech develops.[5]

While the objective/subjective distinction has served to advance both the study of syntax, phonology, and morphology as well as the study of speech utterances, it has in many ways camouflaged the dynamic relation between the "system" of language and its verbal and social production. Although Saussure maintained that language is in and of itself a social phenomenon, he in fact negated its public character by severing the social from the individual, denying its historical antecedents and opposing its collective productive connections.

> In separating language from speaking we are at the same time separating: (1) what is social from what is individual; and (2) what is essential from what is accessory and more or less accidental. Language is not a function of the speaker; it is a product that is passively assimilated by the individual. It never requires premeditation, and reflection enters in only for the purpose of classification. . . . Speaking, on the contrary, is an individual act. It is willful and intellectual. (Saussure 1959:14)

While Saussure's counterposing of the social from the individual and the public from the private have been widely accepted, it is not without critique. One of the most articulated of these is that of Volosinov[6] (Bakhtin) who, as early as the 1920s, exposed the oppositional contradictions:

> Signs can only arise on interindividual territory. It is territory that cannot be called "natural" in the direct sense of the word: signs do not arise between any two members of the species Homo Sapiens. It is essential that the two individuals be organized socially, that they compose a group (a social unit);

> only then can the medium of signs take shape between them. (As cited in Sinha
> 1977:87)

Bakhtin's conception of language enables a dialogic opposition, unaccounted in the work of Saussure. For Bakhtin, language is not a passively assimilated product but a dynamic reflective process that emerges from the sociohistorical setting and from within social exchange. Whereas Saussure perceives the tension between the social and the individual, Bakhtin assumes the individual is constituted by the social—that it is individuals who actively create the society in which their discourse occurs (Emerson 1986). The distinctions between *langue* and *parole* are thus considered by Bakhtin to be illusory since they negate the inherently social reality of language as communication, as a dialogue between self and society mediated through inner consciousness.

Similarly, Bakhtin rejected the distinction of synchrony and diachrony promoted by Saussure and rooted in both Cartesian rationalism and Leibniz's conception of a universal grammar. As he stated in *Marxist Philosophy of Language*, "Formal, systematic thought about language is incompatible with living, historical understanding of language. From the system's point of view, history always seems merely a series of accidental transgressions" (Volosinov 1973:78).

In her discussion of Bakhtin's work, Susan Stewart (1986) points out how such systematization leads not only to a denial of history but also results in conceptions of speech as a series of "accidental transgressions" such as that put forth in Chomsky's dichotomy of competence and performance. She quotes Chomsky to illustrate this point:

> Any interesting generative grammar will be dealing, for the most part, with
> mental processes that are far beyond the level of actual or even potential
> consciousness; furthermore, it is quite apparent that a speaker's reports and
> viewpoints about his behavior and competence may be in error." (1965:8)

Yet, as Bakhtin contends, seldom do speakers apply the criterion of correctness to their utterances; when this does occur it is usually in a contrived situation, such as language instruction.

Stewart emphasizes the practical consequences of this dualism and how it serves to limit collective action. In this regard, she is worth quoting at length:

> In such domains as the exclusion of bi- (and multi-) lingual education,
> language requirements attached to immigration restrictions, tensions between
> nonstandard and standard "dialects" (these terms themselves the necessary
> frictions by which a transcendent "standard" is created), and the language of
> state apparatuses in general, the Cartesian position functions to reinforce state
> institutions and to trivialize change and everyday linguistic creativity. To

silence the diversity of the powerful "unsaids" of actual speech in favor of an opaque and universal form of language is to strip language of its ideological sign—a stripping that is itself strongly and univocally ideological. (1986:44)

Gramsci's emphasis on the historicity of language bears interesting parallels to the work of Bakhtin. Influenced by the Durkheimian and Sausserian perspectives of the time, Gramsci also perceived language as a social collective phenomenon. However, his interest was in neither the subjective analysis of language's social character nor in its objective, phonetic, morphological or syntactic development. Rather, Gramsci's concern was with the cultural content and history of language from the standpoint of politics and ideologies. He saw language's potential as a force for hegemony and as a tool for transformation. Within this perspective, Gramsci argued that language assists in the development of social unity "through the welding together of a multiplicity of dispersed wills in a common conception of the world" (Salamini, 1981:34). He gave credence (along with Bakhtin) to the dialectical character of language and the relation it posits between the collective and the individual:

> It seems that one can say that "language" is essentially a collective term which does not presuppose any single thing existing in time and space. . . . At the limit it could be said that every speaking being has a personal language of his [sic] own, that is his [sic] own particular way of thinking and feeling. Culture, at its various levels, unifies in a series of strata, to the extent that they come into contact with each other, a greater or lesser number of individuals who understand each other's mode of expression in differing degrees. (Gramsci 1971:349)

As Gramsci explicates, the relation between the social and the individual is neither purely arbitrary nor traditionally oppositional. Instead, the relation is dialectical and dialogic: individual consciousness evolves from language while, at the same time, language evolves through the actions and deliberations of individuals brought together out of common interest. Voice is fashioned from this process—from the individual consciousness acquired through language in social practice and from what Caryl Emerson (1986) refers to as the selective appropriation of the voices of others. Involved are the processes of externalization, objectivation, and internalization to which Berger (1967) referred.

At the level of consciousness there is an internalization of one's sociocultural world, a personalizing or subjectivizing of language that occurs as a sort of subconscious dialogue between the individual and her/his community. But, since it is the people themselves who form the cultural community, one's inner linguistic consciousness (the product of internalization) is socially rather than individually determined. Culture provides a framework through which individuals are socialized into the language forms and meanings of the community; thus, in a sense, culture obliges us to see the world in specific ways. However, because the sociocultural group exists within a social structure composed of dominant/subordinate relations, society objectifies the social/individual interaction by creating and legitimating new oppositions that are primarily economic in nature. Thus, while culture may act as a unifying force in bringing people together (giving language its social or public character), culture does not dispel or conceal the hegemony of particular groups or classes. Examples of the tensions hegemony brings to culture were evident in Chapter 1. There, we could observe how U.S. colonial authorities, through the social practices of schooling, Operation Bootstrap, and other economic policies, set out to establish a national bourgeoisie that could assume and implement colonial policy. In a relatively short period of time this emergent Puerto Rican bourgeoisie became a dominant (hegemonic) force on the Island. Although they too were Puerto Rican and spoke the Spanish language, their alliances were more often with the U.S. colonizer than with Puerto Rican workers.

Tensions between hegemony and culture can also be witnessed daily in public schools in the United States where bilingual programs mainly serve children of the working (and under-employed) classes. Upper- and middle-class Puerto Rican (as well as other mid to upper class language minority) parents tend to opt for all English "mainstream" schooling even when their children speak little or no English. The rationalization behind this choice is clearly based on economics; the more privileged classes frequently assume that assimilation rather than remediated segregation, as bilingual education is too often viewed, will afford their children the same opportunities (economic and otherwise) in the United States as Anglos, opportunities to which these classes would have been privy to in their native land. Many times it is these same parents who denounce bilingual education for all language minorities, demonstrating their lack of understanding of the goals and purposes of bilingual education and of working class parents' struggles and demands for bilingual education legislation and programs.

Hegemony thus presents an opposition in language that is socioeconomic in nature. This opposition does not solely signify a struggle between antagonistic classes but rather suggests a broader positioning of "collective wills" that are composed of an ensemble of social groups fused around a particular class formation (Mouffe 1979). The opposition is thus tied to the appropriation and control over the means of communication that certain groups or classes of individuals exercise over other groups or classes and implies a clashing force that arises from the dialectical connection of the individual and society. In contrast to the traditional oppositions presented, class offers the possibility of struggle and of (antagonistic) exchange. This is the struggle that could be seen in Puerto Rican worker, student, and teacher strikes and in the masses' resistance to English language assimilation. It is also the struggle that can be witnessed in U.S. schools over Puerto Rican and other language minority parents' and children's rights to bilingual education.

In the pages that follow, I elaborate on the tensions of class and on the impact these tensions can have in the formulation of voices. Recognition of the oppositional presence of class is particularly important because it enables linguistic struggles to be seen as social struggles as well. Furthermore, it helps to make clear the interaction between consciousness and lived conditions and to demonstrate how voice thrives on the dynamic tensions of language and everyday existence and on the opposition hegemony presents. It is to a discussion of this opposition that we now turn.

CULTURAL HEGEMONY AND THE OPPOSITIONAL FORCE OF CLASS STRUGGLE

Language represents and constructs the personal and the social reality of its speakers, but it also reflects, refracts, and positions another reality outside of itself—the reality of the overall power structure in which it exists. While language unites individuals in a speaking, sociocultural community, language does not diffuse the tensions that may exist between people nor does it equalize the interests of particular classes. It is rather in and through language that we see an intersecting of these variously oriented interests. In language we see the expression of class struggle.

The realization of language-based class struggles can take various forms, some more overt than others. In Chapter 1, for example, we saw how the colonizer (i.e., the ruling class) used the foreign medium of English as a way to dominate and control the Puerto Rican populace. The imposition of English is usually depicted as a battle between two languages (two peoples and two interests). However, at stake is not just the replacement of one language by another, but the taking over of both the public and personal functions of language, that is, the means of communication and the consciousness behind this communication, including self-concepts, identities, and voices. Language serves as an instrument of the ruling class in that language is the site for the internalization of a colonized (English) mentality that acted externally to domesticate the people and thus objectivate a new (colonial) reality. It is in this opposition that we observed the ruling class efforts at hegemony and the oppositional struggle of the subordinate classes.

For a time, the Puerto Rican people remained fairly united against their oppressor with the middle and working classes joining force (as subordinates) in opposition to the ruling class's language policies. However, as the middle class saw the possibility of their own economic advancement (especially with Operation Bootstrap), they became more ideologically aligned with the colonizers, still speaking Spanish but a Spanish permeated with different interests. New oppositions were formed: that between the bourgeois bilinguals who saw the economic and political benefits of maintaining two languages and the Spanish nationalists who viewed any English as foreign imposition; and that of the bourgeoisie, the middle, and working classes, who, while all speaking Spanish, had meanings derived from experiences situated within differential socioeconomic realities.[7]

As Gramsci has illustrated, struggles in the arena of language arise, in part, as a consequence of the hegemony of one class over another, over the power of the dominant class to influence language and the modes of communication. Hegemony was evident in the linguistic class-based oppositions posed by colonialism in Puerto Rico, specifically in the control over language exhibited by the United States and the assumption of this control by the Puerto Rican bourgeoisie who, while opposing the overt U.S. policy of English Only, came to command the colonizer's values and to administer these values in a top-down fashion through their control over institutions like the Church and schools.[8] It was by maintaining this dominion (this anti-dialogic stance) that the bourgeoisie and colonizers assumed they could limit collective action. As Freire notes:

> In order to dominate, the dominator has no choice but to deny the praxis to the people, deny them the right to say their own word and think their own thoughts. He cannot act dialogically; for him to do so would mean either that he had relinquished his power to dominate and joined the cause of the oppressed, or that he had lost that power through miscalculation. (1970:121)

In the realm of language, the power of the dominant class is made evident through the language variety that is given status (e.g., English in the case of Puerto Rico, standard English in the case of the United States) and in the meanings, values, and referents embedded in the linguistic practices and forms. But while this linguistic hegemony has served to oppress the voices of subordinate groups, it has not succeeded in destroying linguistic opposition or silencing antagonistic voices.

At the practical level, it is in the direct confrontation between languages or language varieties that hegemony is most easily understood. Conflicts within one and the same language are less easily described and comprehended for there is little superficial evidence to demonstrate how language actually asserts the interests of a given class. These oppositions can begin to be deciphered through a discussion of the ideological sign.

Bakhtin (Volosinov) maintains that it is in the ideological sign, "the construct between socially organized persons in the process of their interaction" (1973:21), that different class-oriented interests or "accents" come together. That is, while individuals share a sign community (i.e., a language), their class position within that community makes for a differential existence, an existence that is reflected and internalized in the sign—in the meanings and perspectives shaped by experience and mirrored in words. Each class thus has a characteristic way of speaking which reflects similar values and a sense of shared experiences, past and present. However, because language is formed within various sociocultural and ideological contexts, such as the family, community, or the school, the sign is never totally limited to the confines of a particular class. It is rather grounded in what Giroux (1983) has termed a selective affinity to class-specific experiences. In other words, language is impacted by the relations and practices of dominance and domination that take place in the social milieu in which one resides and participates. The force of this impact is particularly evident in schools. Children enter school after having had five to six years of class-oriented experiences that generated a system of values and meanings—of signs. But as both cultural reproductionists (e.g., Bourdieu and Bernstein) and resistance theorists (e.g., Giroux and Apple) have shown, schools, through both overt and subtle mechanisms, tend to legitimate the values and meanings of only the dominant classes. Giroux explains:

> What gets produced and valorized in schools, though not without resistance and struggle, are the values, styles, taste, and culture of the favored classes. Similarly, through the legitimation of certain language practices, the school functions, in part, to both produce and repress cultural identities via the hidden referents of class, gender, and ethnicity embodied in the school curriculum and classroom social relations. (1983:214)

General agreements about meaning allow individuals who speak the same language to communicate across class boundaries. This is not to say that communication presupposes common material conditions but rather that it requires a kind of translation or negotiation of values between speakers (Emerson 1986). Language thus permits interrelation. But, there is also the more subtle, subjective experience of individuals within their social environments that, in contrast to the more objective communication above, linguistically unites a class and determines its orientation of interest or accent. It is because of this intersecting of interests (the "multiaccentuality" of the sign) that the sign (as language in general) is dynamic and capable of change and further development. It is the sign's vitality and mutability that also makes possible its use as a refracting and distorting medium and as a tool of the dominant class in its struggle for power. Bakhtin (Volosinov) explicates:

> The ruling class strives to impart a supraclass, eternal character to the ideological sign, to extinguish or drive inward the struggle between social value judgements which occurs in it, to make the sign uniaccentual. In actual fact, each living ideological sign has two faces.... This "inner dialectical quality" of the sign comes out fully in the open only in times of crises or revolutionary changes. In the ordinary conditions of life, the contradiction

embedded in every ideological sign cannot fully emerge because the ideological sign in an established dominant ideology is always somewhat reactionary and tries, as it were, to stabilize the preceding factor in the dialectical flux of the social generative process, so accentuating yesterday's truth as to make it appear today's. (1973:23-24)

It is in the sign that class struggle can be seen to emerge. Evident in this emergence is a two-tiered opposition: the opposition present in multiaccentuality and the opposition that evolves in the consciousness of the individuals who make up the classes and in the signs and meanings that express this consciousness.

In the former, opposing dispositions are generated through lived social experiences and promulgated by divergent class interests which, in the medium of the sign, come together for the purposes of communication. Although cultural (linguistic) commonality permits the intersecting of accents, the oppositions presented by each of the accents are not permitted equal access. Due to the hegemony of one class over another, it is the dominant power whose collective interests and meanings are validated and given expression in society (as well as in history) and perpetuated through its societal institutions like schools. In Puerto Rico, for instance, we saw how the beliefs and values of the colonizer were embodied in the actions and language of the national bourgeoisie. Similarly, dominant meaning was imparted in schools; instruction in Spanish of U.S. rather than Puerto Rican history negated students' own past as well as the experience and meanings of previous generations.

Because of the dialogic character of the opposition, in the multiaccentuality of the sign there is hope. The dominated class struggles against hegemony, fighting to maintain its own meanings and interests. The oppositional response to the attempted exclusion of its own accent by the dominant group solidifies this accent and enhances linguistic (and cultural) affirmation and solidarity by and through the construction of antagonistic voices (Walsh 1987b). Most teachers in urban schools have witnessed this kind of solidarity among both African American students and Latinos. Michele Sola and Adrian Bennett's ethnographic study of teacher and student discourse in an East Harlem junior high school affords a clear example of this dynamic.[9] There they found teachers had differential success in teaching Puerto Rican students and that this success was often based on the teacher's ability to accommodate the "school official discourse with the peer-community way with words" (Sola and Bennett 1985:107). Puerto Rican students had developed styles of communicating and relating that distinguished them as a unified group. Although these students could communicate with their non-group peers and with teachers, they often utilized their own discourse strategies to emphasize resistance to the dominant modes and solidarity as group members.

Spoken language reflects an inner sign system of meanings and dispositions that are acquired through activity with other human beings. The internalization of this activity comprises what can be referred to as inner consciousness. While inner consciousness evolves primarily through relations in one's surrounding world, it is also effected by the wider forces of hegemony. Inner consciousness thus suggests ongoing tension, for it is there that the contradictory meanings and interests promoted by the dominant class are internalized, struggled with, adopted, re-worked, and/or rejected. In Sola and Bennett's research, for example, the students' communicative styles and intentions resisted the prevailing hegemony; although the dominant force of schooling certainly touched their lives, the students were able to use language to counteract some of its debilitating expression.

Bakhtin (Volosinov) maintains that inner consciousness "can only be understood and interpreted as a sign" (1973:26). That it is specifically in the sign and more generally through voice that inner consciousness—the compilation of subjective experience—finds its articulated expression. According to Bakhtin, inner consciousness retains the same dynamism and dialectical character as do signs; internalization or rejection of meanings is therefore never absolute, thus rendering struggle possible. Evidence for this dynamic tension can be seen in an example from a study I conducted several years ago (Walsh 1984), discussed in further detail in the following chapter. Puerto Rican children were asked to respond to culturally salient words by defining them for me. In describing what the words Puerto Rican mean, a ten-year-old girl named Maria responded as follows:

> Puerto Ricans are sad, Puerto Ricans are dirty, Puerto Ricans are lazy, Puerto Ricans *hace lo que da la gana* (do whatever they feel like). . . . But I'm Puerto Rican, and I'm not sad, I'm not dirty or lazy, and I work real hard. . . . Maybe all Puerto Ricans aren't like that, right?[10] (1987a:203)

Maria's spoken words illuminate her personal struggle with oppositional meanings of "Puerto Rican." On the one hand, the significance of "Puerto Rican" was shaped by the hegemony of societal institutions such as schools; her initial response suggested an internalization of the discourse to which she had probably been subjected. Yet, as her remarks indicate, subjective experience articulated something different.

Socialization in the family, community, and in the overall environment and its institutions like schools shapes inner consciousness. There is thus not one socialization, but many. Individuals internalize through interpretation what they have been taught and told as well as what they have experienced. It is this internalized reality—this inner consciousness—that is echoed in voice. However, as Maria's comments illustrate, consciousness and, as a result, voice hold contradictory realities that enable change. Such reality alludes to what Gramsci (1971) has referred to as contradictory consciousness. As Gramsci explains, hegemony involves a war of positions, a battle over different interests that can be waged in the material world as well as within the individual. It is on this terrain that people come to acquire a consciousness of themselves, a consciousness where the presence of opposing positions may be characterized by tension and contradiction. Maria's definition of Puerto Rican is a powerful example of the presence of contested realities and the capability of people to recognize and work through them. The socializations she had received were in opposition yet she was somehow able to deconstruct these oppressive images. Evident in her deconstruction is how the dialectical character of inner consciousness allows for an inner reality which shifts with new experiences, developing and opposing itself and revealing its partial, incomplete nature. But, as her words also prove, hegemony remains as a constant affront to and influence on one's own social, cultural, and community group consciousness and its articulated voices.

Cultural hegemony lies at the base of class antagonism. Its force can be felt in the oppositions posed in colonialism past and present as well as within the notion of sign, in the oppositions of dialogic character (in that their existence is defined by interaction and by struggle). What has traditionally been present in a majority of the literature on class and language, however, have not been analyses of the lived experience of class altercation. Rather, prevailing in varied forms have been theories that, although still positing the opposition of dominant/subordinate classes, provide a mostly anti-dialectical, objectified view of what has been termed "social class language difference." It has been these differences that have been used by educators and social policymakers to negate the linguistic-based experiences of the masses, and to suffocate their voices in the public schools. It is to a discussion of these static studies and to their dynamic alternatives that we now turn.

Language and Social Class: Static to Dynamic Perspectives

Subjective, language-based analyses have long been used as an indicator of class difference. In the first several decades of the twentieth century, for instance, intelligence tests established definite discrepancies between the aptitude of white middle-class children and children of poor, mostly immigrant homes (Weinberg 1977). Language differences were thought to be caused by "lower intelligence" and not by the circumstances of class or of non-English language background (U.S. Immigration Commission 1911). Comparative studies in the 1940s and 1950s on the communicative practices and uses of language in middle- and working-class families (e.g., Schatzman and Straus 1955; Milner 1951; and Bossard 1945), also found differences in amount of vocabulary and in development and implementation of language structures; poor families were considered to have "less language" than their middle-class counterparts. The deficit notion promoted in these types of studies served as a backdrop to the "disadvantaged" theories of the 1960s most often associated with Arthur Jensen (1967). Jensen and his followers suggested a genetic difference between the races. Other sociologists and psychologists blamed language "deficits" on the home environments of poor, minority students instead of on differences in intelligence. Reference was frequently made to the "cognitive poverty" of lower-class life (Edwards 1976). In response, federally funded education programs such as Head Start and Follow Through cropped up throughout the nation. The explicit goal of these mini Operation Bootstraps was to raise working-class children's language up to the dominant standard.

Although disadvantaged theories are less popular now than in the 1960s many researchers and educators continue to criticize the speech and language practices of white and minority working-class students. They argue that school success requires the learning of "standard" (i.e., dominant) English and Anglo, middle-class ways of interacting. Attesting to this continued deficit notion are the numerous studies conducted and educational reforms suggested in the last twenty years that link poor school achievement to language. Compensatory preschool programs, transitional bilingual education, and English as a second language instructional programs, as well as the reading remediation efforts funded through the Department of Education's Chapter I entitlement all have been implemented as a response.

Transitional bilingual education is a good example of the contradictions inherent in these approaches. While bilingual education legislation was established as a response to language minority parents' struggle for an understandable and equitable education for their children, it has been used by many school districts as a stepping stone for linguistic and cultural assimilation. Rather than reinforcing students' self-concept and language-based experiences, transitional bilingual programs too frequently "remediate" what some researchers have referred to as "semilingualism"—the lack of strong language skills in any language—acculturating students into English and an Anglo view of the world.[11] These transitional programs promote a subtractive bilingualism that places the students' native language (and sociocultural reality) in the subordinate position. The same theories that have been used to support transitional bilingual education and English as a second language programs have been used against developmental (maintenance or additive) bilingual education and against schools providing continued instruction to students in the form of electives in their native language. More recently, they have been utilized as an argument to do away with all native language support in favor of increased English immersion.

The proponents of the "new" deficit theory superficially view language as the avenue to success for both linguistic and racial minorities as well as for white working-class students. The practical implications of this theory can be seen in the remedial practices implemented through language develop-ment kits (e.g., Distar, Peabody), skill-based reading approaches, English immersion, and even speech therapy, which supposedly "rid" white work-ing-class students and working-class students of color of their bad (linguis-tic) habits.[12] The purpose of these remedial practices is not to equalize language abilities (an impossible task since language is grounded in subjec-tive experiences), nor is it to make working-class children as cognitively "superior" as their dominant-class peers. The purpose is rather to submerse students in the language (and as a result, in the values and culture) of the dominant, "standard," white majority, that is, of those in power. Through top-down instructional approaches, through the overt and hidden curricu-lum, and through the meanings and experiences this curriculum values and supports, schools continue to preserve and sanctify inequality by removing, disconfirming, and rewriting the historical and cultural realities of students from (what the dominant group perceives as) subordinate backgrounds. A static view of social class (and of culture and ethnicity) is perpetuated. The powerlessness of the working classes is emphasized, as is a perception of language as the vehicle to bring the masses out of their misery. Class differences are seen not as accents but as structures in traditional opposi-tion.

While the dominant, disadvantaged/deficit hypotheses have served to reify social class language difference, they have also served to heighten interest among sociologists in the intersection of class, culture, language, and schooling. It was from this context that an oppositional response to deficit theory began to emerge, most notably in the work of social and cultural reproductionists (e.g., Bourdieu 1977; Bourdieu and Passeron 1977; Bernstein 1973).

In contrast to the objectified analyses, cultural reproductionists have concerned themselves with the ways in which culture (and language) act to perpetuate class-based societies and class divisions in schools. These cri-tiques have dramatically challenged those that came before in two major ways. First, cultural reproduction theory underlines the importance of the notion of the relatively autonomous institution of schooling in the reproduction of classes. "By appearing to be an impartial and neutral 'transmitter' of the benefits of a valued culture, schools are able to promote inequality in the name of fairness and objectivity" (Giroux 1983:88). Second, cultural reproduction theory actually delineates how it is that schools legitimate and reproduce the dominant culture, putting into context the reproductive force of previous disadvantaged/deficit paradigms. Pierre Bourdieu, for instance, maintains that by valorizing the language-based experiences, styles of language and thinking, and the referents of the mid-dle-and upper-classes, schools exert power over the meanings and modes of thought (i.e., the cultural capital) of the subordinate class. Consequently, school success is dependent on a familiarity with the dominant culture and with the dominant culture's forms of pedagogic communication. Bourdieu notes:

> By doing away with giving explicitly to everyone what it implicitly demands of everyone, the educational system demands of everyone alike that they have what they do not give. This consists mainly of linguistic and cultural competence and that relationship of familiarity with culture which can only be produced by family upbringing when it transmits the dominant culture. (1977:494)

In Bourdieu's analysis, the divergent cultural capital developed in working-class homes and communities is judged in relation to the cultural capital that is given status in society and in school. As with the deficit perspective, the subordinate class's language is evaluated in reference to the standard of the dominant. However, Bourdieu's position differs from the objectified deficit perspectives in two important ways. First, Bourdieu emphasizes that it is schools, which, in their transmission of dominant ideologies, reproduce the distribution of cultural capital between social classes. Second, Bourdieu sees students as consumers of culture—as participants in their own subjugation. That is, the pedagogical and social practices of schools work to structure students' dispositions; thus, in their effort to survive, students internalize and incorporate the (dominant) valued dispositions as if they were their own. The result of this internalization is often symbolic violence toward one's class or ethnic group—such as was evident in Maria's initial description of Puerto Ricans and in many minority students' rejection of their language, culture, and family.[13] It is these same students who then begin, through their own practices, to produce dispositions that reproduce the same inequalities to which they have been privy.

But while Bourdieu considers schools and the people in them as able to act upon their circumstances, this action is very much a one-way phenomenon. In his view, the dominant class imposes its ideology on the dominated and this ideology is incorporated without struggle or resistance. Maria's ability, for example, to reflect upon and contest dominant dispositions is unaccounted for in Bourdieu's work. Lacking is human agency as well as a discussion of how ideological domination is actually constructed and the connections between domination and people's material conditions. Class again is reduced to a static opposition rather than a hegemonic positioning.

Coming out of the same ideological tradition as Bourdieu is Basil Bernstein, whose work is widely recognized as adding to the understanding of social class language difference. Bernstein maintains that middle- and working-class children have "modes of language" that cause them to relate to persons and objects in distinctly divergent ways.[14]

> Class relations generate, distribute, reproduce, and legitimate, distinctive forms of communication, which transmit dominating and dominated codes; and that subjects are differentially positioned by these codes in the process of their acquisition. (1982:304-305)

The codes, which he labeled "elaborated" and "restricted," were initially conceived of as oppositional in a traditional sense (in his 1958 work, Bernstein actually identified a series of linguistic forms, including vocabulary and syntax, to accompany each of the codes). Restricted codes produced a "culturally-induced backwardness, transmitted and sustained through the effects of linguistic processing" (1961:175) and were thought to be counter to the elaborated code emphasized and supported in schools. Articulated in this distinction was an image of language as objectified, static, and devoid of agency.

In 1973, Bernstein began to retreat from the elaborated/restricted dichotomy, criticizing the one-to-one relationship it suggested between syntax and meaning. What he maintained was that his real interest was the social structuring of meanings and their discursive, contextual, and linguistic realizations. Although he continued to use the terminology of elaborated and restricted codes, in recent work they are described as subjective sets of "planning procedures" or sociolinguistic variants that underlie the choice of speech.

> Language is a set of rules to which all speech codes must comply, but which speech codes are realized is a function of the culture acting through social relationship in specific contexts. Different speech forms or codes symbolize the form of the social relationship, regulate the nature of the speech encounters, and create for the speakers different orders of relevance and relation. The experience of the speakers is then transformed by what is made significant or relevant by the speech form. (1977:476)

A restricted code arises under circumstances where speakers share a common history and have common interests, where there is a background of common experience and definitions of that experience are shared. In a restricted situation, speech is particularistic, context-bound and has little meaning outside of the inner group. An elaborated code, on the other hand, is more objective in that there is a boundary between speaker and listener which can only be crossed by explicit speech (Edwards 1976). Meanings are less context-tied, and more universalistic in nature.

For Bernstein, "the code regulates the 'what' and the 'how' of meanings: what meanings may be legitimately put together and how these meanings may be legitimately realized" (1982:322). The realization of these meanings is contingent upon the power structure at work in society. In other words, social and class relations place limits on the manner and ways in which individuals acquire meaning. As such, it appears that the elaborated and restricted codes are not actual traditional oppositions but rather dialogic aspects of the power play within the social structure that have an effect (albeit linguistic) on the individual. However, for Bernstein, as for Bourdieu, the power play is unidirectional in that it is the dominant class who affects the meanings of subordinate groups, not the working class who rejects the advances or places limits on the more affluent. Thus, while Bernstein's recent work suggests a more interactive view of language and class, it still fails to provide a dialectical analysis of how meanings are formed and produced, and how people are the active agents of this process.

In studying social class language practices, it seems researchers have generally neglected to examine the dominance relations that inform these practices and to discuss the numerous oppositions dominant/dominated relations pose. For those promoting deficit theories, working-class children, their environments, communities, and families are thought to be lacking the "rich" language experiences of the middle and upper classes. The system of language as a whole is thereby thought to emanate from the dominant class; not recognized is that class practices are constituted as "different" within the same global system, a system that functions in a social reality that is signified by hierarchical and non-reciprocal relationships (Bisseret 1979). While the cultural reproductionists situate language within the social structure and view the language experience of the dominant class as different from (not better than) subordinate groups, they, too, suffer from the misconception that the dominant class's power (and its language practices, discourses, and voices) cannot be countered. These theories cannot fully account for antagonistic voices since they fail to recognize the dialogic oppositions.

Theoretical positions that can account for voice and the dialogic quality of language are those represented in the work of Bakhtin and Gramsci already discussed and in that of the Brazilian educator, Paulo Freire. Whereas the focus of theorists such as Bourdieu and Bernstein is on cultural reproduction. Freire's analysis is grounded in cultural production. His interest is with "the various ways in which human beings construct their own voices and validate their contradictory experiences within specific historical settings and constraints" (Introduction by Giroux in Freire 1985:xvi).

For Freire (as for Gramsci and Bakhtin), language is intimately connected to a dialectics of both culture and power. Embedded in language practices and meanings are individuals' sociocultural and historical realities that have been shaped by years of living within dominant/subordinate cultural and power relations. While these relations act to control and repress subordinate classes and their systems of meanings, they also present the possibility of tension and contradiction. Because power works through people in their cultural settings and not on them, the relations of power themselves can be recreated and reinvented. As Freire notes:

> This recreation and reinvention of power by necessity passes through the reinvention of the productive act. And the reinvention of the productive act takes place to the degree that people's discourse is legitimized in terms of people's wishes, decisions, and dreams, not merely empty words.... The reinvention of power that passes through the reinvention of production cannot take place without the amplification of voices that participate in the productive act. (1987:55)

Giroux draws from the work of Freire, Gramsci, and Bakhtin in developing an analysis of cultural production and cultural politics in the context of U.S. schools. He argues that schools are arenas of conflict where both teachers and students struggle over different meanings, practices, and readings of the world.

> Schools are one of the primary public spheres where, through the influence of authority, resistance, and dialogue, language is able to shape the way various individuals and groups encode and thereby engage the world. In other words, schools are places where language projects, imposes, and constructs particular norms and forms of meaning. In this sense, language does more than merely present "information"; in actuality, it is used as a basis both to "instruct" and to produce subjectivities. (1986:59)

By examining the ways in which these subjectivities are produced in the linguistic and instructional practices of classrooms, as well as how teachers and students act to sustain and resist the dominant pedagogy, cultural productionists afford a dialectical understanding of language from which an oppositional voice can be seen to naturally emerge.[15] This perspective is critical in promoting a cognizant awareness that schools do much more than teach academics. As class-oriented sites of cultural production, schools help make possible the voices students construct and what students become.

BILINGUALISM IN THE UNITED STATES: WHOSE LANGUAGE IS SPOKEN?

The rudiments of voice lie in the dialogic oppositions that humans create in their daily sociolinguistic and ideologic existence. Class clearly plays a major role in defining the character of this existence, as do the social and cultural relationships and setting in which one develops and resides. Intertwined with class and with these relationships and setting is language—the commonality of meanings, experiences, and words which permit communication.

In Puerto Rico, the linguistic conflict over language became a struggle over values and voice. Similar conflicts over language go on in the United States under the rubric of "bilingual."

The phenomenon of bilingualism—that is, of two-language speakers—is certainly not new to the United States, a nation composed of immigrants, refugees, and migrants from linguistically diverse countries and colonial territories; lest we forget the linguistically diverse indigenous population native to the North American continent. Yet, the United States is one of the few countries in the world that promotes a monolingual populace. The underlying belief is that only one language can be spoken.

While English has never been the official language of the United States, it has served as the common language of government, business, and communication. Until the 1900s, the United States did make efforts to accommodate non-English language speakers. The Germans, for example, who in the 1790 census comprised 9 percent of the population, ran German language schools and used German to conduct local business. The Articles of Confederation and other federal documents were even printed in German (Wagner 1981). In later years, government papers as well as schools appeared in other languages, including French, Spanish, Dutch, and Swedish (Crawford 1987).

Direct English imposition has also been visible at differing points in history, most notably during world wars and economic decline. This imposition has similarly accompanied immigration shifts. It has been most discernible when those coming into the country have had darker skin and more pronounced features or have been racial as well as ethnic minorities. The Americanization campaign of the early 1900s epitomized these English imposition efforts; with it came mass xenophobia. English language proficiency (in the United States and in its possessions) was equated with patriotism. Employers made English language classes compulsory for all foreign-born workers, fifteen states passed laws mandating English as the language of instruction (some even prohibited foreign language instruction in the elementary schools); books in other languages, particularly in German, were burned. The National American Committee (affiliated with the Federal Bureau of Education) advocated the deportation of those immigrants who failed to learn English in three years (Crawford 1987; Higham 1963). During World War II there were similar but less pronounced efforts (see Kloss 1977 and Castellaños 1983 for a detailed analysis).

The 1960s and 1970s appeared to bring a new tolerance for linguistic minorities. With the establishment of bilingual education programs, interpreting services in the courts, hospitals, and other public domains, and voting ballots printed in other languages, it seemed U.S. policy had come around to the idea that diverse linguistic groups were not a threat to sovereignty and were here to stay. Under the Reagan and Bush administrations, however, xenophobia once again has been on the rise. Groups such as "English First" and "U.S. English" flaunt a membership list of over half a million, have representatives in Congress and in local government, and receive financial backing from numerous right-wing organizations and from multinational corporations. Their goals and tactics can be likened to the Americanization campaign of the 1900s (Crawford 1989) and to the efforts to impose English in Puerto Rico (see Chapter 1).[16]

What does history tell us about language and about bilingual and non-English language speakers in the United States? Except for colonial times and brief moments in the present, non-English speakers have not been welcome. Citizenship is predicated on English language proficiency as is success in major institutions including schools. Once English proficiency is obtained, individuals are encouraged to "leave behind" their past and speak English to their children and in their homes. In fact, demographic studies of numerous immigrant groups in the United States have shown there to be virtually no stable bilingualism. By the second generation, most display dominance in English and by the third, most are English monolinguals (Snow and Hakuta n.d.). The Puerto Rican community in the Northeast is one of the few groups that has maintained a bilingualism; schools, however, continue to contribute to its demise: as compared to other members of the community, school-aged children generally have the weakest Spanish abilities (Language Policy Task Force 1982). The linguistic conflict that the United States established in Puerto Rico also exists here at home; English and "minority" languages are placed in opposition.

This opposition is particularly evident in classrooms and schools. While bilingual education programs were established in response to the linguistic mismatch theory—that children cannot learn in a language they do not understand—their underlying philosophy and implementation have been to move students quickly into English. Bilingual education is mandated in eleven states. Most programs, however, are transitional in nature. Students receive intensive English as a second language (ESL) while academic content area instruction is offered in their native language until such time that they are able to perform classroom work in English. In Massachusetts, for example, the transition is usually made within three years and often after one or two. In practice, bilingual classes are sometimes taught by teachers with limited proficiency in the students' language or by English dominant teachers who either personally or pedagogically (or both) just prefer to use English. Those teachers dominant in the students' language (themselves a growing minority in bilingual programs and public schools) are frequently chastised for not having native-like fluency in English.[17] Attitudes toward bilingual education, twenty years after its implementation, remain negative. It appears many of these attitudes stem from both a misunderstanding of bilingual education's original goals and purposes and from xenophobia and classism; most bilingual students are students of color and come from the ranks of the working, underemployed classes. In school buildings, bilingual education teachers and students are isolated and considered "different."

They are told by administrators to speak English in the hallways, cafeteria, and public places of the school (Walsh 1987b). The perception of administrators, mainstream teachers, and English-speaking peers is that students are in bilingual programs because they need remediation. The result is that, in few cases, do bilingual programs promote bilingualism. Instead, they are, as a Puerto Rican bilingual student told me, "to just learn English." This understood purpose positions program participants as deficient and as "other." "Bilingual" thus comes to be perceived as one Anglo boy described: "Those kids that speak Spanish." This divergent naming of "bilingual" makes clear the oppositional status of the language minority student.

Bilingual education has, in fact, eased the transition process for many students, giving them a momentary pause from full scale assimilation and a space within which they can seek the support and solidarity of one another. Opponents of bilingual education maintain students do not learn English quickly enough, that the program segregates children, and that its homogeneous composition promotes a continued maintenance of the native language (see, for example, Porter 1990; Rossell 1990). Apparent in these objections is a fear that bilingual education may somehow retard the assimilation or "melting pot" process, that bilingual education may permit linguistic minority students' language and cultural reality to be spoken, and that someday this reality may supercede the authoritarian white language of schools and of society (for example, Butler 1985). In order to support their position, these opponents cite the poor academic performance of language minority students, particularly Latinos, and maintain that their inability to perform as well as their Anglo peers is in large part due to a limited exposure to English. None have done studies of their own to back up their claims. Research studies that show the insufficient exposure hypothesis to be false (for example, Cummins 1984; Collier 1987; Krashen and Biber 1988) as well as works that demonstrate the impact the societal status of the students' language (and culture) has on both academic performance and on pedagogical practices and on the ways in which this status works to promote differential success (see Cummins 1986; Ogbu 1978; Ogbu 1987), are either ignored by these opponents or discounted.

Recent research in bilingual education shows that students with a well-developed native language learn English both better and faster than students who have little or no schooling in their mother tongue (Cummins 1984; Collier 1987). Educators and policymakers, however, still base their practice on the false premise that increased exposure to English will result in increased English proficiency. Learning to speak English thus assumes an oppositional stance to the overall linguistic/conceptual development that underlies higher order cognitive skills. What becomes primary is that students develop oral English ability, a process that generally takes from one to two years. Their ability to learn through the medium of English, a process that can take as long as five to eight years to develop, becomes secondary. It is therefore of little wonder that so many older linguistic minority students exhibit major academic difficulties.

The linguistic environment of schools not only reflects but constructs and perpetuates the status of bilingualism and of non-Anglo languages in our society. In the educational institution, English is the overwhelming language of authority. The native language is a temporary, remedial, and clarification-designed tool. This dichotomy can be observed on several levels. First, English defines the schools' authoritarian structure. In a majority of cases, it is the language of principals and school administrators: It is the language of power, control, and discipline within the school building. Thus while the native language may be used within the confines of the classroom, students know that the English-language world is clearly in control outside of the classroom door. Second, English is the language of standardized texts, curriculum, and assessment. Native language textbooks are generally used in the first two years of the bilingual program, but by the third year, most students have transitioned into the English "mainstream" or "standard" version. In some programs, English texts are used from the outset, with the bilingual teacher providing a clarification of content in the native language while students read the content in English. The measurement of students' acquisition of this content is also frequently done in English with comparisons made not with other language minority students but with native English speakers. Standardized achievement testing is seldom if ever mandated in the native language, because it is English that provides the standard. Third, English is generally the language of extracurricular activities and of the so-called integrated activities like art, music, and physical education. Because these activities are considered nonacademic and do not rely on strong verbal ability, it is thought that language minority students can somehow get by in English. "Integration" is defined as permitting language minority students to try out the English language environ. No one questions, however, why a language other than English could not be used in these "non-academic" classes as a way to promote bilingualism, biculturalism, and linguistic/cultural understanding.

The choice and use of English in schools are grounded in the beliefs that English, as the common language of the United States, is primary and that the development of other languages are counterproductive and divisive, and that the more English students hear, the more they will learn. Through the practices outlined above, however, schools expose children to and position them with regards to an authoritarian English, an English that does not serve merely as a form of communication but as a language of power, domination, and control.

The reality of bilingualism in the United States suggests an oppositional dilemma, a dilemma that is as much tied to issues of race and class and to a view of the individual and society as it is to issues of language variety (i.e.,

English versus Spanish). In the present historical moment, white European bilinguals are perceived as "interestingly foreign" while bilingual people of color are somehow perceived as a threat. Groups are also played off against one another, oppositions and tensions between groups are constructed and posed; solidarity is inhibited. Southeast Asian refugees are praised for their passivity and apparent assimilation.[18] South American and Central American immigrants and refugees are thought to be more motivated and easier to acculturate (and control) than their Dominican and Puerto Rican sisters and brothers. Even amongst Puerto Ricans, divisions are created between those born on the Island (generally considered the better, more "docile" students) and those raised in the United States.

The low prestige afforded bilinguals in this country has worked to promote practices that attempt to silence bilinguals' voices. The values, meanings, and experiences given credence in schools (in bilingual education as well as in the "standard" curriculum) tell students that their cultural (and linguistic) reality is of little consequence, that their past impedes their future success and integration. Even the words used to name the school policies and practice suggest that the languages and cultures of the bilingual are conceived as truly oppositional, that there can be no coexistence. The word "transitional" in bilingual education, for instance, masks reality by assuming that students can skip over to another context without any psychic pain or suffering. "Standard" places a faith and belief in the English (mostly white and middle-class) ways of learning and talking, while "mainstream" suggests a dominant, prevailing direction of influence. However, despite the oppressive reality projected here, people can and do change their circumstances. They find ways to resist and to speak their language through antagonistic voices. Amidst the hegemony of schooling, voices of struggle and resistance can be seen to emerge. For the language minority student, the struggle is to do battle with implicit and explicit forms of cultural opposition and, in so doing, to both retain a historical, cultural, and linguistic integrity and to construct a compatible present. But, as the subsequent chapters indicate, this struggle is far from won.

CONCLUSION

This chapter offered a theoretical discussion of the tensions and oppositions posed in language study and in languages' social constitution and practiced use. Language is a site for confrontations and conflicts because it is in language that people's histories, lived experiences, perspectives, dispositions, and innermost thoughts are realized and given expression. Relationships of power are embedded in language by way of the social structure in which meaning is also produced. These relationships are made visible in the ways language is used to name reality and in the meanings and voices that emerge from experience and struggle in an ideological and sociocultural world. They are also present in language theories.

For example, in discussing how language is theorized, particular views of agency, knowing, and learning are made evident. The objectivists' conception of language as a set of linear, a priori rules, passively acquired, perpetuates a view of the learner as a vessel into which knowledge can be poured. In contrast, theorists of the subjective school promote language as a product of the individual, actively developed through interaction and impacted by one's background and environment. The metaphors of "disadvantaged," "deficit," and of "less language" prevalent in some of the subjective analyses illustrate whose reality these theories of language actually name. Similarly, in reproductionist accounts like that of Bernstein, particular images of language are articulated through metaphors like "culturally induced backwardness" and "elaborated and restricted" codes. While reproduction theories take the subjective position further by focusing on the ways in which language maintains socioeconomic class distinctions, the learner remains inhibited by the dominant structure. Finally, theories emanating from a cultural productionist perspective perceive language as a dynamic force shaped by cultural and power relations and as holding the possibility for tension, contradiction, and change. It is only through the latter position that agency is fully realized and that knowledge and learning are seen as dialectical processes of both struggle and construction. Here the metaphor applied is "language of possibility."

Discussed throughout this chapter have been the tensions which emerge in the ways language has been thought about, critiqued, used, and spoken. In various forms, we have seen the impact the hegemony of the dominant class has on speech, on inner consciousness, and on the variety of language which is reified and allowed to be heard. However, we have also seen how people actively struggle with and against this force, themselves constituting the power relation. This linguistic and or class struggle is not chosen, it exists simply because of the contradictions between groups (i.e., because of hegemony). It arises not because of external strife or because outsiders want to change, confront, or dominate others, but because of the contradictions inherent within the system. Promulgated by these contradictions are dialogic oppositions, dependent elements within the same relation that are reflected in signs and the systems of meanings, and which are effectuated in individuals' voices.[19] An understanding of linguistic conflict and dialogic opposition affords the possibility of seeing language not as the mere social and cultural expression of a people, but as the active representation and manifestation of the ongoing struggle within people's social, cultural, and political lives. Through voice, realities are spoken and, in conflict, tensions among realities are posed. But, it is in the realm of oppositions that language's dynamic character and its potential and possibility become evident, for it is in a dialectical and dialogic grasp of oppositions that the immutability of hegemony is shown to be untrue.

NOTES

1. This is not to say that people are always aware of how the social structure impacts them as individuals or as a group, but rather to suggest that most individuals do have a general understanding of their place within the sociocultural milieu. Giddens (1979) maintains that every social actor indeed knows a great deal about the conditions of reproduction of the society in which he or she is a member.

2. E. Frances White's article on the voices of Black feminism (1984) illustrates the real life oppositional context of voice. Demonstrated are the multiple ways Black women speak about and define their realities and the conflicts engendered in allying oneself with either color or gender. Elizabeth Ellsworth (1988) also affords a look into oppositional voices in her discussion of students' perceptions of and actions toward racism on a college campus. In addition, Teresa de Lauretis discusses the concept of multiple and shifting identities in feminist writings, identities that are "made up of heterogeneous and heteronomous representations of gender, race, and class and often indeed across languages and cultures; an identity that one decides to reclaim from a history of multiple assimilations" (1986:9).

3. See, for example, Bloomfield (1933), Chomsky (1972; 1975), Saussure (1959).

4. This position was first evident in the work of Wilhelm von Humboldt in the late 1800s, and since has been visible in the studies of Boas, Malinowski, and Sapir in the first decades of the 1900s, Whorf in the 1950s and Bernstein, Gumperz, Hymes, and Fishman, to name just a few in the present.

5. Although Saussure himself never spoke of sociolinguistics or suggested that *parole* might formulate such a field, he did maintain that language (*langue*) was the norm for all other manifestations of speech. As he notes, "amidst so many dualities, language alone appears susceptible to autonomous definition, and it alone can provide the mind a satisfactory base of operations" (1959:24). In its individual sense, parole offered a framework within which to focus on a subjective analysis of speech, such as that reflected in the work of anthropologists and sociologists. By distinguishing speech from the system of language (and glorifying the latter), Saussure relegated the social study of *parole* to a separate (and lower) role.

6. In recent years, Soviet linguists and language theorists in the West specializing in Soviet linguistics have proclaimed that works signed by Volosinov and by Medvedev were actually written by Bakhtin (see, for example, Clark and Holquist 1984). While there is still no absolute evidence to prove this theory either true or false (Bakhtin himself refused to comment on this before he died), its tenet is gaining an increasingly wide acceptance. In keeping with this theory and in respecting Volosinov's signature, citations used here make dual reference.

7. At the time these oppositions were going on in Puerto Rico, similar linguistic class struggles were going on for Puerto Ricans residing in the United States. Here, as on the Island, there were the oppositions of the Puerto Rican people (still the colonized) to the ruling class (still the colonizer) which took place first in the Spanish/English dichotomy, and later in bilingual/English Only confrontations.

With the second and third generations, class-based conflicts within the English language and between English and Spanish for those returning to the Island have also been evident.

8. As Chapter 1 also illustrated, however, the bourgeoisie in Puerto Rico does not really command power but serves as an agent of U.S. interests. Hegemony has permeated their consciousness. A quotation from Paulo Freire brings home this point: "If they come to power still embodying that ambiguity imposed on them by the situation of oppression, it is my contention that they will merely imagine they have reached power" (1970:121).

9. For additional examples of community inclusion strategies in schools, see Walsh's (1987b) discussion of Dominican students, McDermott and Gospodinoff's (1981) analysis of Puerto Rican elementary school children, Gilmore (1983) on African American students, and Deyhle (1986) on Native Americans.

10. It is interesting to note how this young child had not only internalized what mainstream society and its principal institution, the school, think of Puerto Ricans but also the image the colonizer constructs of the colonized. As Memmi (1965:81) notes, "By his accusation the colonizer establishes the colonized as being lazy. He decides that laziness in constituted in the very nature of the colonized." Evident here is the colonial force of U.S. schooling.

11. Use of the term "semilingualism" was fairly prevalent in research about bilinguals in Europe and North America in the late 1970s (e.g., Cummins 1978; Skutnabb-Kangas and Toukomaa 1976). While its connotation was often with regard to the cognitive functions of language and its development in academic settings, its association for practitioners was that minority children somehow had less language; their native language lacked the developed vocabulary of middle-class peers and their second language proficiency was limited. It suggested a deficit view that was clearly class connected. Moreover, it promoted a "blame the victim" philosophy which belies an awareness of the hegemonic context of the term, itself grounded in the superiority of and preference for the class-dominant, class-imposed "standard" and ignored systematic societal efforts to invalidate the language poor children and children of color bring from home. Although these researchers have since chosen not to use the term (see Cummins 1984), it continues to occasionally appear in the literature and in frequent "mainstream" educators' discussions about language minorities. Ana Celia Zentella (1989) makes an association between semilingualism and the dominant group attempts to commit (in the case of bilingual children) a "bilingualcide," the killing of two languages at once.

12. Distar was developed in response to the disadvantaged theories of the 1960s and was widely used throughout the country, particularly in inner city schools. By the early 1970s most school districts discarded the program because of its artificial, skills-oriented style (see Cummins 1984 for a detailed analysis). Distar, however, has made a recent comeback in some urban school districts—now being utilized as a "quick fix" to improve language minority students' English.

13. Iadicola (1981) provides an interesting discussion of symbolic violence as it occurs amongst Latino students.

14. Bernstein's definition of class, particularly in his earlier work, is problematic in that economic strata are defined in terms of two classes only: the middle and working classes. The ruling or dominant class who, as we saw in Chapter 1 controls the means of discourse as well as production, is not in Bernstein's picture.

15. For an enlightening discussion of this production in practice see Carolyn Steedman's analysis of working-class girls' effectuation of meaning and culture in *The Tidy House* (1982). Kathleen Weiler (1984) provides an excellent review of this work. Willis' (1977) and Everhart's (1983) studies of high school and junior high students' resistance and Sola and Bennett's (1985) examination of Latino student discourse practices are also demonstrative of this language of possibility.

16. A more detailed description of the English Only movement is provided in Chapter 4.

17. English as a second language teachers who play a key role in the transition process frequently have limited training. In Massachusetts, for instance, over 90 percent of ESL teachers have "grandfathered" certificates—they have training as either elementary teachers or as high school English teachers and more often than not lack university courses in ESL methodologies and the processes of second language acquisition.

18. For a critique of the "model minority" and Asian success myth see Wei (1986). Asian American Resource Workshop (1987) also offers excellent documentation and anaylsis of racial violence against Asians.

19. Bertell Ollman (1986) affords an enlightening discussion of the dialectics of contradictions.

3

The Power and Meaning of Words

THE WORD, AS the primary means of social interaction, occupies an essential place in our society. But we rarely reflect upon the significance of words or consider the contextual environments from whence this significance was created. In fact, we probably could not remember, even if we tried, how we actually came to understand and employ words in the manner deemed socially and linguistically appropriate within our language community. Yet, somehow such process occurred. We also do not frequently think about the multiple ways our identity is enmeshed with our native language, or about how it is that language determines not just the common labels we share as words, but acts as a determinant of thought. However, if we were to contemplate the import of words in our lives, our minds would probably wander to significant moments or particular contextual situations in which language in some way seemed salient. What would most likely occur is that we would be unable to separate out words from language from social existence.

The study of words by linguists and psychologists in the United States has traditionally neglected their social character. In the field of cognitive psychology and information processing, for example, words are often treated as neutral symbols, morphological or lexical representations for referents divorced from the dynamics of the social setting. However, as Soviet psychologists have taught us (and our own experience verifies), words can also be thought of in a much broader sense, as the means through which we absorb and rework the histories of our ancestors, the sociocultural design of our surroundings, and the political and economic moments in which we (and our antecedents) reside.[1] In the dialogical flow of communication with others and reflection within one's self, words exude much more than a dictionary definition; they become socially inscribed entities imbricated with context and intentionality:

> In language, there is no word or form left that would be neutral or would belong to no one; all of language turns out to be scattered, permeated with intentions, accented. For the consciousness that lives in it, language is not an abstract system of normative forms but a concrete heterological opinion on the world. Every word gives off the scent of a profession, a genre, a current, a party, a particular work, a particular man [sic], a generation, an era, a day, and an hour. Every word smells of the context and contexts in which it has lived its intense social life; all words and all forms are inhabited by intentions. (Bakhtin in Todorov 1984:56)

Bakhtin suggests the interconnectedness that is maintained in the word between our social and psychological existence. Words are acquired in the social world; their meanings are constructed, borrowed, and accommodated through interactions with more experienced members of the speech community. In taking on the "scent," the context, and the intentions of both the moment and the relations in which meaning was developed, the word assumes a more internal character. It is in this internalization of the word that psychological connections are made to other words and a complex system of signs is established. The meaning of the word is always partial and always considered in relation to other words and to the various social and contextual references that both elicit.

The site of this social and psychological connection is inner consciousness. This has been referred to in previous chapters as that which is spoken in voice. Although inner consciousness is a product of social interaction, it also has the potential to be constitutive since, through voice, its contents can influence (and be influenced by) others' interpretations.[2] It is thus by moving beyond the superficial "generalized" meaning of words and unveiling both their social and psychological significance that we can come to understand the various realities that constitute individual consciousness and that shape individual and group voices. The works of Lev S. Vygotsky and Mikhail Bakhtin are essential in this regard.

This chapter draws upon the theoretical perspectives of Bakhtin and Vygotsky in examining the tensions at play in both inner consciousness and in the voices of Puerto Rican children. Analyzed are the power and meaning of their words. It is in talking about what particular Spanish and English words mean to them that this group of fourth grade students makes evident the salience of their sociocultural community and the hegemony of U.S. schooling. Brought to the fore are issues of bilingualism, social and ethnic status and identity, and internal colonialism.

Schools generally consider Puerto Ricans to be problematic "newcomers" to the United States, mostly because of their maintenance of cultural ties, retention of the native language, and perceived refusal to succumb to the "melting pot." The unique situation of Puerto Ricans is seldom recognized. The past and present history lived under U.S. colonialism on the Island and its more subtle perpetuation here in the metropolitan social structure cannot be compared to that of immigrant populations. It is this social, economic, and political reality that names Puerto Ricans as colonized minority "Americans," offering the false hope of inclusion while perpetuating the policies and practices characteristic of exclusion. Language has consistently been one of the key elements in the polemic of assimilation. Education has been its primary site of implementation.

Students are told by teachers and administrators that the English language affords access to the larger society and facilitates academic success. Touted is a requisite trade of native language competence for English development. While these efforts of English imposition have clearly had linguistic and psychological effects on children (as they did on children in Puerto Rico), their underlying theoretical assumption, that Puerto Rican communities only use Spanish, is mistaken. In fact, in comparison to other Latino groups, Puerto Ricans speak 35 to 40 percent more English (Zentella 1989). The daily life of many Puerto Ricans outside the school shows an active use of English (in varying forms) as well as a maintenance of the Spanish language (Language Policy Task Force 1982, 1984; Zentella 1985). This dynamic bilingualism is described by Juan Flores, John Attinasi, and Pedro Pedraza:

> In contrast to the traditional immigrant pattern of transition from the foreign language to English over three generations, with grandparents and grandchildren being virtually monolingual in one or the other language, nearly all Puerto Ricans are bilingual to some degree, with second language skills acquired, for the most part, outside any formal language instruction. There seems to be a life cycle of language use in the community. The younger children learn Spanish and English simultaneously, hearing both languages from those who use them separately and from those who combine them in various ways. The older children and adolescents speak and are spoken to increasingly in English, which accords with their experience as students and as members of peer groups that include non-Hispanics. In young adulthood, as the school experience ends and employment responsibilities begin, the use of Spanish increases, both in mixed usage and in monolingual speech to older persons. At this age, then, the Spanish skills acquired in childhood but largely unused in adolescence become notably reactivated. Mature adults speak both languages. (1981: 197-198)

This seems to indicate that despite the hegemonic conditions of schooling and of other societal institutions, the Puerto Rican community in the United States continues to define its own character. Passed from adults to children are the linguistic norms of communication; accompanying these norms are words and the cultural frames of reference surrounding them. However, as the following pages demonstrate, the maintenance of a community voice is not without struggle.

Unearthed in this chapter are the sociocultural and ideological tensions of the school and the community's ways with words. The relations of power and authority and the contradictory models of representation inscribed in monolingual and transitional bilingual education and in schooling as a whole are made evident. Also brought to light are the ways both institutional structures and home and community relations work on and through children's consciousness, coloring oppositional realities. By demonstrating how children perceive, internalize, and contest these realities, this chapter gives voice a lived significance and words a powerful presence.

UNCOVERING CHILDREN'S WAYS WITH WORDS

Words are an active part of our lives; they provide us with a means to articulate that which we observe, perceive, and experience. Although a large part of each day is consumed in the productive and receptive use of words in communication, we do not often consciously reflect on the multiplicity of meanings that are created and imbued in talk or on the social and cultural circumstances within which meanings are constructed and adjusted. That is, in the natural flow of communication, we generally assume parallel realities and common linguistic understanding. This assumption is probably most reified in schooling; there, students' language is interpreted within the authoritative discourse and sociohistorical experience of teachers and of authors of curriculum and texts. While this may be fine for those students who share similar backgrounds with these adults, students from divergent class, ethnic, cultural, and linguistic backgrounds are expected to somehow accommodate themselves to an imposed "standard."[3] When this "standard" represents a reality which contradicts the reality to which the child has been socialized, the result is frequently social and cultural frustration and alienation. The contradictory realities, however, generally go undetected since teachers often assume (as do standardized tests and competency-based examinations) that students' words signify a native English speaking, middle-class understanding. The subtleties of meaning that constitute their voices are neglected and misunderstood.

For a number of years, I have worked with language-minority and working-class children, their parents, and their teachers. This experience has made me witness to the social and linguistic anxieties produced within the English-speaking, class-oriented environment of the school, and the psychological and cultural traumas that are too often its result. As I observed children struggling to adapt to the sociocultural and language-based norms of English as a second language (ESL) and mainstream classrooms, and struggling to hold on to the limited security of bilingual education, I became interested in the ways their language—specifically their words—reflected and refracted the cultural, historical, economic, and political realities in which they lived. This curiosity led to the design of a participatory study with Puerto Rican children (Walsh 1984). The focus was on how the sociocultural and ideological environment actually impact children's meanings of words, and how this impact is realized in English and native-language speech, in voice and in the inner linguistic world. In concrete terms, I wanted to coax out and to understand what goes on within children's consciousness.

Participants included 54 fourth grade Puerto Rican students of varying levels of English proficiency and thirteen Anglo students who served as points of comparison. All were of working-class background. The methodology was grounded in the use of continuous word association tasks. The utilization of the task, however, did not involve the typical presentation of a word stimulus by the researcher and a passive subject response; the words were also not neutral dictionary entries. Rather, the children were asked to teach me the meanings of various Spanish words, chosen for their cultural saliency and significance in day-to-day life, and their English translation equivalents. The children were thus considered to be the experts—the teachers with knowledge to share. My role was to tell them the words I wanted to learn about and to listen. In order to ascertain their understanding both within and between languages, the children were sometimes asked to respond in Spanish to English words and in English to words in Spanish. Intralanguage (Spanish-Spanish and English-English) conditions were also practiced.

Use of word associations goes back to the time of Freud (1924), who believed that associations, continuous ones in particular, reveal the content of minds in a way that propositional language does not. The character of spontaneity inherent in associations and their freedom from the syntactic and morphological demands of overall discourse help produce responses reflective of subjective meaning, meaning that is personally attuned to the individual's sociocultural world. The central issue in association is not the single connection between a word and a referent but the meanings of the stimulus nested in a matrix of knowledge. It is social experience and culture that in major part define this matrix. For example, in their use of word associations with Korean and Colombian undergraduate students residing in the United States, Lorand Szalay and James Deese found associations to English words often reflected a cultural experience which was different from that of native English speakers. As they note:

> It is cultural experience that produces the unique distributions of associations to particular words in particular languages. Because of the close relation between association distributions and cultural experience, the degree of asso-

ciative similarity between a word in one language and its translation equivalent in another has captured the spirit of the original. Associations reveal nuances that might otherwise be detected only by someone who was intimately acquainted with both languages and cultures. (1978:88)

Associations thus help provide a window into the social and cultural contexts that frame word meanings.

In undertaking this study my intention was, like Szalay and Deese, to uncover cultural nuances in meaning. However, I was also interested in using word associations to understand how the divergent social and ideological environments of the home/community and the school shape children's significance of words. I believed this approach could allow insight into how these conflicting realities are internalized in voice. Word associations thus became a medium through which to detect the socializations and conditions that form the stuff of children's innermost lives. It is to an analyis of these associations that we now turn.

The Cogency of a Community Connection

As in many urban centers where there is a concentration of Puerto Ricans, the Puerto Rican community in the city where I conducted my research was densely settled and tightly knit. Despite a number of odds, members strived to maintain a sense of belonging and to raise their children within the cultural norms. Many of the children's word associations resonated with this influence. Nuances were particularly evident when responses of the Puerto Ricans were compared to those of Anglos.

For example, in responding to the English word "respect," Puerto Rican children most often spoke of concrete relationships of authority:

Respect is when a little child come and the mother tell him not to do it, they have to respect her.

Respect is if the teacher say to you shut up, you have to respect. The same thing with your parents, the teacher, the pastor; if they say to you, you have to respect.

When my mother talk to me, I don't talk back. . . . When she hit me, I go to my bed and I let my mouth shut as I should because if I'm smart to her, she will smack me.

These same type of definitions were also visible in children's response to the Spanish *respeto*:

Tu tienes que respetar tu mamá (That you have to respect your mother).

Que un niño tiene que ser caso el papá, el tío, o algo (That a child has to put attention to his father, his uncle, or something).

In their associations to "respect," Anglo children made no direct reference to the sense of authority and honor for elders obvious in Puerto Rican children's comprehension. For them, "respect" generally suggested behavior:

> Like you don't do anything bad to it or bother it.
> Having manners.

Several Anglo children described "respect" as appropriate treatment due them, for instance, that children should also be respected:

> Respect is when like your mother respects you and stuff, she takes care of you. And like when you go to your aunt's house you expect her to respect you.

Absent from all of the Anglo responses was the association of "respect" with age, status, and cultural dominance.

Sonia Nieto has identified the values of authority, respect, dignity, *capacidad*, and mutual responsibility and obligation as cornerstones of Puerto Rican child rearing practices:

> Through them, children are raised, probably with quite a few more restrictions than North American children, to view the family, not the individual as the most important unit. From infancy, children are taught to respect elders, to expect dignity from others, and to develop a strong commitment to family and community. (1979:42)

The influence of these home-instilled values was clearly evident in associations to "respect" (and *respeto*) but also permeated many of the Puerto Rican children's responses to other value related words. *Vergüenza*, for instance, which can be roughly translated as "shame," brought answers in English and Spanish such as:

> That you pay respect to the teacher if she's talking. If you get in trouble she punish you.
> Cuando mi hermano dio una pata a una maestra, mi mamá vino y dijo; "Vergüenza! ¿por qué tu no respeta? ¡Yo te cojo!" (When my brother kicked a teacher, my mother came and said: "Shame! Why don't you have respect? I'll smack you!")

"Shame," in contrast, had no significance for these children.[4]

When asked to teach me about the Spanish word "*confianza*," descriptions focused on an instilled sense of confidence embedded in familial and community relations, for instance, "En la casa de mi tía, yo entro con confianza (At my aunt's house, I can enter with confidence)." "Trust," its dictionary translation equivalent, reflected more of a sense of faith between individuals. As a Puerto Rican child explained: "You trust people, they don't take nothing." The response of an Anglo was similar: "Trust is like when you let somebody borrow something and you trust them to give it back." One mainstreamed Puerto Rican child seemed to have adopted this significance of "trust" in his interpretation of *confianza*: "Una persona que tu creas que no va divulgar que tu dices algo a ello (A person that you believe won't divulge what you tell them.).." For others, however, "trust" and *confianza* clearly had divergent significances.

Illustrated in the examples of *vergüenza* and *confianza* are cultural saliencies which, while explainable in English, have no equivalent English language terms. "Respect," on the other hand, found an equivalency in the Spanish *respeto*; its significance, however, engendered a Spanish rather than English reality. It seems that although the word and its definition were spoken in English, children tuned into the cultural context of their native language.

Studies by Gearhart and Hall (1979), Ramsey (1981), Szalay and Deese (1978), and Walsh (1983) indicate that in speaking English, non-native speakers often rely on the cultural frames of reference established in the mother tongue. An initial reliance on one's past is, in fact, a natural part of the second language acquisition process. Second language learners structure and interpret new experiences in the second language world in terms of categories derived from their native language and culture together with their perceptions of phenomena, linguistic and cultural, in the English language environment (Strick 1980). It is this combined context that forms initial word meaning in the second language, for example, English. While contact in Anglo contexts expands the English as a second language learner's understanding of English language words, the native cultural saliency of some words remains dominant regardless of English oral proficiency. Consequently, the child may have a concept in mind when communicating in English that is quite different from that of a native speaker (Ramsey 1981). Christian explains further:

> The meanings which have been given to him [*sic*] in one culture do not exist in other cultures, and therefore cannot be replaced. It is a fallacy, for example, to assume that there is an English equivalent for the Spanish word "mamá"—or that there is a Spanish equivalent for the English word mama. These and hundreds of other words which give to the child his existence in terms of his relation to others and to the world occur in cultural contexts which do not coincide. (1978: 161)

Christian's words corroborate the findings of Puerto Rican children's associations thus far: Children draw upon their lived experience in the world to garner meaning. This is not to imply that meaning is determined simply by what happens to us, but rather that meaning is inherited, constructed and reconstructed in the process of becoming experienced (Donald 1982) and in coming to understand the ways these experiences relate to those that have come before. In the case of many culturally salient words, for instance, the translation equivalent affords little more than a morphological representation; sociocultural specificity remains embedded providing an understanding different from that rendered in the intentions of the native speaker. These divergencies of meaning were also visible in Puerto Rican children's interpretations of other words' meanings. One which was particularly pronounced was that of *educación*/"education."

In Spanish, *educación* signifies aspects of breeding and manners taught in the home rather than the formal schooling usually attached to its translation equivalent "education."[5] As with all of the words, some Puerto Rican children were asked to teach the meaning of *educación* while others were limited to education in order to ascertain differences in their understanding of the words in Spanish and in English. Virtually all the Puerto Rican children, regardless of language proficiency, interpreted both the Spanish and English version in terms of respect, politeness, and other-home oriented values:

> Educación quiere decir que no dice malas palabras, ni nada. Eso quiere decir educación, todo eso. (Education means not to say bad words or anything. That is what education means, all that.)
>
> Education means respect.

For Anglos, "education" was always reflective of formal schooling.[6]

Reflected in the divergent understandings of *educación* and "education" were, as with the previous words, a saliency of home/community socialization through which children had come to consider the preparation of education as that of becoming good, respectful children. For them, this was clearly different from the instruction of formal schooling.

"Neighborhood" also produced a significance for Puerto Ricans that was clearly divergent from that of Anglos. When asked to teach me its meaning, Anglos generally made associations to buildings, for example, "Where there's a lot of houses," while the Puerto Rican children referred to people, community, and family:

> It's something the people lives. There's a lot of people there. There's a lot of Puerto Ricans there. There's more Puerto Ricans than Americans there.
>
> A place where there's a lot of family.

In a parallel vein, "family" generated responses among Puerto Rican students that almost always made mention of an extended group:

> You have a lot of families—uncles, aunts, grandmothers, grandfathers, cousins.

Evident was a more collective sense of unity (both in the family and in the neighborhood) that contrasted sharply with Anglo children's conception of neighborhoods as peopleless and the family as parent and child relationships only. Puerto Rican's holistic vision of their surroundings and their affinity to culturally based values carried over to their understanding of other key words as well, such as "church" and "school." "Church" signified a community joined together in prayer and brought mention of the authority and respect promoted through its teachings.[7] Similarly, "school" engendered discussion on the respect students owe teachers and on the people-oriented activity of pedagogy. Anglo children described both as places or buildings. As compared to the Puerto Rican students, the Anglos appeared alienated from the humaness of words.

As these as well as the previous word associations illuminate, the sociocultural context in which words are acquired assumes a powerful influence in meaning relations. Context plays a major role in determining word significance for it offers the milieu for language's development as well as providing the external link to an internal representation. In the examples above, children had internalized the meanings of words as derived in a specific community environment. The cultural saliency of these words for the Puerto Rican child resulted in generalized meanings that spanned languages but that reflected a Spanish, that is, Puerto Rican, context. Even for those children who were dominant in English, meanings for these particular English words differed from that of their Anglo peers. These meanings did not prevent them from speaking or communicating in English (in fact, they probably would never even be detected in normal conversation), but rather gave a distinct flavor to words that only other Latinos might corroborate.

By conceptualizing words in terms of their own reality and not that imposed by the Anglo society or its principal institution, schools, these children seemed to maintain a semblance of voice—of "Puerto Ricaness"—even though this maintenance was undoubtedly subconscious in origin. However, voice, as language itself, is not monolithic. There is not one Puerto Rican (or one Anglo) voice nor are there single interpretations of culturally salient words that are forever prevalent. Through their actions in the world, children create a multiplicity of voices; however, underlying these voices are the lived sociocultural realities from which meanings evolve and words are spoken. The choice of which voice to employ or, conversely, the reality of which voice emerges at a particular moment is most often governed by context. The selection of meaning fits a similar pattern. However, the examples provided so far seem to indicate that the sociocultural context of the home and community was the sole source for these children's determination of word significance. At least in relation to these particular words, Anglo contextual influence was not present. Does this mean that Puerto Rican children who come from Spanish-speaking backgrounds always rely on the experiential and community-based (Spanish) interpretations of salient words when speaking English? Or, with exposure to English, to the Anglo environment, and to the contextual use of specific English words, do they develop context-dependent meanings? Are these meanings context- and language-specific or is there a system of generalized meanings with contextual (and linguistic) denotations? What implications does context have for the development and maintenance of individual and group voices? Insight into these questions can be garnered from examples taken from a second part of my study, which employed a variation on the word association.

The Import of Sociocultural Context

In Part 2 of the study, photographs that reflected school and home/community contexts were utilized along with words.[8] Children were given a photograph to look at and then asked to respond to a key adjective within a sentence, such as, "This boy is very *educated*. What can you tell me about him?" For the more English-proficient Puerto Rican children, response differed according to the context presented in the picture. With the adjectives "educated" and *educado*, for instance, a photo of a Latino child in a school context signaled a reference to being smart and knowing the answers. When the picture displayed a Latino child in the context of the home and community, however, both "educated" and *educado* assumed the definition of politeness (as was visible in the association to the noun *educación*). Spanish-dominant children tended to always utilize the latter definition, regardless of picture context. *Educado*, combined with a school-related photo of a female student, for example, resulted in a Spanish-dominant Puerto Rican girl interpreting the picture in terms of her own subjective situation, reflective of native language-oriented meaning:

> Que quiere mucho los libros para leer y no los tocan y no los hace daño (She likes books alot, especially to read, and she doesn't touch them or do anything to destroy them).

Similarly, in responding to "educated" in an interlanguage condition with a school picture, a Spanish-dominant boy answered:

> El es educado porque lanza la mano y porque hace lo que la maestra diga (He is educated because he raises his hand and because he does what the teacher says).

An Anglo boy, in looking at the same picture, also made a reference to hand raising but his meaning was derived from a totally different conceptual reality:

> Because lots of time he puts up his hand in the room and wants to answer the question.

Evident in the Puerto Rican children's responses to *educado*/"educated" were notions of respect and authority—a respect for school property as well as respect for the authority of the teacher. The focus of response was not, as with the Anglo child, on the reason why the boy had his hand raised (i.e., to tell something to the teacher) nor was it what we might typically expect in Anglo culture, that is, the relating of books to intelligence. Instead, the Puerto Rican children maintained a clear adherence to the cultural values that for them define an *educated* child. This contrasted with the Anglo student's conceptual association of "educated" with school-related knowledge.

Experience in the linguistic and cultural environment promotes an understanding of the contextual appropriateness of certain words and their meanings. Bilingual children demonstrated more flexibility in crossing the contexts of meaning, in moving between the portrayed Puerto Rican and Anglo environments. This was in stark contrast to the monolingual children (both Anglo and Puerto Rican) whose meanings remained generally the same regardless of the visual context. This is not to say that the monolingual children do not make use of context in deciding the meanings for words. In fact, one Anglo girl drew from the context of the picture instead of from her generalized understanding of the word in interpreting the sentence "This girl is not very 'educated.' " Her response was more in the form of a story:

> She's either talking fresh or something. Or walking away when somebody's talking to her.

Although an adherence to authority is clearly suggested in her response, this understanding appeared to emerge from a visual interpretation of a photo rather than from the significance of a single word. In general, contextual associations for Anglos were monocultural, reflective of their own individual experience in Anglo homes and Anglo dominated schools and the result of limited contact in and grasp of the other (in this case, Puerto Rican) cultural world. The photographs provided a contextual setting from which significance could be elaborated. The conceptual understanding of the word, however, came from children's subjective impressions.

The example of "educated"/*educado* illustrates that context-dependent meanings do emerge as language-minority children become more socialized into and aware of the distinct ways words are used in English-dominated settings. It was this cognizance of contextual appropriateness that sparked significance; the particular language variety in which the word was spoken or defined, that is, Spanish or English, appeared to be of little concern.

The influence of context on meaning determination derives from a linking of the social and the psychological in the inner consciousness of the individual. The development of this internal relation and its role in the overall conceptual development of the child was a primary area of study for the Soviet psychologist Lev S. Vygotsky. His analysis affords a theoretical framework in which to ground the children's associations.

In *Thought and Language*, Vygotsky argues that the conceptual development of children entails a growing ability to use language for both abstract reflection and for internalized speech, that is, to be able to decontextualize words and their meanings on the one hand and to form abbreviated contextual referents on the other. In the process of coming to conceptual thinking, young children move from a dependence on the extralinguistic context or concrete moment to an eventual focus on the interrelated categories or sign-sign relation characteristic of adults. It is this advanced stage of conceptual thought that allowed the children in my study to make associations to words like *respeto*, *vergüenza*, *confianza*, and *educación* when no concrete context was present. The socioculturally appropriate meanings, which they voiced in reference to Spanish words, mirrored a generalized linguistic significance obtained through adult social interaction.[9]

Paralleling the development of a conceptual use of words is the establishment of an internalized, personal system of language that reflects both outward (extralinguistic) experience and semiotic or sign-like (intralinguistic) relations. Here, social and collaborative forms of behavior are transfered to "the sphere of the individual's psychological functioning" (Vygotsky 1962:48); speech displaces action. Vygotsky refers to this as inner speech, which he maintains is rooted in contextualization—an increasing dependence on the part of humans to use context in the interpretation and structure of linguistic signs (Wertsch 1985). This contextualization permits the comprehension and utilization of words within the specific entourage of a sentence or in combination with other words. Enabled, as well, are distinctive understandings and uses for words depending on the intralinguistic situation. Vygotsky describes the latter as a word's "sense" which is different from its more generalized meaning. In inner speech, sense is considered to take predominance over meaning. As he details:

> The sense of a word . . . is the aggregate of all the psychological facts emerging in our consciousness because of this word. Therefore, the sense of a word always turns out to be a dynamic, flowing, complex formation which has several zones of differential stability. Meaning is only one of the zones of the sense that a word acquires in the context of speaking. Furthermore, it is the most stable, unified, and precise zone. As we know, a word readily changes its sense in various contexts. This change in a word's sense is a basic fact to be accounted for in the semantic analysis of speech. The real meaning[10] of a word is not constant. In one operation a word emerges in one meaning and in another it takes on another meaning. This dynamism of meaning leads us to . . . the problem of the relationship of meaning and sense. The word considered in isolation and in the lexicon has only one meaning. But this meaning is nothing more than a potential that is realized in living speech. In living speech this meaning is only a stone in the edifice of sense. (1962:146)

Understood in Vygotsky's conception of "sense" is the subjective, inner nature of meaning. Sense is derived from the relation within the individual between his/her psychological and social worlds. It is this inner personal and contextual meaning that permits varied interpretations of words—interpretations that are deduced from individual, cultural, and group experiences and that form abbreviated word references. These senses, or what Bakhtin (Volosinov) (1973) calls the "themes" of words, emerge from their use in an utterance or sentence. In my study, pictures produced an additional point of context from which sense could materialize.[11] Children's responses to the adjectives "educated" and *educado* provide an example.

The circumambiency of these adjectives engendered divergent interpretations in the bilingual Puerto Rican children as compared to their Spanish monolingual peers. As the responses previously cited show, the formal schooling sense of both "educated" and *educado* was prompted through the presentation of a school context photo. In contrast, the home-related picture prompted the sense instilled by parents and reinforced in the community and the home. This distinction was not apparent when children were asked to teach about the isolated nouns, *educación* and "education"; there, the primary language significance was consistently paramount.

Of the various adjectives used with pictures in the study, however, all did not produce the same clear duality of contextual significance that "educated" elucidated. Demonstrated with the adjectives *popular/*"popular," *respetado/*"respected," *capaz/*"capable," and *familiar/*"familiar" were relations to the native language cultural environs that superseded picture context, language proficiency, and language of presentation.

Take, for example, the adjective "familiar." In Spanish, *familiar* is usually considered indicative of a familial relation but, according to the *University of Chicago Bilingual Spanish-English Dictionary,* it can also assume the meaning that "familiar" most often takes in English, well known. In reference to the sentence: "Estos niños no son *familiares. ¿Por qué?* (These children are not familiar. Why?)" matched with a school-related picture, Puerto Rican children described the pictorial representation in a distinctly Latino fashion:

> They are not family.
>
> No se parece (They do not look alike).
>
> His mother isn't the same mother like the other boy and the other girl and that's why they ain't family.
>
> Because one is whitest and one is a little bit black. And the girl is a little bit black, too. And that's how we could tell they are not familiar.

All Puerto Rican children chosé the Spanish significance even when they were heard the sentence spoken in English: "These are two *familiar* children." Here, the picture was of children in an out-of-school context.

> They are like brothers and sisters.
>
> Son familia (They are family).
>
> El papá y este no son hermanos pero el papá de el y la mamá son hermanos. Ellos [los niños] son primos (The father and that one are not brothers but his father and the mother [of that other one] are brother and sister. They [the children] are cousins).

Only one bilingual child adopted an interpretation more typical of the English significance:

> Nope, they're not familiar because I don't know them.

Although his association in English paralleled that of a Puerto Rican child who did not know Spanish (e.g., "Maybe some other people know them but I don't"), his association in Spanish made reference to the family. For this one child, language of presentation clearly had a contextual significance. With other children, however, language of presentation, as with "educated," appeared to be generally unrelated to associations.[12]

Reflected in the majority of associations to "familiar" was a propensity for Spanish meaning which, at first glance, could be likened to the earlier examples of "respect," "neighborhood," "family," and *education*. Even though the contrasting pictorial environments of home and school appeared to have little or no effect on children's sense of the word, they did provide a contextual setting that prompted associational elaborations that were more extensive than response to words alone. Moreover, made evident in the responses to "familiar," as well as those to "popular," "capable," and "respected" was the lack of home/school contextual distinction present in the words themselves which contrasted sharply with that exuded in the word educated.[13]

Illustrated in the numerous examples presented thus far is the exigency of sociocultural context on children's understanding of word meaning. This context was not described as an external factor outside the child (Urwin 1984), but as a multiplicity of relations within which the child actively participated in her/his socialization. While the socialization of formal schooling was evident in interpretations of "educated," all other words generally drew upon lived significance in the home and community. Although each child's sense of the word was subjective in that it reflected her/his own understanding, there was an overwhelming similarity among all Puerto Ricans, suggestive of a community sense that had become internalized in consciousness.[14] Thus echoed in their words was a community voice, a voice that had been derived from both lived experience and a selective appropriation of the voices of older members. As their associations demonstrated, this voice was not language specific; neither the language in which the word was presented nor the language spoken by the child appeared to act as a meaning determinant. Children had not, at least with regard to these particular words, adopted an Anglo-like voice when speaking English or relating to English words. Their use of English instead appeared to be an extension of the voice(s) they had already established. It was context not language that stimulated significance.

The primacy of semantic context over language in inner speech seemed, for the majority of these children, to be pretty much universal. In their work with bilinguals, Norman Segalowitz and Wallace Lambert (1969) also found a prevalence of what they termed semantic generalization. As with the children here, the subjects in their investigation focused on the semantic content of a word before examining the actual language of the word itself. Other studies on the semantic interrelation of a bilingual's two languages have had similar findings.[15]

The issues of semantic generalization and community voice have several implications, particularly when applied to linguistic interactions and language-based performance in the classroom. Language proficiency tests, curriculum, and classroom instructional practices seldom touch the inner meaning of words, that subtle yet salient meaning, reflected in the associations made by children here. It is generally thought that once children learn to speak in English, they think in English. In other words, it is presumed that English acquisition and an Anglo-like familiarity with the environment occur simultaneously. It is also presumed that, within a short period of time, children learn to not just speak English words but to grasp their significance, use, and contextual appropriateness in varying situations.

Those concepts learned through social experience and cultural interaction in the second language environment do take on the significance of that contextual moment as could be seen in children's school-based reactions to "educated"/*educado*. However, children's inability to make a language association to the concept demonstrates a continued influence of the interrelated sign system of the mother tongue. For abstract translation equivalents which have little or no specific contextual function in the second language (or, at least, none perceived by the child) but whose saliency in the native language is quintessential, meaning, as was demonstrated in a number of the associations, may always retain a characteristically native flavor. This predominance of a community-based perspective on meaning is generally ignored by English-speaking school officials. Presumed is that the two worlds of the child coincide and that words, concepts, and meanings are equated naturally. Christian refers to what may result:

> Teachers who do not know these meanings usually find the response of the pupil who knows no others baffling, annoying, and exasperating. Then, when the child begins to discover that the teacher does not understand, he [*sic*] develops negative reactions not only to the teacher but to the educational process, and finally to the entire culture and language which the teacher represents. Or, conversely, he [*sic*] may decide that his parents have provided him with an inferior world, and subsequently attempt to reject entirely what they have provided for him as a cultural base upon which to develop a meaningful life. This may mean that the life he [*sic*] chooses will lack the essential meanings which have their roots which are nourished by the words his parents have taught him. (1978:161)

This disaccordance in meaning is indicative of much more than a cultural mismatch between home and school. It is reflective of the dominant/subordinate context that places the school in opposition to the sociocultural and linguistic realities of language-minority students, particularly those of color. The inner voice, which had previously defined the child's existence, is invalidated in the environment of school. There, a different reality is portrayed—one that negates rather than supports earlier socializations. As a result, the child internalizes pieces of reality from two opposing worlds. What can occur is a kind of cultural schizophrenia or clash of voice, propagated by instructional policies, practices, and personnel who neglect to consider the exigency of the native sociocultural context and the ubiquitousness of a community-oriented consciousness. Children's associations to some additional words demonstrate the pervasiveness and repercussions of this clash in the school district where my study was conducted.

"You Have to Speak a Different Language if You're Black or Something"

This Anglo child's response to the word *Hispanic* renders visible a cultural, linguistic, and racial perspective, clearly monolithic and hegemonic in nature. Although almost half of this girl's school population was Hispanic, a sizeable portion of whom were English-dominant speakers in the mainstream, and even though there were Black (non-Hispanic) students in the school, *Hispanic* was understood only as non-Anglo—of nonwhite skin and non-English speaking ability. By equating all students of color, this girl's meaning reflects the hegemonic appeal to the denial of diverse histories, cultural and linguistic influences, and divergent struggles. Such perspective has much deeper roots than a naive school-based observation.

The language of this child in many ways reflects the attitudes, inaccuracies, and stereotyped notions that Puerto Rican (and other Latino) children confront in U.S. schools. It is within this contextual ambience that the Spanish-speaking Puerto Rican child attempts to construct English meanings and adapt to Anglo ways of speaking. However, often mirrored in their inner speech are not just cultural contexts but also socially produced tensions in meaning that arise from hegemonic relations. These tensions are illuminated in associations to the words "bilingual" or *bilingüe*, "Hispanic" or *hispano*, and "Puerto Rican" or *puertorriqueño*.

"Bilingual" and *bilingüe* were presented to the children as isolated nouns. But even without the context of a picture to direct their association, children consistently drew upon their school-based experience in formulating a response. Forty-four percent of the Spanish-dominant children, most of whom were recent arrivals from the Island, associated English with the stimulus *bilingüe*. Common were responses like: *Aprender inglés* (To learn English)." No English proficient or near-proficient students made this same association. Instead, most defined "bilingual" or *bilingüe* in terms of Spanish, as did all of the Anglos:

> Bilingüe es una clase de español (Bilingual is a Spanish class). —Bilingual student
>
> Those kids who speak Spanish. —Mainstreamed Puerto Rican student
>
> Bilingual is something like if you talked Spanish you'd go to a bilingual class and you'd have a Spanish teacher. —Anglo student

Fifty percent of the Spanish dominant children also made this same association to Spanish. However, in contrast to those who made references to learning English, most of these latter students had come from New York or other U.S. cities and not from Puerto Rico. Their experience in and perception of U.S. schools was thus different from newly arrived children.

An association of "bilingual" and *bilingüe* with two languages was evident in the definitions of only about half of the children who were midway in their acquisition of English. Just two English-proficient children made such associations. Responses from both groups included the following:

> I'll tell you in English or Spanish.
> Una persona que habla español e inglés (A person that speaks Spanish and English).
> Una bilingüe class in Spanish and English.

Made evident in a majority of the children's treatment of these words were experiences with and perceptions of bilingualism in the school context that placed it in a less than positive light. For a sizeable portion of the Spanish-dominant students, the sense of *bilingüe* or "bilingual" was a class that would provide a means of transition into the English language. For most of the English-dominant children, it was a reminder of their native tongue, and of a time when they were thought less of and segregated physically and psychologically from English speakers. Only a small group of students immersed in the process of becoming "bilingual," and not yet identifying with the transition in or out, saw it as the ability to speak two languages. Reflected in these multiple conceptions was the dominant societal connotation of bilingual in the United States—a language minority of limited or low prestige. Such perspective was in contradiction to children's language use outside the school where a dynamic and complex bilingualism functioned on a daily basis.[16]

Studies by Flores, Attinasi, and Pedraza (1981), Language Policy Task Force (1982; 1984), and Zentella (1981; 1985) have shown, and my observations within this particular community corroborated, that many urban Puerto Rican children use Spanish, English, Spanish/English code-switching, and sometimes Black English in varying forms and in varying domains. While bilingualism is a fact and a necessary condition of their existence, the context for being bilingual in the classroom is the transitional bilingual education (TBE) program and the goal of school (and state and federal) officials is to get children out of that environment as quickly as possible.[17] To be bilingual, as the majority of the children's responses indicate, is just a passing phase in the movement towards school-based English and Anglo assimilation. The bilingualism promoted in the community was not included in the terms "bilingual" or *bilingüe* most probably because it was connected in the minds of children to natural communication. In the school, "bilingual" implied imposed language conditions, reflective of (past and present) colonial and hegemonic circumstances. Bilingual students were thus a labeled "class." Contradictory realities were constructed as a result of this arrangement, imbricated with others' intentions, internalized in consciousness and externalized in voices.

The contradictory realities confronting Puerto Rican students can be further witnessed in their responses to the words "Hispanic" and *hispano*. But before examining these associations, it is important to dismantle the cultural and ideological connotations of "Hispanic" that extend beyond its dictionary definition or its significance as a translation equivalent of *hispano*. The word "Hispanic" is, in fact, a contrived term designed by U.S. government officials as a catch-all category in which to lump Puerto Ricans, Chicanos, Mexicans, and other Latin Americans. Its connotation provides links between Spanish colonialism and modern day imperialism. Ethnicity, culture, and linguistic variation as well as historical and present day struggles of diverse people are denied. Although many Puerto Ricans as well as other Latinos do not call themselves "Hispanic," many do utilize *hispano*. In schools, however, Puerto Ricans are classified both on paper and in speech as "Hispanic." It was thus the cultural saliency of the Spanish word as well as an interest in both how children would respond to its English equivalent and whether they would include or exclude themselves in the definitions that prompted the use of these words. As it turns out, definite patterns of inclusion and exclusion were highly evident.

Eighty percent of the children identified as English proficient or near proficient associated *hispano* or "Hispanic" with someone other than themselves who was Spanish speaking. In contrast, almost three-quarters of the Spanish dominant children made self or family associations. While the latter group demonstrated a pride in their ethnic and linguistic heritage, those with some proficiency in English tried to disassociate themselves from the terms. One light skinned, mainstreamed Puerto Rican boy went so far as to define "Hispanic" as a "Black man that speaks Spanish."

Some children's responses actually paralleled associations to the words *bilingüe* and "bilingual." A Puerto Rican boy, for example, explained "Hispanic" as:

> When the people knows Spanish they don't know English. Some people speak Spanish and some people speak English.

The response was similar for an Anglo child:

> Hispanic is a different kid. He knows a different language, like ... um ... what's it called ... not English ... Spanish.

Evident in many children's words was a perception of "Hispanic"/ *hispano* as a language-minority classification. It was only for Spanish-dominant children that ethno-cultural identification was manifest: "Hispano quiere decir 'you Puerto Rican' (Hispanic means you Puerto

Rican)." Bilingual children generally chose to distance themselves and respond as if they were Anglo. A mainstreamed boy even tried to blame his inability to respond in English to the word "Hispanic" on his lack of knowledge of Spanish. Interpretations of the words "Hispanic" and *hispano* thus serve as a further example of the dominant society's ability to influence children's conceptions of themselves and those around them.[18] Yet in contrast to other words, quite a few Puerto Rican children did not respond at all to the words *hispano* and "Hispanic," possibly because of an unfamiliarity with the words, especially the English "Hispanic." Their silence itself was significant. Through it a resistance was spoken—to either the internalization of the words' meanings and/or to its utilization in the school context as a colonial category. Somehow these children had not absorbed the dominant interpretations or, if they had, they chose not to articulate it.

Manifest in the overall associations to "Hispanic"/*hispano* and "bilingual"/*bilingüe* were the ubiquitous power relations at force in the school.[19] The hegemony of meaning is made even more discernable in children's interpretations of "Puerto Rican." Paired with the adjective were alternating pictures of Latino children in a classroom and Latino youth and adults in a community environment. All children generally reacted the same regardless of picture context. Differences in response, however, were most striking between the bilingual and mainstreamed students and those who were Spanish dominant. Seventy-three percent of the former group made reference to stereotyped characteristics: speaks only Spanish, member of a gang, dirty, drinks and smokes a lot, lazy. For instance, in examining a picture of a teenage boy in an urban neighborhood and hearing the sentence—"This boy is 'Puerto Rican.' What can you tell me about him?"—responses among bilingual and mainstreamed children included the following:

> He looks like he's in a gang or something. He looks tough. Parece .. se parece malo (He looks like he's bad).

> No sabe inglés (He doesn't know English).

> El fuma. Está en una ganga. Se crea que es tope (He smokes. He is in a gang. He thinks he's the best).

> He talks Spanish and only he talks Spanish. He could talk English but mostly he talks Spanish. And he does bad things sometimes.

Anglos' associations focused on the characteristics that distinguished Puerto Ricans from themselves, as "other":

> He talks different. He goes to a different school. A school that teaches Spanish. He has different language, lives in a different... was born in a

different place. He does Spanish work. He has different mothers and different fathers that talk different.

Spanish-dominant children reacted to the same picture and sentence in a manner totally divergent from that of both Anglos and more English-proficient Puerto Ricans. As with *hispano*, there was a personal ethnic and cultural association:

> Es puertorriqueño igual que yo (He's Puerto Rican just like me).
>
> Habla español y respeta mucho (He speaks Spanish and he is respectful).
>
> Se ve . . . como nosotros (He looks like us).

Virtually all of the Spanish-dominant students who related the word "Puerto Rican" and the picture context to their own lives were children born on the Island. Zentella maintains that place of birth often acts as a superficial cultural determinant within Puerto Rican families.

> Most parents raise their children to believe that those who were born in Puerto Rico are Puerto Ricans, and those who were born in the U.S. are Americans. This cleavage within families, often based on accidents of birth, given the massive back and forth migration, contributes to the confusion of the children, especially when they find they are rejected by other Americans. . . . In addition to the confusion about race and nationality, the Puerto Rican second generation is confused by too simplistic a link between culture and place of birth. (1985:45)

Obviously, parents' own perceptions of race, nationality, culture, and place of birth stem from the hegemony they, too, have experienced in schooling and in other societal institutions. Many Puerto Rican parents' hope is that things will somehow be better for their children if they assimilate and become North American in their language and in their own self-perceptions. Children's internalization of these beliefs could be evidenced in the response of Juan, for example, a U.S.-born Puerto Rican, who defined "Hispanic" as a Black man that speaks Spanish. Enrique, also U.S. born, made the same association to "Puerto Rican." Because they were not born on the Island, both children considered themselves absolved from their ethnic/racial and linguistic heritage. Blackness, for them, was associated with being foreign—different than and separate from the Anglo controlled majority. Spanish was also thought to be a foreign characteristic.

The oppositional associations of many of the U.S.-born students appeared to reflect both the reality to which Zentella speaks as well as the dominant societal attitude toward Puerto Ricans. Yet, when *puertorriqueño* was utilized, their associations changed character. Whereas 73 percent of the bilingual and mainstreamed students had made negative responses to

"Puerto Rican," 73 percent of this same group made positive references to family, to the Island, and to differences and similarities within their ethnic group (e.g., skin color and language), to values like authority and respect, or to social relations within the community like the playing of dominoes in their definitions of *puertorriqueño*. Self-identification, however, occurred only amongst those considered Spanish dominant.

Mirrored in the diverse senses of "Puerto Rican" and *puertorriqueño* were discordant contextual realities which, in contrast to most other words, were clearly language specific. In speaking about *puertorriqueño*, children seemed to naturally fall back on a cultural significance lived and maintained within the Spanish-oriented context of the community and the home. This seems to be in keeping with Maldonado-Denis' (1976) contention that, for Puerto Ricans born on the Island, or who maintain strong community ties, *puertorriqueño* signifies a social and cultural identity. "Puerto Rican," on the other hand, connotes an ethnic minority. For the children here, "Puerto Rican" exposed an oppositional voice apparently grounded in and influenced by experiences endured and words heard in the English language context of school and the world outside the community. Language itself was not the determinant of these dualistic perspectives; it was the historical, cultural, and ideological settings that defined the linguistic domains and infused these individual words with meaning. Embodied in the significance of the words and realized in children's talk was the lived reality of racial, ethnic, and class dominion.

The negative and self-denying reactions of bilingual children to "Puerto Rican" and to "Hispanic" and "bilingual" are the concrete result of the hegemonic power exerted by the educational institution. This hegemony has its parallels in the colonial policies imposed in Puerto Rico. One effect of both has been to destroy solidarity and to pit Puerto Rican against Puerto Rican. Through school-based policies and practices, through the images and language portrayed and supported in texts, and in the overt and hidden curriculum, children learn that racial/ethnic, cultural, and linguistic differences are not tolerated. Inclusion thus becomes predicated on the perceived need to identify with the dominant group. As this hegemony is internalized, it comes to shape meaning and alter self-image. Hegemony, Raymond Williams explains, is

> a whole body of practices and expectations . . . our senses and assignments of energy, our shaping perceptions of ourselves and our world. It is a lived system of meanings and values—constitutive and constituting—which as they are experienced as practiced appear as reciprocally confirming. . . . It is, that is to say, in the strongest sense, a "culture," but a culture which has also to be seen as the lived dominance and subordination of particular classes. (1977:11)

Advanced through this culture of dominance are contradictory consciousnesses, articulated in dualistic voices, a voice that speaks to the reality of the community and home and a second voice that manifests a disavowal of the former. Such was evident in the facility of children to talk with pride about *puertorriqueños* at one moment and with disdain about "Puerto Ricans" the next. It is by fostering this metaphoric "forked tongue" that schools commit what Peter Iadicola refers to as symbolic violence:

> It commits symbolic violence by promoting the dominance and superiority of the cultural or knowledge system that supports the political economic order over others that are defined as illegitimate or inferior because they may threaten the political economic order, thus promoting the students' rejection of their own ethnicity and the acceptance and striving for conformity to the capitalist Anglo cultural norm. The differentiating and ranking mechanisms within the school perform this function. They serve to isolate the culturally foreign, as determined by the cultural arbitrary, and define them as inferior to the culturally dominant. (1981:380-381)

While this symbolic violence is realized and perpetuated in schools in a myriad of ways, it is not passively consumed or absorbed by the children who are its object. In fact, the children themselves are generally aware of the subordinating mechanisms of schooling, that is, they can identify the conditions and circumstances in schools that make them feel uncomfortable and left out. It is out of a desire to do away with these feelings and somehow make things right that many succumb to violence against their own and demonstrate an apparent cultural and ethnic rejection. But in doing this, children often experience tension. A discussion I had with Jorge, one of the children in the study, illuminates this friction.

Jorge was in a fourth-grade mainstreamed classroom. It was his first year out of the bilingual program. As I had done with all the children I worked with in the study, I entered Jorge's class and asked the teacher if he could accompany me to the library. The teacher's initial response was a blank stare; she then proceeded to tell me there was no Jorge in her class, only a George. Since the last names were the same, she presumed I wanted George and sent him with me. In the hallway, I spoke to the child in Spanish asking him which was his real name. His words were enlightening:

> She just did it. She told the kids and everybody else that my name's George. That I don't speak Spanish, too. But it's okay 'cause my family still calls me Jorge and I know my name isn't really George.

While the teacher's renaming of Jorge may have had the simple intention of making him feel a part of the Anglo environment, the significance of her actions are not so naive. In fact, names have been used as a measure of the dominant society's control in a number of different countries and with a number of different subordinated populations for generations.[20]

As one of the children who defined "Puerto Rican" as "those Spanish kids," and *puertorriqueño* in terms of family, Jorge was caught in the midst of opposing realities. His description of the teacher's action of naming demonstrates a cognizance of these tensions and a struggle to live with them. Thus while it appears Jorge had internalized the dominant view of Puerto Ricans and was adding to their subordination by denying he was one of them, it seems instead that, although probably subconsciously, he had adopted a strategy of survival.

The dialectical character of inner consciousness that made Jorge's struggle with voice possible is made even more evident in the language of Maria, first discussed in the previous chapter. Although Maria had only been in the bilingual program a year and a half and was still essentially Spanish dominant, she too had internalized the low status afforded Puerto Ricans, the symbolic violence, and the colonial image Anglo society perpetuates. However, in speaking this perspective, she seemed to come to terms with the words for the first time, arriving at a realization that they did not describe her own situation.

> Puerto Ricans are sad, Puerto Ricans are dirty, Puerto Ricans are lazy. Puerto Ricans hace lo que da la gana (do whatever they feel like). . . . But I'm Puerto Rican, and I'm' not sad, I'm not dirty or lazy, and I work real hard. . . . Maybe all Puerto Ricans aren't like that, right?

CONCLUSION

Through words we can discover the historical, cultural, social, ideological, and psychological fabric of people's existence. Echoed are both reconstructed interpretations from past generations and new elucidations constructed and created concurrently. These conceptions are in dialogic relation with subjective experience, forming the meanings and contextual senses of words that are internalized in consciousness and then spoken in voices.

For children, the contexts of home and school provide some of the many socializations that shape this inner consciousness. As was illustrated through a discussion of Puerto Rican children's associations to words, the sociocultural influence of home and community continues to position the meanings of some culturally salient words—whether these words are spoken or described in English or the native language. This influence perseveres even after children have acquired proficiency in English. For other words, the social, cultural, and ideological context of the school takes an eminent role, shaping children's meanings and self-perspective and asserting limits on their community-grounded voices. It is not the contexts themselves that impact language, however; it is children's own active experiences in and perspectives gleaned from interactions with individuals in these dual environments that determine the multiple senses and significances that are given expression in their words. As Emerson so eloquently explains: "One makes a self through the words one has learned, fashions one's own voice and inner speech by a selective appropriation of the voices of others" (1986:31).

For many of the bilingual children described in this study, the predominance of "the voice of others" was evident. This was particularly discernable for mainstream students who, as the example of Jorge illustrated, confront an everday life in the school governed by an overt but hidden agenda.[21] In an apparent desire to name which reality is valid by touting the Anglo culture as cardinal and remolding children to fit that image, students' names are changed and the use of Spanish discouraged. Cultural ways of perceiving and interacting are disavowed. While the children are told such efforts will help gain them access to school success, the reality of class and ethnicity stand as ever present obstacles in the path of educational and civic inclusion.[22] The school practices, which work to co-opt the voice of Puerto Rican students and denigrate their image, have their effect on Anglo children as well. Muriel Saville-Troike explains:

> While minority students are learning to disvalue their language, their culture, and their social group, the majority students are likewise learning to disparage their fellow students and to believe in the inferiority of the minority language and culture, and the inherent superiority of the majority culture and its linguistic medium, standard English. Such beliefs, though founded in ignorance, become deeply engrained to the point that they acquire an almost religious tenacity and become the basis for perpetuating inequities and inequality of educational opportunity. (1980:354)

While the hegemony of schooling is most evident in education's monolingual/monocultural orientation, it is also inscribed in the transitional nature of the bilingual education program. As the use of the English language and Anglo-oriented texts becomes increasingly prevalent, children come to perceive their own backgrounds as less significant; success in the school—and in the world—becomes associated with white skin and English language facility. Bilingual teachers' reference to the poor study habits, low attendance, depressed home life, and lack of motivation of many of their Puerto Rican students contributed to low self-esteem; even in the bilingual program, Puerto Ricans were being compared to Anglos. In an effort to belong, some children attempt to do away with the ethnic/cultural obstructions. Common is a refusal to use Spanish with parents and relatives at home, further altering their identity and increasing their own self, social, and cultural disengagement.[23] Although the influence of the home remains with certain cultural values that have been inculcated in the child since infancy, the overall result is self-denial and the legitimation of what Apple (1982), Bourdieu and Passeron (1977), and Bernstein (1977) have called cultural capital—the symbolic and communicative resources of the dominant group. For Puerto Ricans, this legitimation of cultural capital is not limited to the reality of schools or to the boundaries of the United States, it is the result of nearly a century of colonialism and imperialist relations. Certainly the struggles of the children here are not so separate from those of their ancestors on the Island.

Present in voice and emanating from the inner consciousness is a dialogical relation that enables children to question and reflect upon their situations and to develop internal or external stategies that work toward change. Cultural attributes, dispositions, and meanings are thus not merely acquired and absorbed nor are they ever complete. They can be struggled with, transformed and sometimes even rejected (Apple 1979). In laying bare their inner worlds, children taught us about the cogency of community ways of understanding and they made clear to us hegemony's curse. By listening to their voices, we could hear the assimilation of the dominant "other's" words, we could discern the negotiation with and struggles around identity, and we could feel the oppression, frustration, alienation, cultural conflict, and colonization. The power of words of children like Jorge and Maria illuminate these lived contradictions yet also bear witness to inner struggle. In their meanings we witness hope, are encouraged by contest, and see possibility.

NOTES

1. See, for example, Bakhtin (Volosinov) (1973); Vygotsky (1962); Vygotsky (1978); Galperin, Zaporozhets, and Elkonin (1987); and Davidov and Markova (1987).

2. Henriques, Hollway, Urwin, Venn, and Walkerdine maintain that feminism has introduced "the necessity of understanding consciousness as something produced rather than as the source of ideas and the social world—as constituted but not constituting" (1984:8).

3. Certainly the existence of any imposed standard should be questioned whether or not it coincides with that of the teacher and the majority of her/his students. That is, all children should be permitted to utilize their sociocultural realities as the base from which school instruction can build, but until texts are rewritten and practices changed, teachers should encourage students to critically view the realities portrayed in texts and perpetuated in practices as well as to interrogate their own realities in a critical manner. See Chapter 4 for a more detailed discussion of this issue.

4. Anglos tended to adopt a self-centered or individualistic interpretation, such as: "Like when you don't feel good about yourself, you feel ashamed of yourself."

5. Because of the deviancies in translation, both "manners" and "education" were alternately tried with different children as the translation equivalent of *educación*. Response to "education," however, was of most interest.

6. Szalay and Deese (1978) also used the word "education" as a stimulus in their study. They found both Colombian and Korean students made associations to "politeness" while native English speakers most often referred to "intelligence."

7. Not discussed is the significant effect of the evangelical movement on the Puerto Rican community, its influence on the subjective meaning of the word "church," or its hegemonical antecedents.

8. Since limited English-proficient children have been found to rely on context in producing messages (Walters 1980), it was thought that the use of photographs might stimulate children to expand on their associations as well as to relate to the diverse contexts of home and school. All of the photos depicted Latino children and adults in various home/community and school situations; boys and girls and men and women were equally represented.

9. In fact, native Spanish-speaking adults recruited to help categorize the data had similar meaning interpretations.

10. According to Wertsch (1985), the literal translation from the Russian is "signification" rather than "meaning."

11. Research by Hogaboam and Pellegrino (1977) and Szalay and Deese (1978) found that pictures can access the same underlying semantic knowledge base as words. In my study, a kind of dual contextual significance was created by both embedding the adjective in a sentence and combining it with a visual image.

12. A sixth pair of adjectives, *puertorriqueño* and "Puerto Rican," also engendered distinct responses based on language of presentation. These associations are discussed in detail in a subsequent section.

13. The decisions to use these adjectives in the study was based on the supposition that the contextual significance of the school might trigger an English semantic orientation. However, this was generally not the case.

14. Gender differences were evident. While there were several Puerto Rican mainstreamed boys who demonstrated an Anglo influence in their response, Puerto Rican girls always voiced a home/community understanding. Girls' responses in English were also much more limited than were boys, possibly reflective of the fact that many Puerto Ricans girls assume familial responsibilities from an early age. Males, on the other hand, tend to spend more time outside of the home in wider social interactions.

15. See Glanzer and Duarte (1971); Gulden, Martinez, and Zamora (1980); Lambert, Ignatow, and Krauthamer (1968); Lopez and Young (1974); and Magiste (1979).

16. In their ethnographic study in New York's El Barrio, Language Policy Task Force found Puerto Rican children's reporting of their language use to be contextually dependent. When speaking about their linguistic interactions with parents and older relatives, children said they accommodated to the elders' language preference, usually Spanish or Spanish and English together. When speaking about school, however, reported language use was largely tied to the program in which the child was enrolled. As they note:

> This language choice is reinforced by the perception of the teacher as author-

ity figure. The fact that her/his language preference corresponds to that of the program, and the relative homogeneity of language use of students in each class which constrains the interactional possibilities given that most school friendships are among classmates. These patterns continue even during recess, as playground social groupings tend to reflect those in the classroom. (1982:432)

17. Massachusetts Transitional Bilingual Education Law, Chapter 71A, suggests that children be mainstreamed from the TBE program within three years' time. Pressure from the state Board of Education as well as from some state and local officials has resulted in school districts endeavoring to mainstream students before three years. As a result, English as a second language (ESL) instruction often takes priority over content instruction and the development of literacy skills in the native language. The effect is that language minority children become proficient word callers in English but frequently lack the semantic and literacy based understandings required for academic success in the mainstream. As their responses to "bilingual" demonstrate, they internalize this push for English and the neglect of the mother tongue. The rapid transition policy both adds to minority students self-denigration and goes counter to research in the field of second language acquisition that shows it generally takes language minority children upward of five years to develop the English language skills necessary to function on par with native English speakers (e.g., see Cummins 1984; Collier 1987).

18. As this push and pull for voice and for one's sense of self illustrates, identity is not stable or fixed but must, as Deborah Britzman (1989) points out, be negotiated with others within situational and historical constraints. For further discussion on this view of identity see Linda Alcoff (1988), Teresa de Lauretis (1986), and Homi Bhabha (1987).

19. Poststructuralist analyses afford discussions of power as multiple relations rather than as a deterministic property or force, see Michel Foucault (1980) and Cathy Urwin (1984).

20. In the United States, for example, Native American children in state-controlled schools have been required to maintain Christian names. Similarly, the children of Black slaves in the South were often obligatorily named after slave owners. In Latin America, the Spanish invaders have, throughout history, maintained control over the naming of indigenous populations. In Ecuador, for instance, where over half the population is Native American, the state requires that all indigenous children be given a Christian name and that it be documented in the civil register; cultural/ethnic naming is considered invalid.

21. In his study of Portuguese language-minority children, Jose Ribeiro (1983) also found self-esteem to be lower outside the bilingual program. When involved in competitive situations with Anglo peers in the classroom or when rejected in their attempts to be fully accepted by Anglos, Portuguese students could be seen to develop serious feelings of inferiority. Adeline Becker (1990) discovered that the longer Portuguese students are in the United States the more they attempt to take on Anglo-like characteristics. In her study, students were found to even change their own names.

22. See Walsh (1987b) for a detailed discussion of the ways schools promote both an educational and a civic exclusion of Latino students.

23. In fact, upon seeing my Anglo face, several of the children who had been in the bilingual program two or three years told me they spoke very little Spanish. But by speaking to them informally in Spanish and, in the context of the word association task, asking them to teach me the meaning of some Spanish words, their use of the language blossomed.

4

Bilingualism, Pedagogy, and Voice

We have had to be in your world and learn its ways. We have
had to participate in it, make a living in it, live in it, be mis-
treated in it, be ignored in it, and rarely, be appreciated in it. In
learning to do these things or in learning to suffer them or in
learning to enjoy what it is to be enjoyed or in learning to
understand your conception of us, we have had to learn your
culture and thus your language and self-conceptions. But there is
nothing that necessitates that you understand our world; understand, that is, not as an observer understands things, but as a
participant, as someone who has a stake in them understands
them.

Lugones and Spelman 1983:576

MARIA LUGONES AND Elizabeth Spelman elucidate both the unequal vulnerability and the ongoing compliancy which derive
from lived oppression. It is only those who must struggle with
and against domination and for voice who truly comprehend this reality;
they are the "experts," the insiders who know what oppression is and feels
like. They are also the ones who must adapt because the dominant group
seldom endeavors to find them out or to listen to their speaking voices.

Bilingual students know this pursuit for they are also "experts" on their
own lives. They are the only authentic chroniclers of their own experience
(Delpit 1988) because they alone have lived it. While not always able or

willing to verbally express their expertise, these students are aware of the people, experiences, and environments that have touched them and they are cognizant of the multitudinous relationships, both social and linguistic, that constitute their daily existence. This awareness stems not from being passive objective observers but from actively involving themselves as subjects—agents capable of making and being made. It is through this continuing human activity or production (itself grounded in history) that knowledge is constructed, language is formulated, voice is fashioned, and meaning is created.

The previous chapter concretely demonstrated the notion of students as subjects and the effect activity, in the divergent sociocultural contexts of home/community and school, has on thought and language. It also demonstrated children's ability, under the proper conditions, to express their thoughts, understandings, perceptions, and knowledge of the world and of themselves within it. By listening to the students' voices and to the significance they gave to specific words, we learned about the conceptual connections triggered by language and by context, and about the relation between language and subjective experience. The students also revealed a lot about the lived reality of bilingualism—its linguistic, cultural, social, and historical antecedents, and its contemporary realizations. While this insider knowledge offers numerous possibilities for classroom pedagogy, it is seldom utilized or valued in school. The transmission of knowledge is separated from its production. Teachers play an active role in shaping and maintaining this separation by relying on the directives of prepackaged curriculum and purchased texts; commercial authors, publishers, and in-house specialists are thought to know best even though their experience and knowledge base are far removed from that of language-minority communities. This dependency on "outside" expertise derives from the dominant conception of formal education in the United States and of its hegemonic functions. Pedagogy is assumed to be a one-way mechanical process of imparting knowledge, that is, of reproduction—dialogue between teachers and students is virtually nonexistent.[1]

Poststructuralists have demonstrated the partiality of knowledge, that the knowledge portrayed through texts and discourse represents interests, particular points of view and understanding, that are unfinished, imperfect, and limited precisely because they project the interests of one side over others (Alcoff 1988; Aronowitz 1987; Weedon 1987). The dominant perspective is that children and oppressed groups have a deficient knowledge base because they lack the same lived experiences and socialized perceptions that the privileged have been provided. What this perspective fails to recognize is that the process of coming to know involves a shifting and a rebalancing of information. It also precludes an acceptance that there may be some things that will never be known regardless of privilege, if one lacks an "insider's" vision. A number of educators have suggested that this partiality of knowledge can in part be alleviated by a more collaborative pedagogy that pools the collective knowledge of both students and teacher. Pedagogy, in this sense, becomes not a transmission oriented process but a productive, transformational process that involves, as David Lusted (1986) has pointed out, the interaction of three agencies: the teacher, the learner, and the knowledge they together produce. Teaching becomes inseparable from what is being taught and how it is learned. Lusted explains:

> This concept of pedagogy . . . denies notions of teacher as functionary (neutral transmittor of knowledge as well as "state functionary"), the learner as "empty vessel" or passive respondent, knowledge as immutable material to impart. Instead, it foregrounds exchange between and over the categories, it recognizes the productivity of the relations, and it renders the parties within them as active, changing and changeable agencies. (1986:3)

Calling children experts, as I have done above, goes counter to the dominant meaning where an expert is typically understood as someone who dispenses power and polices conduct. In this version of expertise, knowledge becomes dichotomized as either valued for its capacity to control or devalued because it is idiosyncratic. Children's ability to act as knowledgeable subjects is not esteemed or recognized nor is the knowledge that they have developed in the community and home placed at the center of school instruction. Yet, ample opportunities are provided for some children rather than others to sharpen and reproduce their subjective positions. Thus while the discourse of teachers and texts may recognize, reinforce, unequally position, and support the values, beliefs, and reality of white, middle-class families, the lived expertise of children of color and of poor white children is most often negated, ignored, subordinated, and misunderstood.

In counterdistinction, the conception of expertise that I am promulgating recognizes the valor of lived experience and respects an insider's perspective and understanding. This expertise is grounded in the productive capacity to construct and reconstruct knowledge and meaning, that is, the ability of students to become the professional authorities on their own lives and of their collective and isolated struggles for understanding (Lusted 1986). In actuality, it is this kind of cultural production that shapes the way schools deem children's knowledge as objective and "unofficial." The contents of this knowledge are determined as either supporting or countering the dominant "official" standard. As a matter of policy, schools do not generally promote unofficial knowledge production nor, in practice, do they formally recognize or provide a pedagogical forum for children's inside perspectives. What would it mean for schools and for the teachers in them to see children as experts? And, does this expertise also reflect children's voices? In this chapter, I advocate that the various forms of knowledge and experience brought to schools be the point of departure for pedagogies of student voices, pedagogies that are grounded in students' expertise and that interrogate the conditions, contexts, and relations therein. Central to these pedagogies is a recognition of the contradictory nature of schooling for Puerto Ricans.

Bilingual education programs have, at least at a superficial level, brought Puerto Rican students' language and culture into the classroom. They have also awakened some awareness on the part of monolingual English educators of the importance of lingistic and cultural inclusion. However, as has been previously discussed, bilingual education's transitional nature also promotes a compensatory or remedial association. Students' linguistic and cultural expertise is only momentarily valued. Emphasis is not on constructing a bilingual/bicultural environment where students can naturally explore the conceptual, semantic, and sociocultural connotations of each language (and extend their expertise) but on replacing the native language with English. This environment promotes what has been referred to as a cognitively disabling, subtractive bilingualism (Cummins 1984; 1986). It constitutes symbolic violence because it cultivates self-denigration.

By means of the pronounced and subtle messages, orientations, and practices in bilingual as well as monolingual education, dualities are constructed both in the classroom and in students' consciousnesses between the world of the community and the world of the school, and between the divergent knowledge bases and language varieties promoted in each context. The effects of these dualities can be seen in students' attitudes, motivation, and achievement in school, as well as in the voices that they develop. They can be further witnessed in teachers' attitudes, perceptions, and pedagogical approaches.

Alberto, a Latino high school student with whom I worked on a recent dropout prevention project, had experienced this schism. As an inside expert, he knew how students' behaviors and intentions are sometimes misinterpreted. He also knew that one of the major reasons Latino students drop out, or tune school out, is because their history, culture, language, and experiences are devalued and excluded. After only ten months in the United States, he had developed a tacit understanding that school bears little relation to the rest of existence.

> Teachers think we come to school just to be with our friends, to fool around. They think we don't care about school, that we don't want to learn and study. We do but it's not so simple. When I'm in school I am also thinking about what happened last night, what I have to do today, the fight with my cousin, about other problems and worries. The teachers, they need to understand who we are. They need to understand that our lives are much more than just what they see and control in school. Our real lives are the family, our friends, the street, jobs, and all that we came with from before. (Translation from Spanish mine)

Alberto's words, as the words of the Puerto Rican children in the previous chapter, make clear the dualities that are promoted in school and students' awareness of their operation. Yet they also suggest strategies for change.

This chapter draws upon these voices, upon students' expert understanding of their own words, contexts, and experiences, and the tensions, conflicts, and contradictions these understandings engender and suggest. Its project is to make dualities problematic, to discuss ways students and teachers can come to recognize and interrogate these dualities and develop a more critical awareness of the conditions promoting them. Examined are the lived condition of bilingualism and the multiple phenomena embedded in this condition that impact students' performance in school. Through a discussion and analysis of a project conducted in a Massachusetts high school, bilingual students' perceptions of their realities both inside and outside school are illustrated. Highlighted are the myriad actions, resistances, and voices that make up their responses to the tensions and pressures in their lives as well as the ways particular pedagogies permit these responses to be identified, reflected upon, talked about, and interrogated. Emerging from this discussion is a recognition of a need for specific pedagogies (inside and outside of bilingual education) that address the social, cultural, linguistic, political, and ideological contexts of the community, school, and the broader society in ways that encourage questioning, active engagement, knowledge production, and work toward transformation. It is by situating these pedagogies in the past and present history and reality of Puerto Rican students, by acknowledging the impositions and struggles that they and their peoples have faced, and by giving value to lived experiences, that bilingualism itself can extend linguistic boundaries and take on a critically empowering character.

BILINGUALISM AS A LIVED CONDITION

Language is interwined with culture and with identity. It is embedded in how we think about ourselves and others and in how our thoughts are constructed, positioned, and defined. It would seem that having more than one language would therefore afford diverse experiences and broaden one's perspectives and understandings; bilingualism should thus be valued. In fact, in most other nations of the world, bilingualism is a prerequisite skill for active societal involvement and for daily public as well as home and community-based communication. Its development is often promoted and supported by the state and its public institutions. The United States is one of the more parochial and paranoid nations in this regard, for here, while the English language is exalted, other languages are thought to be divisive, detrimental, and unpatriotic. Bilingualism is equated with minority status and with an inability or unwillingness to assimilate to the dominant norm;

the possibility that English could co-exist alongside other mother tongues is disregarded.

Support for English over all other languages has fluctuated throughout our nation's history, becoming most apparent during times of political conservatism when overt racism and xenophobia have also been more prevalent. The contemporary disdain for and fear of bilingualism has been primarily directed toward Latinos who are rapidly becoming the largest racial and ethnolinguistic "minority." Already numerous cities in the Northeast and Southwest have a Latino majority. Fear that Spanish will come to assume co-equal status and that the dominant white English speakers will somehow lose their authority is voiced in both public and private sectors. A recent policy paper written for the Council on Interamerican Security reflects this paranoia:

> Hispanics in America today represent a very dangerous and subversive force that is bent on taking over our nation's political institutions for the purposes of imposing Spanish as the official language of the U.S. and indeed of the entire Western Hemisphere. . . . They represent a serious threat to our cherished freedoms and our American traditions . . . if we desire to preserve our unique culture and the primacy of the English language, then we must so declare rather than sitting idly by as a de facto nation evolves. (Butler 1985)

The move to eradicate bilingualism has, in the last decade, become both a multimillion dollar and a ballot box struggle. "U.S. English," the lobbying organization formed in 1983 by Senator S. I. Hayakawa and Dr. John Tanton, an opthalmologist and population control activist, to place stricter controls on immigration and to fight for an English language amendment to the Constitution, had an annual membership in 1988 of 350,000 and an annual budget of $7 million. Their message, as presented by former president Gerda Bikales, is that English is the bond, the "social glue" in this nation of immigrants and it is now threatened by the "mindless drift toward a bilingual society" (Crawford 1989). Their agenda, however, extends beyond linguistic unification. In a 1986 memo recently made public, Chairman John Tanton echoes the paranoia of a Hispanic takeover:

> "Gobernar es poblar" translates "to govern is to populate." In this society, where the majority rules, does this hold? Will the present majority peaceably hand over its political power to a group that is simply more fertile? . . . Can "homo contraceptivus" compete with "homo progenitiva" if borders aren't controlled? . . . Perhaps this is the first instance in which those with their pants up are going to get caught by those with their pants down. . . . As Whites see their power and control over their lives declining, will they simply go quietly into the night? Or will there be an explosion? . . . We are building in a deadly disunity. All great empires disintegrate; we want stability. (Crawford 1989:57)

While the publication of Tanton's memo along with disclosures of the ties of two of U.S. English's larger contributors to eugenic sterilization groups has resulted in an upheaval in the organization, including the resignation of President Linda Chavez and board member Walter Cronkite, and caused Tanton himself to step down, the U.S. English movement's impact continues. By 1989, seventeen states had passed official English proposals.[2]

Another example of the racist and xenophobic arguments against bilingualism is that of Lloyd Dunn, the principal author of the Peabody Picture Vocabulary Test. Dunn maintains that the Spanish spoken by Latinos in the United States is inferior, that they do not understand either Spanish or English well enough to function adequately in school (the semilingualism argument), and that they do not "have the scholastic aptitude or linguistic ability to master two languages well, or to handle switching from one to the other at school, as language of instruction" (1987:71). He also argues that Mexican American and Puerto Rican students' academic difficulties stem from both environmental factors and racially determined genetic differences:

> Most Mexican immigrants to the U.S. are brown-skinned people, a mixture of American Indian and Spanish blood, while many Puerto Ricans are dark-skinned, a mixture of Spanish, black, and some Indian. Blacks and American Indians have repeatedly scored about 15 IQ points behind Anglos and Orientals on individual tests of intelligence. (1987:64)[3]

Within this present environment, native speakers of languages other than English[4] are forced to conceal their bilingualism behind closed doors.[4] Even there, parents are often told by sometimes well-meaning school administrators and teachers that their children would be better off if English were to become the home language.

Mario, a ten-year-old Puerto Rican boy, is a product of the above described context. Exemplified in his words is a desire to cover up his linguistic reality—to deny his lived bilingualism.

> I don't speak no Spanish. I just talk English. . . . Yeah, my mother only talks Spanish so I has to talk Spanish to her but with my brothers and sisters we talk mostly English. With my grandmother, Spanish. And in school, well, English is the language. . . . But I just speak English. I don't know no Spanish.

Mario is acutely aware of the various language domains he encounters in his daily life and, as his words demonstrate, is able to move between these domains, switching languages as appropriate. But, while he is able to talk about with whom he uses each language, the condition of being bilingual is one he staunchly denies. The status associated with each of his languages is both perceived and experienced as manifestly unequal.

Mario is not so different from many Puerto Rican children in U.S. schools. Although he had been through the bilingual program (entering school as Spanish dominant), he quickly internalized the negative societal status associated with Spanish.[5] While he had told both his Anglo classroom teacher and me that he did not "speak no Spanish," he could be heard conversing in Spanish outside of the classroom—on the playground and informally with peers. Access to the Anglo controlled "dominant" world (which we, as whites, in fact represented) was, in his perception, clearly predicated on English monolingualism, bilingualism could only hold him back, perpetuating his (and his community's) dominated reality. The allegation to Anglos of an English Only repertoire thus afforded him the false hope of inclusion in their environment. With a group of Puerto Rican friends it was permissable (and, in fact, valued) to use both Spanish and English in a natural code-switching style. This was indicative of group membership and solidarity. But outside of the peer group, English became a way to assume power (i.e., domination) over other Spanish dominant individuals, including members of his own family. A further example illustrates:

> My mother, she don't speak no English. Sometime I talk English to her anyway. Me and my brothers, we talk English mostly and she don't know what we're saying. She get mad and sometime she cry. She say talk Spanish but she can't do nothin 'cause we knows English and she don't.

Through his words, Mario makes evident the way language usage and language practices reflect lived experiences and shape social relations. English had come to assume a prominent position in his life as well as in the lives of family members. At one level, this effect can be witnessed in his (and his brother's) choice of English for communication. However, also made clear is the control and sense of superiority English affords him.

School was the primary context for Mario's acquisition of English and it was there he interacted with adult and child native speakers, constructed meaning, and began to develop subjective understanding. However, as his attitudes toward English demonstrate, this experience was by no means neutral but was governed by the power relations expressed in and through the language forms at work in the classroom. As Giroux describes,

> One of the most important elements at work in the construction of experiences and subjectivities of schools is language. . . . Language intersects with power in the way a particular linguistic form is used in schools to legitimate and structure the ideologies and modes of life of specific groups. Language, in this case, is intimately related to power and functions to both position and constitute the way that teachers and students define, mediate, and understand their relation to each other and to the larger society. (1988:99)

The example of Mario raises interesting questions about the lived relations of language, power, and gender and their interplay with culture. Also brought to the fore are questions about children's perception of these relations. Was Mario, for example, always conscious of his choice of language with particular individuals and was intentionality shaped by linguistic preference, issues of authority, and/or by perceived sociocultural norms? How did English act to position him in relation to others in the community and in the broader social world?

At the time I met Mario, his ability to communicate in both oral and written form was greater in English than in Spanish, typical of most students who have been "mainstreamed" out of the bilingual program. School records classified him as fully English proficient and, as he himself described, English was his preferred language. While he did not articulate (and was probably not totally conscious of) the intersection of power with his language use, it was made evident in the passage about his mother. It seems he had not learned to simply speak English words, but had learned the power of its cultural capital. English was his source of authority. His utilization of English with his mother was thus not so much a linguistic phenomenon (especially since he could speak Spanish if he wanted) as psycho-emotional, a product of the hegemonic circumstances that had shaped his English acquisition. In this sense, the English language had come to symbolize domination, that which he used over his mother, that which had been used over him, and that which had been used over his ancestors in Puerto Rico. It thus appears that, as Freire (1970) has noted, the oppressed often themselves come to be oppressors. But upon closer examination, it becomes evident that Mario's linguistic oppression was at best superficial. While he seemed to have assimilated into English, Mario's ways of thinking about many of the English words that were presented in the word association tasks described in the last chapter demonstrated more of a Spanish than an Anglo orientation. (These responses came after his above quoted comments.) Of particular note was his constant reference to the values of respect and authority. This seems peculiar since adherence to these values in his own life appear to be absent, that is, if we believe that his described treatment of his mother really did happen.

In Puerto Rican homes (and throughout Latino culture), there is a strong tradition and vision of matriarchy. While "machismo" positions the father in specific relations of domination in the home (and in society), the mother retains control over the household and authority over the children. Culturally, she is revered in an almost saint-like fashion. At first glance, Mario's behavior seems to go counter to this norm. Could it be that since there was no father in the home, he had begun to assume a father-like role? Or, could it be that the action of disrespect exemplified through words somehow confirmed or validated a perceived Anglo male identity? In other words, by not showing respect for his mother's authority and identity, by putting down her Spanish dominance, and by telling me, an Anglo woman, about it, was Mario not using language both figuratively, conjuratively, and selectively as both a form of cultural disassociation—as a way to somehow negate what was ever present in his consciousness, and of (Anglo) gendered domination? Was he not also demonstrating the reality of U.S. bilingual/ biculturalism as cultural struggle and as lived contradictions?

Because language is an obvious marker of in-group and out-group differences, it becomes one of the primary social constructions available for group identification (Hurtado and Gurin 1987; Giles 1977; G. Williams 1979). De la Zerda and Hopper (1975) found, in their study of Mexican-origin populations, that variation in ethnic identity is systematically related to attitudes toward language and dialect. Those who think of themselves as "American" favored standard English; Mexican and Mexican-American identification resulted in an acceptance of minority speech styles but a preference for English, while Chicanos looked down on English in favor of Chicano dialect. Parallels between these findings and Mario's comments as well as the responses of other Puerto Rican students (detailed in Chapter 3) can be witnessed: mainstreamed students exhibited a preference for English and for American status while recently enrolled bilingual program students accepted their Spanish but at the same time showed a strong desire for English language use and inclusion. Aida Hurtado and Patricia Gurin (1987) maintain that attitudes toward bilingualism among Latinos are not so much a reflection of ethnic identification but of particular meanings their ethnicity has assumed. For Chicanos, ethnic identity has become politicized and their bilingual dialect form thus valued. A political consciousness, a sense of solidarity, and a predilection for a bilingual dialect is also present among many Puerto Rican students and adults who reside within the community. In general, however, the subordinate status given to Puerto Ricans in U.S. society encourages negative associations, particularly among children and those who aspire to the values and life style of the dominant class. For these individuals, the obstacles placed on socioeconomic mobility, on quality education, and on societal inclusion are often associated with bilingualism and with what they perceive as Puerto Rican ways of being. While bilingualism in general is not supported by the native English-speaking populace or by state structures, tolerance and opinion of different varieties vary depending upon the group's racial/ethnic roots and its class position. Colonial status also appears to play a role since, in the hierarchy of Spanish/English bilingualism, Chicanos and Puerto Ricans fall at the bottom of the ladder. It seems that negative attitudes toward Puerto Rican bilingualism derive first from historical race and class biases (that were in fact perpetuated through colonial practices in Puerto Rico and continue in many urban areas in the United States). These biases are then realized through judgments made on the quality and character of the language varieties and speech forms that comprise their bilingual repertoire. Juan

Flores, John Attinasi, and Pedro Pedraza are worth quoting at length in this regard:

> Puerto Rican Spanish, with its admixture of indigenous, African, and peasant qualities, is stigmatized to this day as a corruption of the pure mother tongue and its supposedly more faithful Latin American variants. The class basis of this judgement is obvious. Unfortunately this kind of purist condescension toward Puerto Rican Spanish is very much alive among many bilingual educators intent on the maintenance and cultivation of Spanish. Thus the very idiom that Puerto Ricans bring to the bilingual arena as their own is one that has historically been viewed as inferior, and associated with deviance and ignorance. (1981:198-199)

Derogatory opinions of Puerto Ricans' language use are not limited to the Spanish/English dichotomy, however. Most Puerto Ricans in the United States are not simply bilingual, but gravitate toward an integrative use of both languages when involved in in-group communication. It is this complex, rule-governed utilization of code-switching, or what has been disparagingly called "Spanglish," that is frequently attacked by North American as well as some Latino educators as a sign of a lingusitic, and therefore cultural, deficiency. As Flores, Attinasi, and Pedraza further explain:

> Code-switching is viewed as the tragic convergence of two nonstandard vernaculars, and thus is assumed to epitomize the collapse of the integrity of both. It is in this context where practical bilingualism occurs most spontaneously and expressively, that the charge of alinguality has gained its widest currency. For many observers, Puerto Rican and American alike, code-switching amounts to contamination and interference, an easy recourse to compensate for incomplete resources in either idiom. (1981:199)

In schools, value judgments are placed on Puerto Rican students' communicative behavior. Recent arrivals from Puerto Rico are viewed as less problematic than Nuyoricans. Their language is considered more developed and legitimate and their ways of speaking absent of, what school officials perceive as, on the one hand, a deficit-oriented language mixing and, on the other, a form of social and linguistic resistance. The deficit notion derives from the belief that students' movement between languages is detrimental and that cognitive and lingusitic confusion are its result. Puerto Ricans' disproportionate school failure thus becomes attributed to a lack of standard language development. Blamed are the linguistic and sociocultural environment of the home and parents' own inability to speak the language "correctly." As one teacher told me:

These poor kids come to school speaking a hodge podge. They are all mixed up and don't know any language well. As a result, they can't even think clearly. That's why they don't learn. It's our job to teach them language—to make up for their deficiency. And, since their parents don't really know any language either, why should we waste time on Spanish? It is "good" English which has to be the focus.

The bilingualism that children bring with them thus becomes perceived as a deficit condition; the experiences, biculturalism, and "unofficial" knowledge acquired in its wake are perceived to be impediments to be silenced and somehow eradicated. These attitudes and misconceptions about code-switching have been transferred to Puerto Ricans themselves, with new migrants and those still on the Island criticizing the "mainland" way of speaking. Another understanding of Puerto Rican students' communicative behavior is also prevalent among educators. In contrast to the belief that people code-switch because they do not know the word or the grammatical construct, some contend that code-switching is a conscious rejection of standard English and a way to "latinize" the language. This perceived linguistic resistance is thought to be two-fold: parents' resistance to using standard English among themselves and with their children, and children's resistance to assimilate to the dominant standard. In this sense, code-switching is considered a conscious reaction against the taking up of English as the common language. That it might be a lived condition of bilingualism remains discounted. As both negative and unnatural, it is perceived as an act of defiance, a practice that must be subjugated:

I never mix languages in class and I don't allow my students to do it either. We have our English time and our Spanish time and now that they are used to it, they are pretty good about keeping to it. But I still have problems with them during informal times, when they are playing at recess or talking to one another in class. They still go back and forth and I know where it comes from. Their parents do it all the time instead of trying to be a model and speak "good" Spanish or English. It's the kind of way they talk in New York and on the street. But with the kids, it will only get them into trouble.

For a majority of educators, school success is predicated on standard (i.e., white) English language proficiency.[6] Deviations from the standard are thought to impede achievement. Such is the reason typically given for why African-Americans who have spoken English for generations, for instance, continue to experience disproportionate failure. And why non-Spanish-speaking Puerto Ricans also do less well in school than Puerto Rican students who have had several years of schooling in Puerto Rico. Success in school thus becomes contingent upon silenced or highly controlled voices. Class and cultural differences contribute to failure precisely because they represent a divergence from the standard Anglo-English model.

Language is situated within the various forms of cultural production and reproduction that take place within the context of school as well as in the wider society and provides the mode, expression, communicative interaction, and relation through which knowledge is produced, meaning is constructed, and voices are formed. Language thus cannot be isolated from the contexts in which cultural production occurs or from the sociocultural, political, ideological, and pedagogical relations that are embedded in this production. Bilingualism cannot be considered as separate from lived experience. The debilitating condition of bilingualism and biculturalism in U.S. schools and the differential school success of many Puerto Ricans must therefore be linked to factors beyond language variety. How have educational researchers understood these factors? Three major directions exist in the recent research literature that are worthy of examination and critique.

Cultural Borders

The first is reflected in applied ethnographic studies that have looked at the forms of interaction, the cognitive styles, and ways of nonverbal and verbal communication that poor minority students bring to the classroom and have contrasted them with those of white students from the middle-class (see, for example, Heath 1983; McDermott 1987; Trueba 1986). Investigations have examined how particular communicative styles and/or cultural forms affect both students and teachers' behavior and expectations in the classroom. The misinterpretations of these expectations and behaviors and the resultant miscommunications that follow need attention.

The cultural border or cultural difference position does not place the cause of educational failure with the individual student or with the school as an institutional structure. Rather, failure is thought to derive from incompatibilities between the home and school cultures. As Luis Moll and Stephen Diaz write:

> There is nothing about the students' language or culture that should handicap their schooling; the problems some language minority students face in school must be viewed as a consequence of instructional arrangements that ensnare certain children by not capitalizing fully on their social, linguistic, and intellectual resources. (1987:300)

Rectifying these incompatibilities through the specification and implementation of more appropriate and culturally responsive educational practices becomes the major focus (e.g., Au and Jordan 1981; Vogt, Jordan, and Tharp 1987; Moll and Diaz 1987).

Cultural Boundaries

A second approach is typified by the work of John Ogbu (1978; 1987; 1990). Ogbu maintains that while cultural differences exist, social forces in U.S. society give rise to cultural boundaries which, in part, are determined by the minority group's relation to and ability to adapt to the larger society. The causes of school failure are thought by Ogbu to be outside the school itself and beyond home and school cultural differences. In his widely cited ethnographic study in Stockton, California, Ogbu (1978) found immigrant minority students, for instance, to have better school success than domestic minorities (i.e. Chicanos and Blacks), even though both groups exhibited cultural differences from the Anglo majority. Differential achievement thus became attributable to the groups' status in U.S. society and their ability and willingness to accommodate to the dominant ways. The status of Chicanos and African-Americans as well as Puerto Ricans and Native Americans stems from their position as caste-like or involuntary minorities, people "originally brought into the United States society involuntarily through slavery, conquest, or colonization" (Ogbu, 1987:321). Caste-like minorities have, historically, been oppressed by U.S. society. As a result, they tend to be more fatalistic about their chances for success in school or in the labor market; their poor school performance tends to be "both a reaction and an adaptation to the limited opportunity available to them to benefit from their education" (Ogbu, 1974:12).

Ogbu's distinction between minority groups helps explain why it is that some language minority students have more academic success than others. South and Central American students, for example, tend to do better in school than Puerto Ricans and Chicanos even though they share a similar linguistic and cultural heritage. The impact of being a colonialized minority clearly defines and positions the latter group's lived reality. Adding to this history is the development of an oppositional identity that further sets off this group from immigrants and from the dominant ethnic class.

> They develop a new sense of social identity in opposition to the social identity of the dominant group after they have become subordinated, and they do so in reaction to the way that the dominant group members treat them in social, political, economic, and psychological domains. (Ogbu, 1987:323)

Both the cultural borders and cultural boundary perspectives offer insight into the multiple factors that impact Puerto Rican students' school success and that define their lived realities. Applied ethnographic studies that have focused on the incompatibilities between the home and school cultures, for example, illuminate how teachers' use of language in instruction, their pedagogical orientation, and instructional style can work to silence language-minority children, diminish their self-esteem, and promote both learning difficulties and cognitive dissonances. But, because teachers and students are understood to be capable of acting upon their contexts, these cultural borders can be challenged and diffused. Absent from a majority of these studies, however, is an analysis that locates cultural contexts within a sociopolitical, economic, and ideological frame. That is, issues of race, ethnicity, class, language, and gender are primarily conceived as factors of difference rather than as ongoing historical relations reflective of institutional structures.

The cultural boundary position affords an historical as well as labor market explanation for Puerto Rican students' disproportionate school failure. It is evident that the force of history has determined present-day conditions and relations. Advocates of the cultural border or difference approach, however, have criticized Ogbu's position as deterministic, ignorant of the cultural significance of language and of the impact of educational intervention. Ogbu, on the other hand, maintains that sociopolitical and economic factors wield much more power than cultural differences. Nevertheless, lacking in his work is an analysis of the individual and collective action of students, teachers, and communities in forming history and defining lived reality (i.e., in cultural production). Educators' efforts toward more meaningful and culturally appropriate instruction are viewed as helpful but relatively insignificant.

Debates between the cultural borders and boundary approaches have appeared in recent educational literature (see Jacob and Jordan 1987, and Trueba 1988). While these critiques are helpful in elucidating issues in each prospective camp, they suffer from the same weaknesses detailed above. Both serve to isolate culture from broader societal forces, that is, from hegemony, instead of highlighting their productive interaction.

A third approach to the study of minority students' disproportionate school success incorporates aspects of the two previous positions but also takes into account the socially constructed relationships between and among minority and majority groups.

Borders, Boundaries, and Beyond

Jim Cummins (1986; 1988), for example, draws from both the cultural difference oriented studies and from Ogbu's work in establishing his theoretical framework of disablement and empowerment. While more concerned with policy than daily classroom life, Cummins argues that educators can make a difference. He suggests that the generalized school failure of language-minority students is directly related to the relationships between majority and minority groups, specifically between educators and minority students, and between schools and minority communities. The interactions that occur in these various configurations are governed by relations of power; they predispose some children to failure before they even come to school and, once there, they cause students to develop an insecurity and ambivalence about the value of their own linguistic and cultural identities.

Cummins maintains there are four structural elements in the organization of schooling that can contribute to the empowerment of students or lead to their disablement. These include: (1) the incorporation of minority students' language and culture into the curriculum; (2) the inclusion of minority community participation as an integral part of children's education; (3) the utilization of pedagogical approaches that promote intrinsic motivation on the part of students to use language actively in order to generate their own knowledge; and (4) the promotion of assessment as advocacy—by "focusing primarily on the ways in which students' academic difficulty is a function of interactions within the school context rather than legitimizing the location of the 'problem' within students" (1988:138).

The incorporation of minority students' language and culture into the classroom has been found in numerous studies to have a positive impact on academic success (e.g., Cummins 1983; Campos and Keating 1988). In fact, it was to improve the academic performance of children from diverse language and cultural backgrounds that bilingual education programs were established. The context and purpose of native language use, however, greatly determines the ultimate success of the approach. As Cummins explains:

> Educators who see their role as adding a second language and cultural affiliation to students' repertoire are likely to empower students more than those who see their role as replacing or subtracting students' primary language and culture in the process of assimilating them to the dominant culture. (1988:139).

Cummins contends that students are further empowered when their parents are actively involved in their education and when teachers make an effort to collaborate with the family. This inclusion validates students' (as well as parents') identities and provides for more of a connection between the worlds of home and school. However, as Cummins emphasizes, the pedagogical orientation of the classroom is also key. The transmission models of instruction found in most classrooms tend to maintain unequal relations of power and control; emphasized are surface features of language, literacy, and recall of content. A reciprocal interaction model, on the other hand, is based on dialogue, guidance, and facilitation (Cummins 1986). Students' own background knowledge assumes a key role and is integrated with meaningful language use and involved in curricular content. Assessment is viewed as an ongoing, supportive component.

While not stated as such, educators' incorporation of these elements may well require teachers to begin to work with a notion of agency—their own as well as those of their students. However, in the way he explains it,

Cummins' framework offers a process oriented approach to reversing the educational failure of language-minority students. Although the incorporation of the four elements listed above are key in making schools more relevant to and responsible for bilingual students and should therefore not be easily dismissed, the naivete of these proposals threatens to simplify domination and structural inequalities. Many of the same inadequacies are present in other current process oriented approaches (e.g., whole language).[7] What these approaches do is focus on the inclusion of students' sociocultural and linguistic experiences as essential components of the curriculum. All experience is valorized and supposedly treated as equal. Students are not encouraged to question lived realities nor are these realities examined within the context of dominant and dominated relations. Instead, the assumption is made that the process method of experiential inclusion will somehow remediate racial/ethnic, linguistic, and class inequalities. Ignored are the multiple ways power relations permeate students' language, meanings, and voices and the internal and external struggles and resistances these lived relations promote.

Cummins' most recent work (1989) makes broader connections between the power relations at work in society and the limits placed on the equality of educational opportunity for class, racial, and ethnic minorities. A large part of this effort is dedicated to making parallels between the disempowerment of dominated groups in the United States and in the Third World:

> Violations of human rights (e.g., destabilizing the economies of weaker nations, destroying the personal and academic development of minority students) are veiled in the rhetoric of equality and justice, as they always have been by dominant groups everywhere. The rhetoric is no different in essence than the rhetoric of "the white man's burden" used to justify colonialization and exploitation of developing nations under the guise of promoting democracy, civilizing the natives, saving heathen souls, etc. (1989:124)

Cummins expresses the need to challenge debilitating structures (whether in the Third World or at home) and, in so doing, the need to develop a conscious awareness of both the nature of subjugation and the means through which it is achieved.

While Cummins (1989) affords a more developed political analysis of bilingual education and of the collaborative actions of educators, policymakers, and community members, the human agency of students remains absent. As in his previous work, his overriding assumption is that students passively accept domination, it is adults who must rescue them from its effects. The multiple ways that students struggle with and contest ongoing power relations are neglected.

Frederick Erickson (1987) provides a more critical analysis of minority student failure by locating aspects of the cultural borders and cultural boundaries positions within the framework of theories of resistance. As he explains:

> One way to reconcile the two positions is to consider school motivation and achievement as a political process in which issues of institutional and personal legitimacy, identity, and economic interest are central. To do this we must also consider as well the nature of the symbolic discourse through which issues of legitimacy, identity, and interest are apprehended and formed by individual students and teachers in local communities and schools. (1987:341)

Erickson maintains that success or failure in school thus cannot be limited to a cultural determinist perspective in which difference produces conflict and similarity rapport or to an economic determinist perspective that negates the human agency of students and teachers. Instead, school success and failure reflect the learning or not learning of what schools deliberately teach. This knowledge is not made equally available to all students but is distributed along lines of class, race, ethnicity, and language background. As Erickson describes, learning is thus a form of political assent—a trust in the legitimacy of this knowledge. Not learning is characteristic of mistrust and involves a witholding of assent, that is, political resistance.[8] To get beyond this resistance means establishing

> trust in the legitimacy of the authority and in the good intentions of those exercising it, trust that one's own identity will be maintained positively in relation to the authority, and trust that one's own interests will be advanced by compliance with the exercise of authority. (Erickson 1987:344)

What does Erickson contribute to furthering an understanding of the lived condition of bilingualism and the school situation of Puerto Ricans? While not speaking directly to the experience of language-minority students or to Puerto Ricans, Erickson highlights the interconnectedness of hegemony, of knowledge, and of schooling and makes clear the import of collective teacher and student agency. In contrast, Cummins makes reference to the power of the dominant society but views educators as able to empower students rather than students confronting (and transforming) domination themselves. Both Cummins and Erickson underline the importance of culturally responsive pedagogy. For Erickson the basis of this pedagogy comes not solely from the inclusion of language, culture, and parents in the classroom or from more interactive instructional approaches, but from addressing the politics of legitimacy, trust, and assent and their multiple functions and interrelations (both institutional and existential) in the classroom, community, and the wider society.

As these three movements in the literature demonstrate, minority students' academic difficulties in school cannot be simply explained through arguments of language deficency or language difference. Both teachers and students bring to the classroom culturally developed ways of communicating and interacting that are shaped not only by home socialization but by the dominant political structure and the relations it supports and fosters. Because bilingualism is conceived to be a "detrimental condition" that limits school success, teachers and administrators often unknowingly treat language as the cause. Language thus becomes a tangible variable that can be treated and corrected; the multitudinous effects of structural and institutional inequality are less easily identified and measured. Yet, as previous discussions have shown and as the literature just reviewed suggests, it is this inequality that impacts students' performance and influences their internalization of meaning and their interpretation of linguistic valor.

The lived condition of bilingualism thus emerges from the dominated reality of Puerto Rican and other language-minority students of color. While the ability to utilize two languages in communication and thought has been demonstrated to have cognitive benefits (Hakuta and Diaz 1985; Peal and Lambert 1962), these benefits have been both ignored and treated as themselves a threat to the monolingual Anglo dominion. There are arguments for the creation of a harmonious, integrated society, to be achieved if English is the only language. Disregarded, of course, is the continued segregation and unequal treatment of racial/ethnic minorities in schools, housing, employment, and in a myriad of other societal institutions.[9]

Even though bilingualism has come to be both seen and endured as a debilitating state, many students continue to maintain a semblance of voice—to keep a sense of their linguistic, cultural, and social identities and to struggle against the forces and people who attempt to oppress them. The resistances that result from this struggle are treated as academic and behavioral disorders, manifestations of problem students. Put another way, inappropriate behavior, academic difficulties, disinterest in English, and low motivation are attributed to individual and (cultural) group inadequacies rather than expert responses to oppressive conditions. This is not to suggest that all resistance reflects expertise or that all responses to oppression are necessarily expert in the sense that I have defined it. When students themselves assume a capacity to control or begin to dispense power over others, then expertise loses its critical character. In this case, what needs to be interrogated is why this need to control is occurring and where it is coming from. For students to become the experts of their own lives, they must come to recognize and understand the contexts and contents of lived experience that produces their resistances. The next section makes clear what these resistances are and the varied ways students struggle for voice. It also affords examples of how both resistance and voice can inform pedagogy.

STUDENTS' PERCEPTIONS OF THEIR REALITY–ASPECTS OF VOICE, PEDAGOGY, AND RESISTANCE

> Our real lives are the family, our friends, the street, jobs, and all that we come with from before.
>
> Alberto

For Alberto, as for many other Latino students in U.S. schools, the instruction and relations of the classroom exclude both daily reality and personal and community history. As he makes clear, the past is an integrated part of one's identity. While numerous educational studies have demonstrated the connection between a positive identity and school success, few if any efforts are made to foster Latino students' identities or to talk about their lives in positive ways. Teachers too often presume that the community holds no place in the classroom, that students can somehow forget who they are outside of school and conform to Anglo norms and expectations while within. Obscured from the curriculum and from written, oral, and nonverbal expression are students' culture and lived contexts as well as the social, economic, and experiential conditions that they confront (Fine 1987). At school, when references are made to the community, they most often highlight the negative, for example, welfare, drugs, and poverty, or these references include blaming the victims, and talk about how education and the English language can help students "get out." Critical discussion is absent. Within this environment Latino students' voices become silenced; their interest and motivation in school are extinguished. As one of Alberto's peers put it, "Why should we bother anyway? We know they don't want us here."

Silencing is easily associated with authority and control; in essence, it is a way to quiet and subordinate minority students, to devalue their backgrounds, and, as Michelle Fine (1987) has demonstrated, to push them out of school. But silencing can also be viewed from another perspective, as a choice by students not to engage with teachers or with school officials. A silenced voice can therefore be an active, momentary (and safe) response to oppressive conditions within the classroom or school, or a conscious and/or unconscious decision not to risk self-disclosure. Thus, while classroom conditions may greatly contribute to the silencing of minority students, silent voices do not necessarily result in permanently voiceless individuals. In fact, the perceptions of many so-called silenced students of the school environment indicate a complex understanding of the goings-on within. As inside experts on schooling and school-based relations, they can tell us what works and what does not work in the classroom, how they feel included or excluded in the curriculum, the instructional approaches, and in the linguistic, cultural, and social ways of speaking, learning, and acting. This awareness was made clear to me by Alberto and his peers, with whom I worked on a classroom video project over a four month period.

As in many urban cities, there was a disproportionate percentage of Latino dropouts (primarily Puerto Rican and Dominican) in the city where this project was undertaken. More than half of the bilingual students at the secondary level were considered "at risk"; attendance was infrequent, grade repetition was common, and academic grades were often failures. Teachers both in and out of the bilingual program often blamed the students and their families. I was told they lacked motivation and were lazy and that high mobility, unstable homes, and the influence of drugs made the education of these students an impossibility.[10] Administrators made little effort to understand, support, or even listen to the students; the rate of suspensions were more than twice what they were for whites and reprimands for speaking Spanish in the halls were not uncommon. When one vice-principal was questioned as to his habitual demand that Spanish not be spoken, he replied:

> They need to learn English and speaking Spanish will just hold them back. I have their best interests at heart when I tell them to talk in English and I try and integrate them ... split them up from their friends ... force them to speak English ... because that's the only way they will ever get ahead.

Through their involvement with parents in a lawsuit against the city several years before, some of the older students were able to talk about the oppression and negative attitudes, speak of their rights, and suggest ways to improve the environment.[11] Moreover, as the court-appointed monitor, a key component of my efforts to improve the school environment included the active integration of high school students in the identification and development of institutional remedies, which provided a way for students to gain some power over and through their education. Their recommendations formed the base for curricular and staff changes and augmentations. Meeting as a group, seniors in the bilingual program cited a lack of appropriate English instruction as the biggest impediment to their future success. Untrained, disinterested ESL teachers had neglected to provide the academic environment through which students could fully develop the abilities to read, write, and comprehend. As one student explained:

> I speak English okay and I get pretty good grades in my bilingual subjects. I want to take regular classes and I want to go to college. I tried a couple of times to take some classes in English but I couldn't keep up. I couldn't do the reading. I didn't understand and nobody seemed to care. The English I know, I learned it on the street. My ESL teacher would just read the newspaper and drink his coffee. Now what am I going to do? It's too late. I'll graduate but I can never make it in college. (Translation from Spanish mine)

The remedy was the hiring of trained ESL teachers and the establishment of transitional ESL content area courses, including a transitional English class with a primary focus on reading and writing.

Some students spoke of the irrelevancy of courses, particularly the fact that Spanish as a native language courses focused only on grammar. All mentioned that the reality of their lives (and of their communities) never seemed to be a part of school, nor was it recognized or deemed important. More often than not, it was publicly put down, made to look degenerate in the eyes of white administrators, teachers, and students. The lack of a bilingual counselor and the students' sense of overall exclusion from the context of the curriculum (many books came from Spain), contributed to dropping out, poor grades, behavioral problems, and frustration. As a result of their suggestions, new Spanish language courses were developed to reflect students' lives, culture, and interests (e.g., Current Issues of Latinos in the United States, History and Culture of Santo Domingo and Puerto Rico, Latin American Literature). A bilingual counselor was hired. Texts were bought from Puerto Rico, Santo Domingo and from U.S. publishers with a Caribbean focus. The students began to see their perceptions and ideas valued; their voice did in fact matter.[12]

Younger students, however, maintained the colonial traits as internal, blaming themselves and their families for their absenteeism, disinterest, and failure. The focus of the project was therefore to create a classroom environment where they could talk about and reflect upon their realities both inside and outside of school, and begin to recognize and interrogate the underlying conditions and relations. The hope was that silenced voices would emerge and that, tangentially, the teachers would come to realize the value and power of a pedagogy based on students' sociocultural perceptions, and on their words and actions. The medium of the project was sociodrama and video. The participants included fifteen male bilingual students, all termed by teachers and administrators as "at risk" of dropping out. Academic problems were common, as were frequent absenteeism and discipline-related reprimands. According to one teacher, these kids were "beyond salvation." All were members of a class entitled The History and Culture of Puerto Rico and Santo Domingo. While the curriculum of the class had been designed to reflect the title, the focus of instruction had been Spanish grammar. According to the teacher, this was because the students had very low literacy skills and an inability to comprehend texts and written materials. The class was handed over to me to teach. During the course of four months, I spent approximately three hours a week in the classroom.

Although there were a number of girls in the school who also had academic and attendance problems, none were in this class. According to the counselor, this was because girls would not be able to tolerate this particular group of male students and, because of the boys' domineering behavior, the girls' interests and needs would be neglected. This revealed a macho conception of the boys and a perception that Latino girls are easily silenceable.[13] The boys in the class in fact thought it strange that there were no girls and mentioned it to me, asking if we might bring in some girls for the project. But since the dynamics of the group were already well-defined by March when the project began, I thought it best not to alter the composition. Instead, we occasionally talked about the diverse perspectives female students may have brought to the project.[14]

After some initial discussions and dialogues with the students, it became evident that they were not willing to talk directly about their own lives. The use of sociodrama permitted the students to step out of themselves and take on the persona of someone else. Thus, while they were not able or willing to talk openly about the conditions that contributed to their own difficulties in school or how they felt in the school environment, they were able to articulate their experiences, perceptions, and feelings through sociodrama. As facilitator, I presented general situations to the students that had emerged from informal discussions with them around the generative theme (Freire 1970) of "dropping out." The students took these situations and, over several days, worked out among themselves the specifics of the situation and how it might be enacted. They negotiated roles and discussed the development of an oral script; a written script was not permitted since the goal was to capture the students' language and meaning at the moment of action, thereby avoiding a contrived and controlled presentation. Basic props were identified and the responsibility for their acquisition was shared. Over the course of the four months, three interrelated thematic situations were filmed by the student camera crew (trained by a Puerto Rican technician). Group discussions on the scenes were also filmed; it was here that the students themselves began to make connections between their own lives in the school and the community, the roles they had assumed, and the perspectives and situations they had presented in the sociodrama.

The situations evolved around a ficticious student, Carlos, who was contemplating dropping out. In the first scene, Carlos is thrown out of class. The principal and vice-principal call for a meeting with Carlos and his father; the teacher, the guidance counselor, and the bilingual director also attend. Through their actions and words, the actors make clear the ways Carlos is being pushed out of school—including the multiple efforts by the authorities to silence him. In the flashback to what went on that day in the classroom, they also demonstrate the strained relations between students and teacher, futile attempts at transmission-type instruction and classroom control, and illustrate student resistance (i.e., the relation between their behavior and the conditions which they confront in school and in the broader society).[15] In reviewing what they had filmed and reflecting on the disorder, chaos, and oppositional behavior, one student described what he perceived to be the reality: "Part of the problem has to do with respect. A lot of the students don't have respect for the teachers or the school." But then he paused, contemplated for a moment, and added: "But maybe that's because the teachers and principals don't respect them. . . . It's really a problem of *respeto* and *confianza*. They don't have it for us. Then, how can we have it for them?" (Translation from Spanish mine)

By being able to step back and view the dynamics of his own classroom, this student was able to judge the reality in a more critical light. No longer was the culpability that of the students alone. Instead, it was generated by the teacher and the other school authorities. Through the relations of resistance propagated in this context, a "them" and "us" was created. The divisive alliances were characterized by power but also by ethnicity and language. The alliances were further witnessed in the meeting in the principal's office. There, the vice-principal comes out of his role of disciplinarian for a moment and identifies with the student, referring to *nosotros hispanos* (we Hispanics). His words suggest the dominated condition of bilingual education and of bilingual students and bring to the fore the age-old circumstance of oppression: gratitude to the *patrón*—to the boss or slave owner.

> We have to act better than them. They have given us a special program so we have to act better. We have to show them that we deserve it. It's a special program for us. It is the bilingual program. They have given us this so we have to act better. (Translation from Spanish mine)

While the vice-principal returned to his administrator persona after these comments, this momentary association with lived reality corroborated a powerful identification with the "them" and "us" categorization. Certainly it is not just by chance that, in "real" life, all of the administrators and all (except one) of the teachers in the high school at the time were Anglo. Nor was it probably play-acting when Carlos, the fictitious student, said his problems in school were mainly related to the fact that the teachers did not like or understand him.

The second scene was called "On the Street." Here, the students again underscored the push-out phenomenon. Carlos' frustration with school and his feeling of helplessness over controlling his life is made evident as he speaks to a group of friends:

> They suspended me, *loco*. They suspended me. . . . They won't let me go to school. They just keep throwing me out. What can I do? I am always suspended. . . . My future, its a factory or something. What am I going to do? I can't attend school even if I want to. (Translation from Spanish mine)

Carlos looks for support in his peers. A group involved in selling drugs attempt to sway him to their side with promises of money, girls, and prestige. Two others argue for the importance of a diploma and having something better. Carlos is literally pulled by each arm. Then, the police appear on the scene and his drug friends are busted. Carlos stands by and watches, contemplating his future.

Scene 3 focuses on the tensions at home when Carlos makes the decision to leave school and go to work in a car repair shop. Both the good pay and the shop owner's interest in Carlos' skill are incentives for the adolescent—he now has something to offer, a prized expertise that will be rewarded. His parents, however, argue that he must stay in school. Their authority gives them the right to make the decisions. While Carlos respects his parents, he knows he has little future in the school and therefore feels he has little or no choice. He accepts the job and is thrown out of the house. Eventually he returns home and complies with his parents' wishes, vowing to return to school, to be a good son, and make an effort to do well and study. Never does he mention the oppression he feels there. He dredges up hope that even with all the odds against him, somehow he will make it.

In later reflecting on what they had enacted, the father talks about his obstinance and unwillingness to allow his son to give up on schooling. While he is no longer acting the part, he seems to have internalized the persona:

> In the first place, a job is only for some days, some years. A profession lasts a lifetime. I think about my father and I think about me. I wouldn't want my son to work in a factory all the time or be in a repair shop all his life. There has to be something better. School offers the only chance to do something with one's life. I'll tell my son this and others should also listen. (Translation from Spanish mine)

Critical Reflection

Through the medium of sociodrama, the students recreated the environments in which they live and struggle. They took on the personas of the various actors and assumed their voices. This amplified their own perspectives and understandings, helping them see beyond their immediate realities. A crucial element in this process was the time for critical reflection. Initially, I structured questions in a problem-posing manner, asking students what they thought was going on in a particular scene, if they thought there was some kind of problem, whether or not they could identify with it, and what actions could be taken. But, early on, the students themselves took over this function, proudly wielding the microphone, interviewing one another, and attempting to tease out responses. Their questions were not the same as I had asked. Instead, they had much more poignancy: how did you feel playing this particular part? what might you have done in real life? do things like this happen on a day-to-day basis in the Hispanic community? As individual students responded to these queries, the others listened with interest. Both in the questioning and in the reviewing, they discussed the efficacy and delivery of scenes and of the appropriateness of the final outcome. They sometimes talked about parallel situations in their own lives and often ruminated about alternative actions.

The process of critical reflection sparked three major outcomes. First, by reviewing the sociodrama on video, students examined the efficacy of the scene and its delivery as a whole and by individual actor. They become aware of audience and the need to work collectively in order to deliver a message. Second, each student was given the opportunity to contemplate the parallels between Carlos and themselves and between the struggles they individually face in the environments of school, street, and home, the contexts of the sociodrama. Third, they began to see their struggles not as individual, but as ethnic/racial group struggles. Previous demarcations between Puerto Ricans and Dominicans were softened. Linguistic and racial oppression became an issue for discussion.

None of the students had ever been asked to work cooperatively with other students nor had their opinions and perspectives on life ever been the center of the curriculum. Nevertheless, the process of script formation and negotiation required collaboration. After filming several scenes where, because of a lack of intergroup collaboration, chaos was evident, the students themselves began to establish rules of cooperation and designs for synergy. They began to see themselves more as a team and less as singular individuals. They had learned to respect one another's opinion and to appreciate differing perspectives.

During the enactment of the sociodramas, a student "resident photographer" took pictures of what was going on. These were developed on a weekly basis and given back to the students for follow-up writing activities and for further discussion. From these pictures emerged the development of a photonovel. Students collaborated on dialogues to accompany the photographs, wrote them down in a comic book "bubble" format, and sequenced them into a narrative. This also promoted critical reflection. Knowing the dialogue from their own enactment, the students endeavored to move beyond, discussing new dialogues that might also be appropriate to the context, new angles on the problem, and resolutions. They also haggled over the effectiveness of certain words and talked about the words' significance. While they had been diagnosed as low literates, their interest and investment in the topic and activity spawned text. Although there were grammatical errors and misspellings, their meaning and message were fluid.

Critical reflection was also promoted through an additional activity after the final version of the video was completed. Screenings of the video were arranged in school for peers and teachers. Another was held with parents in the community. In both of these contexts, discussions occurred between the students and the viewers. Parents had the most questions and comments. Many exhibited the same perspective that the students had given before the filming: students are to blame for their problems; the school and parents only want to help them. Although it was difficult for the students to speak out in front of these adults (who, according to cultural standards, they should respect and listen to), one found the voice to emphasize the complexity of the problem and its relation not just to the individual but to the conditions within which he has to function. As he spoke, the sociodrama was brought to life:

> While we are still young and not yet adults, we feel alot of the same pressures and responsibilities you do. Many students work. We have to help the family and have a little spare change, too. We go to school but there is nobody there who understands. And many times parents don't either. . . . It's different in this country. We all have to learn and adapt. But we need you to support us and try and understand what we go through. (Translation from Spanish mine)

His words expressed a need for parents to look beyond the video and to think about their relationships with their own children. Also made clear was an ability on the part of this student to promote critical reflection and encourage social transformation. While all students were not as adept at facilitating this process, most were cognizant of the connections between the sociodramas and lived experiences. All took ownership of the project and were aware that it was they who had, during the four months, created the curriculum. The inclusion of the content of their lives in school, and the opportunity to talk about this content in a critical fashion, produced numerous changes in individual students. Let us look at two examples.

Student Transformation

Raymundo, or Ray as he is called for short, played the vice-principal in scene one.[16] Of all the students in the class, he was probably the most at risk of dropping out. He averaged one day a week in school, his grades were all F's and D's, he had been suspended numerous times and, when he was in school, he spent the majority of the day in the vice-principal's office because of what was considered inappropriate behavior. His expertise for the role thus came from personal experience and frequent observation. Ray was actually not enrolled in the class when I first began the project but had a Spanish class in an adjoining classroom. When the teacher was not looking, he would often slip into our class and try and insert himself in the action. Since his Spanish teacher found him to be a major disruption, she did not discourage his leaving. Soon afterward he formally changed classes and joined the project.

Once inside, Ray wanted to control the process, trying to be the camera man, take charge of the lights, and play major characters. He would run from one thing to the next, and, when he did not get his way, would climb on top of desks, hassle others, and disrupt the script development and filming. Somehow, however, he negotiated with the other participants, and one day emerged as the vice-principal. The change in his persona was incredible. On the day of the filming, he borrowed a white shirt and a tie, lowered the tone of his voice, and took on a serious manner. Without any written, preplanned script, he assumed the role and carried on as the typical disciplinarian for more than thirty minutes. His words were well thought out and extremely articulate. No one could believe the shift in character. After reviewing the film several days later, Ray himself even commented on his total assumption of the role and joked about his professional demeanor. In fact, he said he had always been interested in drama and had once participated in a summer program run by the city. In school, drama was only offered in English. He had been told his lack of fluency in English and his disruptive behavior prohibited his participation.

During the process of developing and filming this and successive scenes in which he was involved, Ray's attendance improved by about 80 percent. He was only absent on days I was not in the building. His physical appearance demonstrated more care and he walked with an obvious pride, telling everyone about his new found talent. Teachers said they could see more interest and better control. He began to write about the video project. There were no suspensions.

Ray's fame, however, began to go to his head. He wanted all the major parts and refused to negotiate with the other students. As a group, they began to reject him. His behavior subsequently reverted to its former patterns. I sought ways to give him other responsibilities and tried to actively integrate him into the process when he did not have a part in the sociodrama. These efforts proved to be mostly successful. We also filmed some of his characteristic resistance in a scene that replicated the "typical" classroom environment. Afterward, upon reviewing the film, he commented about his need to always get attention:

> Look at me there. The camera is on me. They know I'm the best, the leader of the band. That's me, the one everyone looks to. I have to keep up my image. That's why I act like I do. (Translation from Spanish mine.)

Ray's reflection on and recognition of his behavior was, for him, a transforming experience. While he found it comical to watch on film, he was also beginning to come to terms with its implications, that is, the way it isolated him from his peers and was individualistically stimulated rather than collectively oriented. Slowly, he began to seek solidarity. Other teachers, however, had lost patience and even the guidance counselor had given up on him. His attendance began to fade and his grades drop. While everyone expressed amazement with his articulate character in the sociodrama, they saw it as only "acting." He was recommended and sent away from the school to a live-in program called Job Corps. There he lasted six months, receiving, according to the guidance counselor, all kinds of awards and recognitions. But now he is again back at the high school demonstrating, says the counselor, "his destructive character and lack of motivation. He'll never make it anywhere," she added. Ray, on the other hand, maintains he returned because he felt isolated and alone. "I didn't like it there. It was too strict and tough. It was like the army or something. I had to get out and try and make it back here." But, since the overall atmosphere of the school and the attitudes of the staff had changed little, it did not take long for Ray to return to his former patterns or to demonstrate his resistance to the dominant school order. He averages one day a week in the building and, two months after his return, had already had several suspensions. His behavior is not without cause. Since the counselor believed he could not make it in the monolingual English classes because of his disruptive character, she placed him in ESL classes he had taken the year before. As he said to the teacher, "I have gone through this book already. Why should I waste my time repeating and repeating?"

While the changes brought about in Ray as a result of the project were momentary, they suggest what can happen when students are given an active role in the classroom, when their voice counts, and their words are listened to and respected. Years of forced silence and denial had promoted forms of lived resistance. The voice that he had thus assumed was not, by his own admission, really his, but the product of frustration and the desire for recognition. The project enabled Ray to begin to come to terms with this reality and transform his behavior in order to recapture his own dignity and demand a different kind of respect, rather than to satisfy the demands of the institution or the teachers. Rather than utilizing this resistance and helping him reflect upon it critically, the traditional curriculum continues to feed its destructive possibilities.

Eduardo was another student who went through considerable transformations during the four months of the project. Before I came to the class, he had not spoken in class once in the previous six months. His chosen seat was in the far corner of the room, and there he occupied himself with a heavy chain, rolling it over in his fingers for the duration of the class. Other students called him fat and dumb and never attempted to include him. When he did not have the chain in his hand, he had a candy bar. The teacher said he was like a big fat lump, adding that she had pretty much given up on him.

During the first two weeks I was in the classroom, Eduardo's behavior remained somewhat consistent. Slowly, however, I began to notice his intent observation of what was going on. While he refused to participate on the camera crew or in the initial development of the sociodramas, he watched with interest and frequently caught my eye, nodding with approval. One day he stopped me in the hallway after class. "You know, I really want to be in the play," he said. "But I'm afraid the other kids will make fun of me." We talked for a few minutes about what role he would like to have and we agreed that the following week he would give it a try. When the time came, however, his fear of the others once again returned and, without speaking, he just shook his head, bowing out of participation. The next class, I brought a camera with me in order to record what was going on and to have pictures for a later photonovel. When I found it impossible to both take pictures and facilitate the group, I passed the camera to Eduardo and asked him to shoot the pictures. He took the responsibility seriously and with pride. From then on, he was the "resident photographer" in charge of documenting the project. As pictures came back after developing, he examined them closely and discussed with me how he might improve his shots. He then shared the pictures with the other students.

Eduardo's prominent function as resident photographer uplifted his confidence, gave him a feeling of worth, and changed his stature among his peers. He showed more concern about his physical appearance, began to interact with others in the class, and even modified his gait from a heavy-footed shuffle to a lighter strut. Teachers commented on the changes. While he continued as photographer throughout the project, he occasionally put the camera down, volunteering to serve as an administrator for one improvisational filming and as an unruly student in another. Although he did not speak out during the process of reflection on the filming, he watched intently, listened to his peers, and smiled at his own performance. As with Ray, Eduardo's attendance also improved dramatically.

Teacher Engagement

During the first couple weeks of the project, Ms. Gordon, the teacher, left me alone with the students, allowing me to develop a relationship with them and giving herself a break from the classroom routine. At times, she would observe from the window in the door, commenting afterward on the disorganization, chaos, and noise level. Her resistance to the pedagogical structure was clear. She consistently questioned how this approach could help the students academically and/or improve their language and literacy skills. Cooperation and discussion among students was viewed as "fooling around," and the videotaping was considered a short-term "fun" activity. She did not witness knowledge transmission nor could she recognize its production. Moreover, my nonauthoritarian role was acknowledged as effective only because I was not really the teacher. She, in turn, could not take the risk of giving up authority since the class was her responsibility as the "teacher" in charge.

As we began to film, Ms. Gordon saw the apparent disorganization transformed. One day she re-entered the classroom as an observer and soon asked how she might keep the project going on the days I was not in the building. While she helped facilitate the development of roles and script, identify props, and encouraged students to write about the project, she also continued to complain about what she perceived as a lack of structure. These concerns were accompanied by an expressed amazement over the seriousness of the students during the filming, the significance of the content and roles they portrayed, and the transformation of individuals. She began to see the project as also hers.

During the course of the four months, Ms. Gordon began to deal with the contradictions between the traditional "banking" model (Freire 1970) of instruction in which she had been educated, trained in, and had followed, and the more cooperative, student-based approach that I was encouraging. She began to theorize about her own subjectivity.[17] While she never spoke to me directly about these contradictions, she exhibited in various ways her weighing of and ruminating about what was going on in the project. She talked about how similar projects might be done in subsequent years and eventually become an actual part of the curriculum. But she also qualified this with the need to involve only the best, most motivated students so that there would be less chaos, noise, and need to deal with problematic individuals. As a derivative of the project, she developed a summer course entitled "ESL Through Photography." Ray and other "disruptive" students were not allowed to enroll. Even though she had begun to move toward more of a process-oriented, student-based approach to instruction, her view of student resistance had not changed nor had her understanding of the multiple conditions in and out of school that serve to promote it. While Ms. Gordon was willing to compromise some of her authority over instruction, she was not yet willing to risk losing control of the classroom situation or having to deal with disruptive and resistant voices. Her engagement in the project was evident. Her understanding of its pedagogy, however, was fragmented; agency and productive capabilities were made contingent upon an objectified compliance.

Pedagogical Conclusions

What did this project offer for the students and how did this specific pedagogy impact language, cultural relations, and the overall conditions of their lives? First and foremost, it afforded the students the opportunity to construct, assume control over, and then take ownership of the curriculum. With the elimination of the textbook and the teacher as "knower," the production of knowledge became a collective process that was in their hands. Second, they became attentive to the various voices in the classroom and to the differences and similarities among them, to the resistances portrayed and present, and to the requirements of collaboration among peers. The students awakened to the common conditions they (and their families and communities) face and the struggles they share. Third, their language, cultural ways of relating and interacting, and lived experiences assumed an essential, "expert" function in the class. The deficit oriented focus on Spanish grammar was replaced by spontaneous, purposeful language use, and a focus on multiple communicative forms. *El relajo,* the playful, fooling around among students, was built upon rather than rejected, and the contents of their lives were made worthy of recognition, discussion, and interrogation. Finally, the project and pedagogy fostered an authentic engagement with and a transformative understanding of the tensions and pressures engendered in their bilingual and Puerto Rican (or Dominican) status. Not only did they come to discern and identify what these tensions and pressures are but they also began to address what might be individually and collectively done to diffuse or abate them. In this sense, the pedagogy was critical in prompting students to reflect upon and take action in their daily lives, to recapture the voices that had been silenced, and redefine those that, because of oppressive conditions, had emerged.

What can this pedagogy offer bilingual education or, more generally, the public schools? Because there is not one all encompassing pedagogy that addresses the linguistic, racial, class, gender, age, sexual orientation, biographical, or historical experiences of all learners, the specific strategies and content deployed may in fact not be appropriate or applicable in other contexts. As Lusted points out:

> Pedagogy in general is always inevitably tied to a historical moment defined within the then current state of knowledge. It is consequently necessary to go on to clarify the nature of "particular" pedagogies in particular instances of theory and teaching. What is required is productive distinctions between pedagogies of theory and teaching at particular moments, pedagogies that release genuine engagement and transformative understanding in the consciousness. (1986:10-11)

The pedagogy described above is therefore not a step-by-step approach to be indiscriminantly implemented. Rather, both the process and the results suggest the overall efficacy of building upon students' inside understandings and expertise, fostering an awareness and a questioning of the conditions and contexts in which these understandings developed, and promoting actions that work toward social change. Given the hegemonic, racist, sexist, and anti-bilingual circumstance of U.S. schooling, however, there is a necessity to develop specific pedagogies that recognize and interrogate Puerto Rican students' past and present realities, to include the experiences, perceptions, and voices that have traditionally been shut out, and to encourage movement toward critical bilingualism—the ability to not just speak two languages, but to be conscious of the sociocultural, political, and ideological contexts in which the languages (and therefore the speakers) are positioned and function, and of the multiple meanings that are fostered in each. Pedagogies that make use of students' voices can help promote critical awareness, an "expert" understanding of reality, and the possibility for personal and collective transformation.

NOTES

1. In her article "Working Across Difference," Uma Narayan discusses the difficulties in establishing dialogue between oppressed "insiders" and "outsiders" who do not share the oppression and suggests ways of alleviating these difficulties. While her analysis is in terms of heterogeneous members of political groups, it provides insight into both the subtle and overt ways all oppressed insiders must struggle to be understood and heard.

2. These states include Arkansas, Arizona, California, Colorado, Florida, Georgia, Hawaii, Illinois, Indiana, Kentucky, Mississippi, Nebraska, North Carolina, North Dakota, South Carolina, Tennessee, and Virginia. Hawaii is, in fact, an officially bilingual state where both Hawaiian and English are co-equal languages. On February 6, 1990, a federal district judge in Phoenix declared Arizona's constitutional amendment making English the language "of all government functions and actions" (the most stringent such an amendment in the nation) to be a violation of federally protected speech rights. This action sets an important precedent for the future.

3. For a more developed discussion of Dunn's position and its implications, see Cummins (1989) and Ana Celia Zentella (1989).

4. The lived effect of this linguistic domination can be illustrated through an example. In Lowell, Massachusetts, a city with a 45 percent minority school enrollment comprised of Latinos and Southeast Asians, the English Only movement has been both visible and vocal. An "English Only" referendum was placed on the ballot in 1989 and voted in with a two-thirds majority. It is an antecedent of this vote, however, that affords a vivid example.

On a memorable night in May 1987, over 100 language-minority parents came to the school committee meeting to express their concerns about the segregation of their children in substandard classrooms and in rented non-school facilities. When their interpreters stood up to speak, a school committee member, an avid, outspoken member of "English Only," shouted that there would be no translation. His explanation was that this was "an English Only school committee, in an English Only city and an English Only country." Non-English speakers therefore did not have a right to speak. Not all members of the committee supported this position and asked for a vote. But rather than compromise his position, the vocal member got up and walked out, preventing a quorum and thus disbanding the meeting. While parents were later to take their concerns about segregated conditions to court, many left that evening with feelings of fear and apprehension. A few days later, one couple asked to speak to the legal advocate who had been actively involved in supporting the parents and who had been present at the meeting. They wanted to know if it was illegal for them to speak Spanish to their daughter and, if so, what were they to do since there were long waiting lists for adult classes in English as a second language. The threat of an English Only mandate is the threat of silence.

5. While the promotion of bilingualism and the maintenance of Spanish among Latinos is both discouraged and suppressed, the emergence of programs of Spanish as a second language and two-way bilingual education for Anglo students suggests that at least some members of the dominant group recognize the benefits of bilingualism. One cannot help but wonder, however, if an underlying motive for support of two-way programs is not the dissolution of ethnic and cultural group solidarity under the guise of "integration."

6. In her essay on the experience of teaching a course about Black English, June Jordan (1988) describes the ways white standards of English control both popular and official judgments of verbal proficiency and correct or incorrect language skills. She also reveals the tenuousness of the concept of "a standard."

7. For a detailed discussion on the ideological tenets of process approaches to instruction, see Walsh (1990).

8. Narayan provides a lucid look at the ways trust and mistrust are tied to power differentials between advantaged and disadvantaged groups. As she explains, while goodwill on the part of advantaged group members may be an important foundation for the beginning of trust building experiences, it "is not enough to overcome assumptions and attitudes born out of centuries of privilege" (1988:35).

9. Christian Niera's (1988) recounting of the dualistic experience of living in a New York City housing project and attending an elite preparatory school makes vivid the social, emotional, and psychological struggles and challenges to one's sense of self and to one's identity.

10. Reflected in the presumptions of laziness and lack of motivation are the traits used historically to describe colonized peoples (see Memmi 1965).

11. Filed by Latino parents against the city, the major focus of the suit was, among other things, the high dropout rate of their community (68 percent), the lack of certified, trained teachers to teach English as a second language, and a failure to provide bilingual guidance counseling.

12. While these changes provided a respite from that which had occurred previously, their effect in reality is limited. Because the administration of the school continues to harbor animosity toward the Latino students and because many of the teachers in the bilingual program and the school believe these students cannot and/or do not want to learn, a negative environment continues. Suspension rates remain twice that of what they are for whites. In 1989, 64 percent of the Latino students in the bilingual program at this one high school were suspended and in the first four months of the 1990 school year, 20 percent of the bilingual program at the high school dropped out. Students' "cultural pecularities," inappropriate behavior, and lack of motivation are blamed.

13. School officials' perceptions of gender issues were made clear at a recent meeting with administrators over the disproportionate suspension rate of Latino boys. According to one vice-principal, a majority of suspensions resulted from a discordance between the traditional forms of male Latino behavior, that is, "machoism," and female teachers' demands and expectations. He maintained that until the boys learned how to behave with women teachers, they would keep getting suspended. This indicated the stereotyped roles of the sexes, the passivity of women, and the lack of recognition of the impact of both racial/ethnic and class differences (all the teachers were white and middle-class) and majority/minority relations.

14. One female student did actually participate in the enactment of the sociodrama entitled "In the Home." Here, the students felt they could not enact a home scene without a mother and none were willing to assume the role. They thus brought in the girlfriend of one of the boys for just one class period. Her dynamic and realistic performance afforded a context from which discussions on the role of the mother in the home and on the relationship of mothers and sons in Latino families emerged.

15. Giroux describes resistance as both a theoretical and ideological construct that ties schools and the behaviors in them to the hegemonic relations in the wider society. As he explains:

> The concept of resistance represents . . . a mode of discourse that rejects traditional explanations of school failure and oppositional behavior. In other words, the concept of resistance represents a problematic governed by assumptions that shift the analysis of oppositional behavior from the theoretical terrains of functionalism and mainstream educational psychology to those of political analysis. Resistance in this case redefines the causes and meaning of oppositional behavior by arguing that it has little to do with the logic of deviance, individual pathology, learned helplessness, and a great deal to do, although not exhaustively, with the logic of moral and political indignation. (1983:107)

16. Pseudonyms are given for the students and the teacher in order to protect their identities.

17. For a discussion of the multiple ways teachers' biographies affect their perceptions of schooling, students, and the curriculum and an analysis of how this subjectivity interacts with the dominant models and myths perpetuated in teacher education, see Deborah Britzman (1986; 1988; in press).

5

Conclusion

and i looked into the dawn
inside the bread of land and liberty
to find a hollow sepulchre of words
words that i admired from my mother's eyes
words that i also embedded as my dreams

Tato Laviera

I BEGAN THIS TEXT by acknowledging the complex interaction of language, culture, and experience as described by a young Puerto Rican girl. Tato Laviera's poetic verse recalls and renames this labyrinthine condition of growing up both American and Puerto Rican. As Buffy, Tato, and the other Puerto Ricans present in this study make clear, there is no simple connection nor static relation for Puerto Ricans between language, culture, and existence. Instead, there is an elaborate multiplicity of meanings and representations that inscribe how Puerto Ricans come to know and what it is to be Puerto Rican. These significances are wrapped up in historical, racial/ethnic, political, economic, and ideological issues that have been, and continue to be, manifest through social and linguistic coercion and exclusion as well as varied forms of resistance and production. They are neither wired to a singular language nor to a unitary experience, but rather construct the multilayered essence of lives lived across languages, contexts, and conditions.

How individuals and communities understand the way they use language elucidates the complexity of the language and culture relation. In their survey of Puerto Rican adults in El Barrio, for instance, Flores, Attinasi, and Pedraza (1981) found a widespread connection to both the English and Spanish languages. Most people they interviewed perceived no conflict between the use of English and Puerto Rican identity or between Spanish use and involvement in American culture. Furthermore, they described the mixing of both languages in discourse as common and judged it to be positive. English was recognized as an asset while Spanish was said to retain a cultural significance.[1]

In their interviews with children, however, Language Policy Task Force (1984) discovered that some children clearly preferred using one language more than the other and that this preference was often related to their programmatic placement in the school. The children who spoke in this text revealed an understanding of language use that, regardless of program placement, tended to be more negatively shaped and positioned by the attitudes and power relations of the dominant society. As the mixed significances of their words suggested, these students were as much struggling with the social, cultural, and political tensions that surround being Puerto Rican in a small U.S. city as they were with language variety—that is, Spanish and English. Most admitted, either directly or indirectly, to being bilingual, yet positioned this bilingualism (at least to me) within the broader social structure in which the institution of school is primary. The reality of lived bilingualism in the community and the home were perceived as irrelevant and, in some cases, even detrimental to "mainstream" schooling. Yet, as with the adults and children studied in New York, the use of both languages in daily life was a reality. Speaking Spanish did not necessarily ensure a high self-esteem or an unproblematic identity. Moreover, fluency in English also did not ensure assimilation or societal inclusion. While language may be perceived as a visible site of contradiction for bilinguals, their own understanding indicates that language is the active expression of a much wider problematic in which social, cultural, and ideological issues are brought to bear on meaning, voice, and consciousness.

The early chapters attempted to frame this problematic. In the Chapter 1, I used the spoken words of the U.S. colonial agents and the Puerto Rican people on the Island to demonstrate the linguistic, sociocultural, and political oppression and the tensions that Puerto Ricans have faced for nearly a century. This history is important because it informs the consciousness of the people who lived it, as well as that of their descendants who continue to live and struggle with and speak about subordination in varying forms. In Chapter 2, I presented a theoretical examination of the oppositions traditionally posed in and through language, oppositions that suggest a static view of language as well as of people. My intention was to afford a more dynamic understanding of language (and of voice) by underlining human agency, that is, the ability of people to produce meaning, to challenge conceptions, and to act on reality. In so doing, the chapter reveals the constant push and pull that underlie the oppositions and tensions that students confront linguistically, culturally, psychologically, and materially—the dialectical interplay that constructs, shapes, and enables voices that are often contradictory and always partial and multiple in character. An awareness of this interplay is important because it requires us to be cognizant of the complex relations and tensions among language, culture, ethnicity, class, and power that shape and position our own as well as our students' understanding.

The remainder of the text illuminates the intricacy and salience of "voice" as a theoretical and practical category of locution and understanding. It renders visible the ways voice constructs and incorporates both the consciousness of individuals and the environments within which they carry on and struggle. It also illuminates how the substance of voice is hinted at, alluded to, and sometimes even fully expressed in the significance of words. What these chapters tell us, in practice, is that when we think about the voices of others and of the meanings expressed by their words, we are obligated to consider how they are thwarted and disorganized, masked and concealed, or encouraged and valued in a variety of lived contexts. This consideration is important because it enhances our capacity to imagine, be sensitive to, and comprehend difference. Finally, in these chapters I suggest that the presentation and interrogation of voices within the classroom can facilitate a more critical awareness on the part of both teachers and students of how understanding actually happens. This seems of particular importance for Puerto Rican students since, as statistics of high dropout rates and low academic performance demonstrate, schools, for the most part, have been unsuccessful in tapping these students' potential.

The aim of this study was to render visible the semiotic tensions and the multifaceted nature of the struggles Puerto Rican students face in the U.S. public school system. "Voice" afforded a means to both express these struggles as understood and articulated by real people and as constructed and incorporated in consciousness. My purpose was to highlight how the past and present intersect in people's voices, infuse pedagogy, and sculpt the conditions and processes involved in coming to know.

Both stated and implied throughout the text is the need for teachers to develop pedagogies that recognize the divergent histories, experiences, and meanings that underlie students' voices. Such pedagogies must also address the complex ways differences are manifest in perceptions, actions, and in communication and are positioned by asymmetrical power relations. We need pedagogies that help people understand how they understand. Since this study exposes much about the substance of the processes involved in this understanding, what I will endeavor to do here is to highlight in more specific terms what is to be done in schools in light of what I have already written.

TOWARD PEDAGOGICAL PRACTICE

Schooling does a lot more than teach academic subject matter. It shapes individuals' consciousness, molds their image of themselves, their community, and others, and positions them in the social world. Paulo Freire argues that one of the major purposes of education should be to encourage learners to believe in themselves; it should invite them to believe they have knowledge (Freire 1973; Wallerstein and Bernstein 1988). Yet, as we have seen in this text, schools often work to do just the opposite—to make Puerto Rican students feel ashamed of and even reject their background, to have a low self-esteem and negative self-image. And, because the knowledge these students have constructed and the meanings they have fashioned are divergent from those who control educational content and process, their inside expertise and their voices are considered either nonexistent or invalid.

What conditions are necessary for schools to value and extend the voices of students? How can teachers learn from their students' words? And how can students understand their own knowledge? What pedagogies help students to critically view their realities? And what does it mean to be critical?

The significance of these questions for Puerto Ricans demands the recognition of three primary contradictions. First is their involuntary political status and colonial situation both on the Island and on the U.S. "mainland." As long as Puerto Rico remains a U.S. possession, Puerto Ricans will be faced with the duality inherent in being both Puerto Rican and U.S. "Americans" with no sovereign homeland and no option of national allegiance. Second is the requisite ability to be able to function in (often oppositional) racial/ethnic/linguistic groupings and divergent contextual settings. While we are all required, to a limited extent, to adapt to the various environments in which we live, work, and study, minorities are expected to accommodate to the "majority" world—that is, to the world of those who wield power.[2] They are forced to struggle with strategies for self-maintenance or risk losing their sense of self in the process. Third is the issue of language—that is, the way language is made into an issue in the schools. The intimacy and value associated with Spanish and with code-switching in some familial and community contexts is often interpreted by non-Puerto Rican teachers and peers as backward and detrimental to U.S. cultural adaptation. Thus, in an attempt to facilitate a belief in oneself in the context of school, many Puerto Ricans resort to saying and sometimes pretending they are English monolinguals.

Because of the tensions they proffer and the limits they place, these contradictions cannot go on unspoken. Moreover, for education to assume Freire's purpose, the incessant persistance of these contradictions in students' consciousness and in the contexts within which they live and struggle must be acknowledged, questioned, and transformed. This action is a first step in creating the conditions necessary for voices to be valued, for students to begin to understand their perceptions, actions, and realities, and for teachers to learn from t..eir students. Thus while the status of Puerto Rico cannot be resolved in a classroom, it can invite interrogation through a discussion, dialogue, or enactment of the interrelations of the past that intersect with and position those of the present and future. Similarly, the dualities and positionings that both political and minority status construct can be identified and analyzed in terms of subjective and collective discourses and experiences, that is, in part, in how students tell stories about themselves, their families, and communities, and the interpretations, meanings, and representations they suggest in the telling. This can help teachers as well as students come to understand that identities are not only social, cultural, and linguistic but are forged within asymmetrical power relations. And, since these contradictions partially constitute what is perceived and felt as "difference," pedagogies need to be concerned with acknowledging and accepting difference and addressing the ways difference is recognized and understood by the bearers and the observers.

Contradictions and tensions in the area of language have, in large part, been the focus of this entire study. Since language forms the basis for how we learn, convey meaning, and express ourselves in words and voices, it is central to what goes on in schools. Educators must be aware of the conditions for language development and use proffered in their classrooms as well as of the linguistic and sociocultural related processes through which bilingual children learn. Most importantly, they need to accept that bilingualism is a necessary circumstance of life for many Puerto Ricans. Language learning in the school must therefore take into account the critical role of the speech community and children's out-of-school interactions; schools must be recognized as only one of many agents for language teaching (Language Policy Task Force 1984). These conditions have much to do with enabling, valuing, and extending students' voices.

In practice, schools must allow students' language(s) to be spoken, and to recognize their varied forms of linguistic expression as a resource. This means accepting students' regional variety of the language and also accepting code-switching as a valid communicative form that is both appropriate and expected in certain situations. It means using the native language as well as English as a medium of learning and understanding. We know from research that students learn best in the language they think in and understand. Learning is enhanced when it builds upon students' cultural styles and ways of interacting, and when it incorporates their family and broader community. Also, the process of developing a second language, to the extent that one can learn in it like a native speaker, can take anywhere from four to nine years. Moreover, we know from this study that there is a community-based salience of language that, for many bilingual children, crosses linguistic variety. Speaking English in no way ensures or suggests a standard significance or interpretation, nor does living in the United States precipitate a singular cultural perspective. Given these dynamics, we must concern ourselves with creating classroom conditions through which languages, and thus bilingualism, can be seen and understood as developmental, multifarious, dialectical, socioculturally inscribed, in flux, and often without borders. We need to create the conditions within which bilingual learners might explore, utilize, broaden, and name their language-based understandings and build upon what Luis Moll (1989) refers to as their "social funds of knowledge." Also important is the alleviation of the power arrangements belonging to the institutional structure and the classroom, working to silence some students more than others, and to position, isolate, and alienate teachers.[3] We must work to establish conditions that, among other things, include an openness and respect for the differences students bring, a genuine interrelationship between the community and the school, a space for life-stories and future visions to be contemplated, written, and spoken in both languages, and the opportunity to connect subjectivities and identities to a history, culture, and wider sociopolitical world. As I will discuss in further detail later, these conditions necessitate pedagogies that encourage an active engagement and dialogue among all of the participants.

Teacher education programs and texts for the most part tell us very little about the students who fill our classrooms. While many of us endeavor to better understand the linguistic and cultural background and the academic needs of these students, we seldom listen to or explore the significance of their words. Carroll Smith-Rosenberg (1986) reminds us that words transpose experience into meaning. And, experience for each individual obviously has its own subjective, social, cultural, and gendered understandings that are constantly shifting and being negotiated. As this study demonstrates, there is much in our students' words that we can learn from. But how do we go about this learning?

One way was illustrated by my examination of children's words described in Chapter 3. Encouraging children to talk about what words mean to them and how this meaning varies across context offers much insight both for us and for them into semantic processes. This "word talk" engendered stories that revealed emotions, frustrations, contradictions, and an awareness of and experience with power arrangements. It also made clear the import of community-based values like respect and authority. Another way to encourage children to talk about and share the significance of their words is through classroom activities like semantic mapping. Semantic mapping, or semantic feature activities, provide a graphic way for students to represent their meanings of particular words, as well as an opportunity for teachers to engage students in dialogue about subjective and collective meaning.[4] Smith-Rosenberg suggests that we can additionally learn from the relations of words to words in written text, of words and social groups, and "of words to specific social relations within the ebb and flow of a particular culture" (1986: 32).

Whether we realize it or not, how we understand the purposes of schooling (itself shaped by personal experiences with schooling and cultural, community, and class socialization) shapes the ways we, as teachers, understand knowledge, the ways we relate to students, the ways we challenge and instruct them, and the ways we encourage (or discourage) them to question and struggle with the world in which they live. Underlying what we do with students are cultural, political, and economic perspectives—our own as well as those of administrators, school boards, and curriculum developers—that our practices with students support. These subjective perspectives also guide and limit how much we can ever really know about those whom we teach and that which we teach them. As Cleo Cherryholmes (1985) asserts, our educational practices are social practices that are shaped and positioned by our own socializations and by the societal structures in which we live and work. The way we understand these social practices suggests an understanding of knowledge, of pedagogy, of ourselves, and of our students. If, for example, we view schooling as the imparting of fixed content knowledge to students, then chances are our teaching methodology is based on passive transmission, what Freire (1970) refers to as a "banking" model of education. Students are treated as mere recipients. If we view schooling as the promotion of interaction through which students generate their own knowledge and, with the assistance of curriculum, build upon their language, culture, and experiences, then our approach is most likely process oriented (e.g., incorporating aspects of whole language and techniques of cooperative learning). Or if, instead, we view schooling as a sociopolitical and cultural process through which students act and struggle with ongoing power relations and critically appropriate forms of knowledge that exist outside their immediate experience, then chances are our classroom is based on dialogue, on the problem-themes of students' lives, on encouraging students to question and to work toward social change.

It is this interconnection between practice and vision that guides the work of teachers, that is, their pedagogies.[5] And, it is the interaction of teacher, learner, and the knowledge they together produce (Lusted 1986) that composes the realization of pedagogy. Yet, how often do classrooms overtly reflect or promote such an interaction? Put another way, do the pedagogies used encourage the knowledge production of all students? And, do these pedagogies assist students in understanding how they undertand? For instance, is the background knowledge Puerto Rican students bring with them from the home and community generally valued in the school environment? Do their lived experiences form the base of the curriculum? Do teachers endeavor to create contexts whereby learners can step back from their personal experience and see it in a more global, critical light? Do they also act as co-learners in class, moving beyond their familiarity with the content and relearning it with the students? Are broader connections made that reveal the relation between knowledge and power? In other words, do we ever question whose knowledge it is that the textbook imparts? Or, do we ever think about the ways knowledge is portrayed as fixed so that students and teachers have no chance to question and change it? Do we question the kinds of knowledge standardized tests measure and validate? And do we reflect upon the ways traditional forms of knowledge have been used to further isolate and denigrate people of color and non-English speakers?

What usually happens in schools is that the knowledge production of some students takes precedence over others because of our vision and pedagogical orientation. White, middle-class students are more often encouraged in dialogue and to discuss and to "produce" knowledge in conjunction with peers and teachers. In counterdistinction, Puerto Rican and other "minorities" are silenced and remediated. However, as interactionist type approaches begin to take precedence over skills-based orientations in many schools, "nonmainstream" students are beginning to be permitted to take a more active role in their schooling. But this is not enough. It is not enough to create an active, creative, sensitive, and stimulating haven in the school when, outside, students and their communities are still confronted and constrained by racism, ethnic prejudice, sexual violence, drugs, crime, poverty, and a myriad of obstacles and forms of oppression. Nor is it enough to include students' language, culture, and community in the classroom, or to encourage them through process approaches to generate their own knowledge. We also need to help students identify the multiple forms of domination that restrict their possibilities and position their understanding. We need to develop pedagogies that encourage students to take action toward transforming that which limits them. What does this mean in concrete practice? What pedagogies help students come to critically view their own realities and, in so doing, help them understand their own knowledge?

The video project described in the previous chapter provided a concrete instance of how the problem-themes of students' lives can be incorporated into the public school environment, and how the use of these themes can help students understand their own understanding. Through a dialogic, participatory, and critical pedagogy, students looked at both the familiar as well as the more global context of why Latino students drop out of schools. This process of "extraordinarily reexperiencing the ordinary" (Shor and Freire 1987:18) permitted the students to transcend subjective experience. They then could challenge the uncritical way they had previously viewed schooling, and consequently could start the journey to break through the opaque reality positioned by normative curricular encounters. They began to read the world. And, tangentially, their desire and motivation to write about this world improved.

Similarly, students' talk about the significance of words, as described in Chapter 3, illuminated portions of consciousness and lived realities that, in a classroom setting, could serve as the basis for dialogue and both group and personal reflection. Through an analysis of meanings within and across languages, students could improve metalinguistic awareness while investigating the ways their language, culture, history, class, and sociopolitical status situate them, their meanings, and their voices.

Just as there has been not one but a polyphony of methods, approaches, and strategies used throughout history to silence and control Puerto Ricans, there is no single technique or pedagogy by which students can suddenly become active participants and critical thinkers. There are many pedagogies depending upon the context, the students, and the teachers. However, we can identify elements common to many critical approaches.

First is a belief in the participatory nature of learning. In participatory classrooms, students do not merely "cooperate" in small groups but are actively engaged throughout the day in collective production, investigation, and interrogation. Second is the element of dialogue. More than conversation or teacher-directed talk, dialogue entails an open exchange among students and teacher that is situated in their language, culture, and themes, and that is centered on helping students actively exchange thoughts to better illuminate and eventually act on their realities (Shore and Freire 1987). In a social world that is clearly unequal, participation and dialogue never just happen. Power relations are always at work, differentially positioning students in relation to one another, to the subject matter, and to the teacher. As Maxine Greene points out, we cannot negate the power we wield as teachers. But as she proposes, we can "undertake a resistance, a reaching out towards becoming persons among other persons."

> To engage with our students as persons is to affirm our own incompleteness, our consciousness of spaces still to be explored, desires still to be tapped, possibilities still to be opened and pursued. (1986: 440)

Teachers who undertake critical approaches must accept their own incompleteness as well as that of students and, in so doing, work toward creating an environment that encourages both subjective and collective awareness of this very condition.

A third element that is common to many critical approaches is the use of generative problem-themes. Here, curriculum is grounded by the themes that concern and interest students. Subject matter content and skills development is connected to these themes rather than vice versa. Fourth is the use of a problem-posing methodology that encourages students to consider these themes in a problematic light, to reach beyond their personal experiences, to concern themselves with what is absent, and to make broader connections with others—together developing strategies for how the problems might be resolved or addressed. This approach invites a questioning of all forms of knowledge and a recognition of its incompleteness. Fifth is the element of reflection. Students are urged to reflect personally and collectively on the material being studied, and to keep making connections to themselves, their communities, and the society at large. Finally, is the essential component of action. This involves the development of an understanding that, as human beings, we have some control over our destinies, and that we can impact the contexts, environments, and world in which we live. Fostered through the element of action is both the need and the responsibility to work toward transforming problematic and oppressive conditions.

In identifying elements common to many critical approaches, I run the risk of being accused of advocating a generic, unproblematic, critical pedagogy. Some educators have understood this to be the downfall of contemporary writers associated with the critical pedagogy tradition (e.g., see Ellsworth 1988). My intention is not to detail what critical pedagogy is or not. Rather it is to imply that all pedagogies are by design complex, artificial, context-dependent, incomplete, and always in transition. Mention of the elements detailed above do not in any way eradicate this reality. However, as good educational practices they can help shift instructional emphasis, teacher authority, and classroom relations and, in so doing, prompt a questioning of, discussion about, and an engagement with these very changes. There are obviously many other practices that could also assist in this endeavor.

Audre Lorde writes that "the master's tools will never dismantle the master's house" (1984: 112). Dominant educational research and practice are neither designed nor intended to illuminate or confront the racial, classed, and gendered relations of classrooms and society. Furthermore, such research and practice will never assist Puerto Rican students in making connections between the colonialism in history and that which weighs upon their consciousness and lived realities in the present. As progressive, concerned, and "critical" educators, we must re-accentuate the purposes and strategies of investigation, documentation, and instruction. This re-accentuation should incorporate participatory modes and methods that engage students in learning about and studying themselves and their relation to the structures, institutions, relations, and world around them. Together with our colleagues and students, we must seek and share practices and strategies that challenge the often oppressive and alienating environments of schools—practices and strategies that invite talk, stimulate thought, and elicit a more critical understanding (within ourselves and our students) of the varied contexts of our lives, the power-knowledge relations that position us, and the cacophonous voices that go on around us and in our heads. To be critical means to grasp how we come to know, to understand, both the partiality and the potential of understanding.

NOTES

1. Because of its large concentration and established character, New York City's Puerto Rican community has been referred to as a culture in and of itself (Ruiz 1989). While many Puerto Ricans, regardless of residence, maintain the connection to bilingualism of which Flores et al. speak, the actual maintenance of a bilingual ability is more likely in urban areas and in Puerto Rican neighborhoods than in isolated suburban or rural situations. In other words, active bilingualism requires a function and purpose.

2. The contradictions inherent in the terms "minority" and "majority" are obvious. At the global level, people of color outnumber whites. And, in an increasing number of U.S. cities, people of color are clearly the majority. The signification of the words lies not in census calculations but in the dominated/dominant relations they suggest, themselves governed by social, political, and economic power.

3. As Ellsworth (1988), Hooks (1986), and Aiken et al. (1987) emphasize, the condition of silence does not necessarily imply a lack of voice, identity, or an inability to express. People who are subordinated because of who they are within particular power arrangements sometimes choose not to speak, not to open themselves up or reveal their perspectives and thoughts to those who are differentially positioned. While this silence should be respected, the arrangements that produce it should nevertheless be countered.

4. For a more detailed discussion about the use semantic mapping and semantic feature activities and the ways these activities can help draw out meaning, see Walsh (1984).

5. Roger Simon provides a detailed discussion of the significance of "pedagogy" as compared to "teaching." As he notes:

> [Pedagogy refers to] the integration in practice of particular curriculum content and design, classroom strategies and techniques, a time and space for the practice of those strategies and techniques, and evaluation purposes and methods. . . . Together they organize a view of how a teacher's work within an institutional context specifies a particular version of what knowledge is of most worth, what it means to know something, and how we might construct representations of ourselves, others, and our physical and social environment. . . . Talk about pedagogy is simultaneously talk about the details of what students and others might do together and the cultural politics such practices support. (1987: 371)

Bibliography

Aiken, Susan Hardy; Anderson, Karen; Dinerstein, Myra; Lesnick, Judy; and Mac-
quodale, Patricia. "Trying Transformations: Curriculum Integration and the
Problem of Resistance." *Signs* 12 (Winter 1987): 225–75.

Albizu Campos, Pedro. *Obras Escogidas*. Compiled by Benjamin Torres. Vol. 1. San
Juan, Puerto Rico: Editore Jelofe, 1975.

Alcoff, Linda. "Cultural Feminism versus Poststructuralism: The Identity Crisis in
Feminist Theory." *Signs* 13 (1988): 405–436.

Allen, Charles H. *First Annual Report of The Governor*, 1900–1901. Washington,
D.C.: Government Printing Office, 1901.

Altbach, Philip G., and Kelly, Gail P. *Education and Colonialism*. New York:
Longman, 1978.

Apple, Michael. *Ideology and Curriculum*. London: Routledge and Kegan Paul,
1979.

Apple, Michael. *Education and Power*. Boston: Routledge and Kegan Paul, 1982.

Apple, Michael. *Teachers and Texts: A Political Economy of Class and Gender
Relations in Education*. New York: Routledge and Kegan Paul, 1986.

Apple, Michael. "Gendered Teaching, Gendered Labor." *In Critical Studies in
Teacher Education. Its Folklore, Theory, and Practice*, edited by T.S. Pop-
kewitz. New York: Falmer Press, 1987.

Aronowitz, Stanley. "Postmodernism and Politics." *Social Text* 18 (Winter 1987/
88): 99–115.

Asian American Resource Workshop. *To Live in Peace: Responses to Anti-Asian
Violence in Boston*. Boston, Mass.: October 1987.

Au, Kathryn H. and Jordan, Cathie. "Teaching Reading to Hawaiian Children:
Finding a Culturally Appropriate Solution." In *Culture and the Bilingual
Classroom: Studies in Classroom Ethnography*, edited by H. Trueba, G.

Pung Guthrie, and K. Au. Rowley, Mass.: Newbury House, 1981.

Bakhtin, Mikhail/Volosinov, V. N. *Marxism and the Philosophy of Language.* Translated by L. Matejka and I. R. Titunik. New York: Seminar Press, 1973.

Bakhtin, Mikhail/Volosinov, V. N. *Freudianism: A Marxist Critique.* Translated by I. R. Titunik. New York: Academic Press, 1976.

Bakhtin, Mikhail. *The Dialogic Imagination.* Edited by M. Holquist and translated by C. Emerson and M. Holquist. Austin: University of Texas Press, 1981.

Beauchamp, José Juan. "Colonialismo, Agresión, y Cambio Cultural Perturbador en Puerto Rico." In *La Agresión Cultural Norteamericana en Puerto Rico,* edited by J. L. Mendez. Mexico D.F.: Editorial Grijalbo, 1980.

Becker, Adeline. "The Role of the School in the Maintenance and Change in Ethnic Group Affiliation." *Human Organization* 49 (Spring 1990): 48–55.

Berger, Peter. *The Sacred Canopy.* Garden City, N. J.: Doubleday, 1967.

Berger, Peter, and Luckman, Thomas. *The Social Construction of Reality.* Garden City, N. J.: Doubleday, 1966.

Bernstein, Basil. "Some Sociological Determinants of Perception." *British Journal of Sociology* 9 (June 1958): 159–174.

Bernstein, Basil. "Social Structure, Language, and Learning." *Educational Research* 3 (June 1961): 163–76.

Bernstein, Basil. *Class, Codes, and Control.* Vol. 2, *Applied Studies Towards a Sociology of Language.* Boston: Routledge and Kegan Paul, 1973.

Bernstein, Basil. *Class, Codes, and Control.* Vol. 3, *Towards a Theory of Educational Transmissions.* Boston: Routledge and Kegan Paul, 1975.

Bernstein, Basil. "Social Class, Language, and Socialization." In *Power and Ideology in Education,* edited by J. Karabel, and A.H. Halsey. New York: Oxford University Press, 1977.

Bernstein, Basil. "Codes, Modalities, and the Process of Cultural Reproduction: A Model." In *Cultural and Economic Reproduction in Education: Essays on Class, Ideology, and the State,* edited by M. W. Apple. Boston: Routledge and Kegan Paul, 1982.

Bhabha, Homi. "Interrogating Identity." In *Identity,* edited by L. Appignanesi. London: Institute of Contemporary Art, 1987.

Bisseret, Noelle. *Education, Class Language, and Ideology.* Boston: Routledge and Kegan Paul, 1979.

Bloomfield, Leonard. "A Set of Postulates for the Science of Language." *Language* 2 (1926): 153–156.

Bloomfield, Leonard. *Language.* New York: Holt, Rinehart, and Winston, 1933.

Boggs, Carl. *Gramsci's Marxism.* London: Pluto Press, 1976.

Bonilla, Frank. "Beyond Survival: Por qúe seguiremos siendo puertorriqueños." In *The Puerto Ricans: Their History, Culture, and Society,* edited by A. Lopez. Cambridge, Mass.: Schenkman, 1980.

Bonilla, Frank, and Campos, Ricardo. "A Wealth of Poor: Puerto Ricans in the New Economic Order." *Daedalus* (Spring 1981): 133–176.

Bonilla, Frank, and Campos, Ricardo. *Industry and Idleness.* New York: El Centro de Estudios Puertorriqueños, 1986.

Bossard, James. "Family Modes of Expression." In *The Sociology of Child Development,* edited by J. Bossard, and E. Boll, New York: Harper International, 1945.

Bourdieu, Pierre. "Cultural Reproduction and Social Reproduction." In *Power and Ideology in Education*, edited by J. Karabel, and A. H. Halsey. New York: Oxford University Press, 1977.

Bourdieu, Pierre, and Passeron, Jean-Claude. *Reproduction in Education, Society, and Culture*. Beverly Hills, Calif.: Sage, 1977.

Britzman, Deborah. "Cultural Myths in the Making of a Teacher: Biography and Social Structure in Teacher Education." *Harvard Educational Review* 56 (Nov. 1986): 442–456.

Britzman, Deborah. "On Educating the Educators." *Harvard Educational Review* 58 (Feb. 1988): 85–94.

Britzman, Deborah. "Who has the Floor? Curriculum, Teaching, and the English Students Teacher's Struggle for Voice." *Curriculum Inquiry* 19 (Summer 1989): 143–162.

Britzman, Deborah. *Practice Makes Practice*. Albany, N.Y.: SUNY Press, in press.

Butler, Rusty. On Creating a Hispanic America: A Nation Within a Nation? Washington, D.C.: Council for Interamerican Security, 1985.

Caban, Pedro A. "Industrialization, the Colonial State, and Working Class Organizations in Puerto Rico." *Latin American Perspectives: Destabilization and Intervention in the Caribbean* 11 (Summer 1984): 149–172.

Campos, Ricardo, and Bonilla, Frank. "Industrialization and Migration: Some Effects on the Puerto Rican Working Class." *Latin American Perspectives: Puerto Rico: Class Struggle and National Liberation* 3 (Summer 1976): 66–108.

Campos, Ricardo, and Bonilla, Frank. "Bootstraps and Enterprise Zones: The Underside of Late Capitalism in Puerto Rico and the United States." *Review* 4 (Spring 1982): 556–590.

Campos, Jim and Keatinge, Robert. "The Carpenteria Language Minority Student Experience: From Theory to Practice to Success." In *Minority Education: From Shame to Struggle*, edited by T. Skutnabb-Kangas and J. Cummins. Philadelphia, PA.: Multilingual Matters, 1988.

Carr, Raymond. *Puerto Rico: A Colonial Experiment*. New York: Vantage Books, 1984.

Castellaños, Diego. *The Best of Two Worlds: Bilingual-Bicultural Education in the U.S.* Trenton, N.J.: New Jersey State Department of Education, 1983.

Cebollero, Pedro. *A School Language Policy for Puerto Ricans*. San Juan, Puerto Rico: Superior Educational Council, 1945.

Centro de Estudios Puertorriqueños. "The Genesis of the Puerto Rican Migration." In *The Puerto Ricans: Their History, Culture, and Society*, edited by A. Lopez. Cambridge, Mass.: Schenkman, 1980.

Centro de Estudios Puertorriqeños. *Bulletin* 2 (Spring 1988).

Césaire, Aimé. *Discourse on Colonialism*. New York: Monthly Review Press, 1972.

Cherryholmes, Cleo H. "Theory and Practice: On the Role of Empirically Based Theory for Critical Practice." *American Journal of Education* (November 1985): 39–70.

Chomsky, Noam. *Aspects of the Theory of Syntax* Cambridge: MIT Press, 1965.

Chomsky, Noam. *Language and Mind*. New York: Harcourt Brace Jovanovich, 1972.

Chomsky, Noam. *Reflections on Language*. New York: Pantheon, 1975.

Christian, Chester C. "The Acculturation of the Bilingual Child." In *Bilingualism and the Bilingual Child*, edited by F. Cordasco. New York: Arno Press, 1978.

Cintron Ortiz, Rafael. "A Colonial Experience: Schools in Puerto Rico as Agents of Domination." *Critical Anthropology* 2 (Spring 1972): 104–112.

Clark, Katerina and Hollquist, Michael. *Mikhail Bakhtin*. Cambridge, Mass.: Harvard University Press, 1984.

Coll y Cuchi, Cayetano. "American Rule in Porto Rico." Living Age 27 (1922).

Collier, Virginia. "Age and Rate of Acquisition of Second Language for Academic Purposes." *TESOL Quarterly* 21 (December 1987): 617–641.

Colon, Jesus. *A Puerto Rican in New York*. New York: Mainstream Publishers, 1961.

Constantino, Renato. *The Miseducation of the Filipino*. Manila, Philippines: Foundation for Nationalist Studies, 1982.

Crawford, James. "The English Language Amendment: Hazardous to Language Minority Children." Paper presented at the Institute on Bilingual Education, Harvard Graduate School of Education, December 11, 1987.

Crawford, James. *Bilingual Education: History, Politics, Theory and Practice*. Trenton, N. J.: Crane, 1989.

Cummins, Jim. "The Cognitive Development of Children in Immersion Programs." *Canadian Modern Language Review* 34 (Dec. 1978): 855–83.

Cummins, Jim. "The Role of Primary Language Development in Promoting Educational Success for Language Minority Children," In *Schooling and Language Minority Students*, edited by California Department of Education. Los Angeles: Evaluation, Assessment, and Dissemination Center, 1981.

Cummins, Jim. *Bilingualism and Special Education: Issues in Assessment and Pedagogy*. Avon, England: Multilingual Matters, 1984.

Cummins, Jim. "Empowering Minority Students: A Framework for Intervention." *Harvard Educational Review* 56 (Feb. 1986): 18–36.

Cummins, Jim. "From Multiculturalism to Anti-Racist Education: An Analysis of Programes and Policies in Ontario." In *Minority Education: From Shame to Struggle*, edited by T. Skutnabb-Kangas and J. Cummins. Philadelphia: Multilingual Matters, 1988.

Cummins, Jim. *Empowering Minority Students*. Sacramento, Calif.: California Association for Bilingual Education, 1989.

Davidov, V. and Markova, A. "La Concepción de la Actividad de Estudio de los Escolares." In *Biblioteca de Psicología Soviética: La Psicología Evolutiva y Pedagógica en La URSS, Antología*. Moscow: Editorial Progreso, 1987.

Davis, George W. *Report on Civil Affairs of Porto Rico, 1899*. Washington, D.C.: Government Printing Office, 1899.

de Lauretis, Teresa. "Feminist Studies/Critical Studies: Issues, Terms, and Contexts." In *Feminist Studies/Critical Studies*, edited by T. de Lauretis. Bloomington, Ind.: Indiana University Press, 1986.

de la Zerda Flores, Nancy, and Hopper, Robert. "Mexican Americans' Evaluations of Spoken Spanish and English." *Speech Monographs* 42 (June 1975): 126–134.

Delpit, Lisa. "The Silenced Dialogue: Power and Pedagogy in Educating Other People's Children." *Harvard Educational Review* 58 (August 1988): 280–

298.

Deyhle, Donna. "Break Dancing and Breaking Out: Anglos, Utes, and Navajos in a Border Reservation High School." *Anthropology and Education Quarterly* 17 (June 1986): 11–127.

Dietz, James. *Economic History of Puerto Rico: Institutional Change and Capitalist Development.* Princeton, N.J.: Princeton University Press, 1986.

Diamond, Stanley, ed. *Anthropological Perspectives in Education.* New York: Basic Books, 1971.

Donald, James. "Language, Literacy, and Schooling." In *The State and Popular Culture*, edited by M. Keynes. London: Open University Press, 1982.

Dunn, Lloyd. *Bilingual Hispanic Children on the U.S. Mainland: A Review of Research on Their Cognitive, Linguistic, and Scholastic Development.* Circle Pines, Minn.: American Guidance Service, 1987.

Edwards, A. D. *Language in Culture and Class.* London: Heineman, 1976.

Ellsworth, Elizabeth. "Why Doesn't This Feel Empowering? Working Through the Repressive Myths of Critical Pedagogy." Paper presented at the Tenth Conference on Curriculum Theory and Classroom Practice, Dayton, Ohio, October 26–29, 1988.

Emerson, Caryl. "The Outer Word and Inner Speech: Bakhtin, Vygotsky, and the Internalization of Language." In *Bakhtin: Essays and Dialogues on His Work*, edited by G. S. Morson. Chicago: University of Chicago Press, 1986.

Epica Task Force. *Puerto Rico: A People Challenging Colonialism.* Washington, D.C.: EPICA, 1976.

Epstein, Erwin H. "School Language: Private Right or Public Mandate?" In *Politics and Education in Puerto Rico: A Documentary Survey of the Language Issue*, edited by E. H. Erwin. Metuchen, N. J.: Scarecrow Press, 1970.

Erickson, Frederick. "Transformation and School Success: The Politics and Culture of Educational Achievement." *Anthropology and Education Quarterly* 18 (Dec. 1987): 335–356.

Everhart, Robert. *Reading, Writing, and Resistance: Adolescence and Labor in a Junior High School.* Boston: Routledge and Kegan Paul, 1983.

Fanon, Frantz. *The Wretched of the Earth.* Translated by Charles Lam Markman. New York: Grove Press, 1963.

Fanon, Frantz. *Black Skin, White Masks.* New York: Grove Press, 1967.

Fanon, Frantz. *Toward African Revolution.* Translated by Haakon Chevalier. New York: Grove Press, 1969.

Fernández García, Benigno. "La Realidad Social y Nuestro Problema Educativo." In *Antología del Pensamiento Puertorriqueño*, Tomo II, edited by E. Fernández Méndez. Río Piedras, Puerto Rico: Editorial Universitaria, 1975.

Fine, Michelle. "Silencing in Public Schools," *Language Arts* 64 (Feb. 1987): 157–174.

Fisher, John C. "Bilingualism in Puerto Rico: A History of Frustration." *The English Record*, 21 (April 1971): 19–24.

Flores, Juan. "The Puerto Rico that José Luis González Built: Comments on Cultural History," *Latin American Perspectives* II (Summer 1984): 173–184.

Flores, Juan, ed. *Divided Arrival: Narratives of the Puerto Rican Migration 1920–1950.* New York: Centro de Estudios Puertorriqueños, 1988.

Flores, Juan; Attinasi, John; and Pedraza, Pedro. "La Carreta Made a U-Turn:

Puerto Rican Language and Culture in the United States." *Daedalus* 110 (Spring 1981): 193–217.

Foucault, Michel. *Power/Knowledge.* Translated by C. Gordon; L. Marshall; J. Mepham; and K. Soper. New York: Pantheon, 1980.

Freire, Paulo. *Pedagogy of the Oppressed.* New York: Seabury Press, 1970.

Freire, Paulo. *Education for Critical Consciousness.* New York: Continuum, 1973.

Freire, Paulo. *The Politics of Education.* South Hadley, Mass.: Bergin & Garvey, 1985.

Freire, Paulo, and Macedo, Donaldo. *Literacy: Reading the Word and the World.* South Hadley, Mass.: Bergin & Garvey, 1987.

Freud, Sigmund. *Collected Papers.* Translated by Joan Riviere. London: Hogarth, 1924.

Galperin, P.; Zaporozhets, D.; and Elkonin, D. "Los problemas de la formación de conocimientos y capacidades en los escolares y los nuevos metodos de enseñanza en la escuela." In *Biblioteca de Psicología Soviética, La Psicología Evolutiva y Pedagógica en La URSS, Antogía.* Moscow: Editorial Progreso, 1987.

Gearhart, Maryl, and Hall, William S. "Internal State Words: Cultural and Situational Variation in Vocabulary Usage." Technical Report #115, Center for the Study of Reading, University of Illinois at Champaign-Urbana, February 1979.

Giddens, Anthony. *Central Problems in Social Theory: Action, Structure, and Contradiction in Social Analyses.* Berkeley: University of California Press, 1979.

Giles, Howard, ed. *Language, Ethnicity, and Intergroup Relations: European Monographs in Social Psychology.* London: Academic Press, 1977.

Gilmore, Perry. "Spelling 'Mississippi': Recontextualizing a Literacy-Related Speech Event," *Anthropology and Education Quarterly* 14 (Dec. 1983): 235–255.

Giroux, Henry A. "Teacher Education and the Ideology of Social Control." *Journal of Education* 162 (Winter 1980): 5–27.

Giroux, Henry A. *Theory and Resistance in Education: A Pedagogy for the Opposition.* South Hadley, Mass.: Bergin & Garvey, 1983.

Giroux, Henry A. "Critical Pedagogy, Cultural Politics, and the Discourse of Experience." *Journal of Education* 167 (Spring 1985): 22–39.

Giroux, Henry A. "Radical Pedagogy and the Politics of Student Voice," *Interchange* 17: 1 (1986): 48–69.

Giroux, Henry A. "Citizenship, Public Philosophy, and the Struggle for Democracy." *Educational Theory* 37 (Spring 1987): 103–120.

Giroux, Henry A. *Teachers as Intellectuals: Toward a Critical Pedagogy of Learning.* South Hadley, Mass.: Bergin & Garvey, 1988.

Glanzer, Murray, and Duarte, Anibal. "Repetition Between and Within Languages in Free Recall." *Journal of Verbal Learning and Verbal Behavior* 10 (Dec. 1971): 625–630.

González, José Luis. *El País de Cuatro Pisos y Otros Ensayos.* Río Piedras, Puerto Rico: Huracán, 1980.

Gramsci, Antonio. *Selections from the Prison Notebooks.* Translated by Q. Hoare and G. N. Smith. New York: International Publishers, 1971.

Greene, Maxine. "In Search of a Critical Pedagogy." *Harvard Educational Review* 56 (Nov. 1986): 427–441.

Gulden, Aleta; Martínez, José E.; and Zamora, Juan Clemente. "Bilingual Memory: The Weak Hypothesis." *Bilingual Review* 7 (January–April 1980): 15–18.

Hakuta, Kenji, and Diaz, Rafael. "The Relationship Between Degree of Bilingual and Cognitive Ability: A Critical Discussion on Some New Longitudinal Data." In *Children's Language*, Vol. 5, edited by K.E. Nelson. Hillsdale, N. J.: Erlbaum Associates, 1985.

Hall, Stuart. "Signification, Representation, Ideology: Althusser and the Post-Structuralist Debate." *Critical Studies in Mass Communication* 2 (June 1985): 91–114.

Heath, Shirley Brice. *Ways with Words, Language, Life, and Work in Communities and Classrooms.* New York: Cambridge University Press, 1983.

Henriques, Jules; Hollway, Wendy; Urwin, Cathy; Venn, Couze; and Walkerdine, Valerie, eds. *Changing the Subject: Psychology, Social Regulation and Subjectivity.* London: Methuen Press, 1984.

Herring, Hubert. "Rebellion in Puerto Rico." *The Nation* CXXXVII (Nov. 29, 1933): 618–619.

Higham, John. *Strangers in the Land: Patterns of American Nativism 1860-1925.* New York: Atheneum, 1963.

History Task Force (Centro de Estudios Puertorriqueños). *Labor Migration Under Capitalism: The Puerto Rican Experience.* New York: Monthly Review Press, 1979.

History Task Force (Centro de Estudios Puertorriqueños). *Sources for the Study of Puerto Rican Migration 1879–1930.* New York: Research Foundation of the City University of New York, 1982.

Hogaboam, Thomas, and Pellegrino, James. "Hunting for Individual Differences in Cognitive Processes: Verbal Ability and Semantic Processing of Words and Pictures." *Memory and Cognition* 5 (March 1977): 189–193.

Hooks, Bell. "Talking Back" *Discourse* 8 (Fall/Winter 1986): 123–128.

Hurtado, Aida, and Gurin, Patricia. "Ethnic Identity and Bilingualism Attitudes." *Hispanic Journal of Behavioral Sciences* 9 (March 1987): 1–18.

Huyke, Juan B. "Americanism," *Puerto Rico School Review* (Oct. 1921): 9.

Huyke, Juan B. *Articulos Pedagógicos.* Bulletin No. 4. San Juan, P.R.: Department of Education, 1929.

Iadicola, Peter. "Schooling and Social Control: Symbolic Violence and Hispanic Students' Attitudes Toward Their Own Ethnic Group." *Hispanic Journal of Behavioral Sciences* 3 (December 1981): 361–83.

Ickes, Harold L. "The Aim of English Instruction." Letter to José Gallardo, Commissioner of Education for Puerto Rico, May 22, 1943. Reprinted in *Politics and Education in Puerto Rico: A Documentary Survey of the Language Issue* edited by E. Epstein. Metuchen, N.J.: Scarecrow Press, 1970.

Jacob, Evelyn and Jordan, Cathie. "Moving to Dialogue," *Anthropology and Education Quarterly* 18 (Dec. 1987): 259–261.

Jensen, Arthur. "The Culturally Disadvantaged: Psychological and Educational Aspects." *Educational Research* 10 (Nov. 1967): 4–20.

Jiménez-Muñoz, Gladys M. "Wishful Thinking vs. Social Reality: Childhood, Class, and Moral Education in Puerto Rico, 1898–1930." Unpublished paper,

SUNY-Binghamton, 1989.

Jordan, June. *Dry Victories*. New York: Avon, 1972.

Jordan, June. "Nobody Mean More to Me Than You and the Future Life of Willie Jordan." *Harvard Educational Review* 58 (August 1988): 363–374.

Kloss, Heinz. *The American Bilingual Tradition*. Rowley, Mass.: Newbury House Publishers, 1977.

Krashen, Stephen, and Biber, Douglas. *On Course: Bilingual Education's Success in California*. Sacramento, Calif.: California Association for Bilingual Education, 1988.

Lambert, Wallace; Ignatow, M.; and Krauthamer, M. "Bilingual Organization in Free Recall." *Journal of Verbal Learning and Verbal Behavior* 7 (Feb. 1968): 207–214.

Lambert, Wallace, and Rawlings, Chris. "Bilingual Processing of Mixed Language Associative Networks." *Journal of Verbal Learning and Verbal Behavior* 8 (Oct. 1969): 604–609.

Language Policy Task Force. *Intergenerational Perspectives on Bilingualism: From Classroom to Community*. New York: Center for Puerto Rican Studies, Hunter College, 1982.

Language Policy Task Force. *Speech and Ways of Speaking in a Bilingual Puerto Rican Community*. New York: Center for Puerto Rican Studies, Hunter College, 1984.

Laviera, Tato. *La Carreta Made a U-Turn*. Houston, Tex.: Arte Publico Press, 1984.

López, Mike, and Young, Robert. "The Linguistic Interdependence of Bilinguals." *Journal of Experimental Psychology* 102 (June 1974): 981–983.

Lorde, Audre. *Sister Outsider*. New York: The Crossing Press, 1984.

Lugones, Maria, and Spelman, Elizabeth. "Have We Got A Theory For You! Feminist Theory, Cultural Imperialism, and the Demand for Women's Voice." *Women's Studies International Forum* 6 (Feb. 1983): 573–581.

Lusted, David. "Why Pedagogy?" *Screen* 27 (Sept.–Oct. 1986): 2–14.

Magiste, Edith. "The Competing Language Systems of the Multilingual: A Developmental Study of Decoding and Encoding Processes." *Journal of Verbal Learning and Verbal Behavior* 18 (Feb. 1979): 79–89.

Maldonado-Denis, Manuel. *Puerto Rico y Estados Unidos: Emigración y Colonialismo*. México, D.F.: Siglo XXI, 1976.

Marqués, René. *El Puertorriqueño Dócil y Otros Ensayos*. San Juan, Puerto Rico: Editorial Antillana, 1977.

Marx, Karl. *The Eighteenth Brumaire of Louis Bonaparte*. New York: International Press, 1963.

Marx, Karl. *The Gundrisse*. Translated by David McLellan. London: Macmillan, 1971.

Mathews, Thomas. *Puerto Rican Politics and the New Deal*. Gainesville, Fl.: University of Florida Press, 1960.

McDermott, Ray, and Gospodinoff, Katherine. "Social Contexts for Ethnic Borders and School Failure." In *Culture and the Bilingual Classroom Studies in Classroom Ethnography*, edited by H. Trueba, G. P. Guthrie, and K. Hu Pei Au. Rowley, Mass.: Newbury House Publishers, 1981.

McDermott, Ray. "The Explanation of Minority Student Failure, Again." *Anthropology and Education Quarterly* 18 (Dec. 1987): 361–364.

Memmi, Albert. *The Colonizer and the Colonized*. Boston: Beacon Press, 1965.

Meyn, Marianne. *Lenguaje e Identidad Cultural: Un Acercamiento Teórico al Caso de Puerto Rico*. Río Piedras, Puerto Rico: Editorial Edil, 1983.

Milner, Esther "A Study of the Relationship of Reading-Readiness and Patterns of Parent-Child Interaction." *Child Development* 22 (June 1951): 95–112.

Moll, Luis. "Community Knowledge and Classroom Practice: Combining Resources for Literacy Instruction." Year One Progress Report to Development Associates/U.S. Department of Education, June 28, 1989.

Moll, Luis, and Diaz, Stephen. "Change as the Goal of Educational Research." *Anthropology and Education Quarterly* 18 (Dec. 1987): 300–311.

Mouffe, Chantal. "Hegemony and Ideology in Gramsci." *Gramsci and Marxist Theory*, edited by C. Mouffe. Boston: Routledge and Kegan Paul, 1979.

Muñoz Marín, Luis. Quoted in *American Mercury* (Feb. 1929): 62.

Muñoz Morales, Luis. "El Idioma y El Status." *El Mundo* 3 (Nov. 17, 1946).

Morson, Gary Saul. "Who Speaks for Bakhtin?" In *Bakhtin, Essays and Dialogues on His Work*, edited by G.S. Morson. Chicago: University of Chicago Press, 1986.

Narayan, Uma. "Working Together Across Difference: Some Considerations on Emotions and Political Practice." *Hypatia* 3 (Summer 1988): 31–47.

Negrón de Montilla, Aida. *Americanization in Puerto Rico and the Public School System 1900–1930*. Río Piedras, Puerto Rico: Editorial Edil, 1971.

Negrón de Montilla, Aida. "Indoctrination and the Educational System." *El Imparcial*, April 1972: 8.

Niera, Christian. "Building 860." *Harvard Educational Review* 58 (August 1988): 337–342.

Nieto, Sonia. "Curriculum Decision-Making: The Puerto Rican Family and the Bilingual Child." Doctoral dissertation, University of Massachusetts at Amherst, 1979.

Ogbu, John. *The Next Generation: An Ethnography of Education in an Urban Neighborhood*. New York: Academic Press, 1974.

Ogbu, John. *Minority Education and Caste*. New York: Academic Press, 1978.

Ogbu, John. "Variability in Minority School Performance: A Problem in Search of an Explanation." *Anthropology and Education Quarterly* 18 (December 1987): 312–334.

Ogbu, John. "Cultural Diversity and School Experience." In *Literacy as Praxis: Culture, Language, and Pedagogy*, edited by C. E. Walsh. Norwood, N. J.: Ablex, 1990.

Ollman, Bertell. "The Meaning of Dialectics." *Monthly Review* 38 (November 1986): 42–55.

Osuna, Juan Jose. *A History of Education in Puerto Rico*. Río Piedras, Puerto Rico: Editorial de la Universidad de Puerto Rico, 1949.

Peal, Eleanor and Lambert, Wallace. "The Relation of Bilingualism to Intelligence," *Psychological Monographs* 76: 546 (1962): 38–43.

Peoples Press Puerto Rico Project. *Puerto Rico: The Flame of Resistance*. San Francisco: Peoples Press, 1977.

Phillipson, Robert. "Linguicism: Structures and Ideologies in Linguistic Imperialism." In *Minority Education: From Shame to Struggle*, edited by T. Skutnabb-Kangas, and J. Cummins. Philadelphia: Multilingual Matters,

1988.

Picó de Hernández, Isabel. "Americanización o proletarización? Comentarios en torno al libro de la Dra. Aida Negrón de Montilla." *La Escalera 5* (Oct.-Dec. 1971): 30-41.

Ponce, Anibal. *Educación y Lucha de Clases.* Havana: Imprenta Nacional de Cuba, 1961.

Porter, Rosalie Pedalino. *The Forked Tongue: The Politics of Bilingual Education.* New York: Basic Books, 1990.

Quintero Rivera, Angel G. "Clases sociales e identidad nacional: notas sobre el desarrollo nacional puertorriqueño." In *Puerto Rico: Identidad Nacional y Clases Sociales,* edited by A. Quintero Rivera, J. L. Gonzalez, R. Campos, and J. Flores. Río Piedras, Puerto Rico: Ediciones Huracán, 1979.

Ramirez, Rafael L. "National Culture in Puerto Rico." *Latin American Perspectives: Puerto Rico: Class Struggle and Liberation* 3 (Summer 1976): 109-116.

Ramos, Moises Rosa. "Analysis of the Church in Puerto Rico." Church and Theology Project of the National Ecumenical Movement of Puerto Rico, 1985.

Ramsey, Robert. "A Technique for Inter-Lingual Lexico-Semantic Comparison: The Lexigram." *TESOL Quarterly* 15 (March 1981): 15-24.

Ribeiro, Jose L. "Self Esteem and School Achievement." *Bilingual Journal* 7 (Spring 1983): 11-13.

Rivera, Pedro Angel. *Manos a la Obra: The Story of Operation Bootstrap (A Study Guide to the Film).* New York: El Centro de Estudios Puertorriqueños, 1986.

Rodríguez, Clara E. "Economic Survival in New York City." In *The Puerto Rican Struggle: Essays on Survival in the U.S.,* edited by C. E. Rodriguez, V. Sanchez Korrol, and J. O. Alers. New York: Puerto Rican Migration Research Consortium, Inc., 1980.

Rodríguez, Clara E.; Sanchez Korrol, Virginia; and Alers, José Oscar. "The Puerto Rican Struggle to Survive in the United States." In *The Puerto Rican Struggle: Essays on Survival in the U.S.,* edited by C. E. Rodriguez, V. Sanchez Korrol, and J. O. Alers. New York: Puerto Rican Migration Research Consortium, Inc., 1980.

Rodríguez Pacheco, Osvaldo. *A Land of Hope in Schools. A Reader in the History of Public Education in Puerto Rico 1940-1965,* San Juan, Puerto Rico: Ediciones Edil, 1976.

Rossell, Christine H. "The Research on Bilingual Education," *Equity and Choice* 6 (Winter 1990): 29-36.

Ruiz, Elaine. Talk given at Parents United in the Education and Development of Others Conference, Holyoke, Mass.: June 1989.

Salamini, Leonardo. "Gramsci and Marxist Sociology of Language." *International Journal of the Sociology of Language* 32 (February 1981): 27-44.

Saussure, Ferdinand de. *Course in General Linguistics.* Translated by W. Baskin. New York: McGraw-Hill, 1959.

Saville-Troike, Muriel. "Cross-Cultural Communication in the Classroom." In *Current Issues in Bilingual Education: Georgetown University Roundtable on Language and Linguistics,* edited by J. E. Alatis. Washington, D.C.: Georgetown University Press, 1980.

Schatzman, Leonard and Strauss, Anslem. "Social Class and Modes of Communication." *American Journal of Sociology* 60 (Jan. 1955): 329-338.

tion." *American Journal of Sociology* 60 (Jan. 1955): 329–338.

Seda Bonilla, Eduardo. *Requiem por una Cultura*. Río Piedras, Puerto Rico: Ediciones Bayoan, 1972.

Segalowitz, Norman, and Lambert, Wallace. "Semantic Generalization in Bilinguals." *Journal of Verbal Learning and Verbal Behavior* 8 (Oct. 1969): 559–566.

Shor, Ira, and Freire, Paulo. *A Pedagogy for Liberation. Dialogues on Transforming Education*. South Hadley, Mass.: Bergin & Garvey, 1987.

Silen, Juan. *We, the Puerto Rican People: A Story of Oppression and Resistance*. New York: Monthly Review Press, 1971.

Simon, Roger. "Empowerment as a Pedagogy of Possibility." *Language Arts* 64 (April 1987): 370–380.

Sinha, Chris. "Class, Language, and Education." *Ideology and Consciousness* 1 (May 1977): 77–92.

Skutnabb-Kangas, Tove. "Multilingualism and the Education of Minority Children." *Minority Education: From Shame to Struggle*, edited by T. Skutnabb-Kangas, and J. Cummins. Philadelphia: Multilingual Matters, 1988.

Skutnabb-Kangas, Tove and Toukomaa, Peritti. *Teaching Migrant Children's Mother Tongue and Learning the Language of the Host Country in the Socio-Cultural Situation of the Migrant Family*. Helsinki, Finland: UNESCO, 1976.

Smith-Rosenberg, Carroll. "Writing History: Language, Class, and Gender." In *Feminist Studies: Critical Studies*, edited by T. de Lauretis. Bloomington: Indiana University Press, 1986.

Snow, Catherine, and Hakuta, Kenji. "The Costs of Monolingualism." Unpublished paper, New Haven, Conn.: Center for Language Education and Research, n.d.

Sola, Michele, and Bennett, Adrian. "The Struggle for Voice: Narrative, Literacy, and Consciousness in an East Harlem School." *Journal of Education* 167 (Winter 1985): 88–110.

Steedman, Carolyn. *The Tidy House*. London: Virago Press, 1982.

Stewart, Susan. "Shouts on the Street: Bakhtin's Anti-Linguistics." In *Bakhtin: Essays and Dialogues on His Work*, edited by G. S. Morson. Chicago: University of Chicago Press, 1986.

Strick, Gregory J. "A Hypothesis for Semantic Development in a Second Language." *Language Learning* 30 (June 1980): 155–75.

Sunshine, Catherine A. *The Caribbean: Survival, Struggle, and Sovereignty*. Boston: EPICA, South End Press, 1985.

Szalay, Lorand and Deese, James. *Subjective Meaning and Culture: An Assessment through Word Associations*. Hillsdale, New Jersey: Lawrence Erlbaum Associates, 1978.

Todorov, Tzvetan. *Mikhail Bakhtin: The Dialogic Principle*. Translated by Wlad Godzich. Minneapolis: University of Minnesota Press, 1984.

Torres Gonzales, Roame. "Democracy and Personal Autonomy in the Puerto Rican School System: A Socio-Historical Survey and Critique of Educational Development." Doctoral dissertation, University of Massachusetts at Amherst, 1983.

Trueba, Henry. "Review of Beyond Language: Social and Cultural Factors in

Schooling Language Minority Students," *Anthropology and Education Quarterly* 17 (Dec. 1986): 255–259.

Trueba, Henry. "Culturally Based Explanations of Minority Students' Academic Achievement." *Anthropology and Education Quarterly* 19 (Sept. 1988): 270–287.

Urwin, Cathy. "Power Relations and the Emergence of Language." In *Changing the Subject: Psychology, Social Regulation, and Subjectivity*, edited by J. Henniques, et al. London: Methuen Press, 1984.

U.S. Bureau of Education. *Report of the Commissioner, 1899–1900*, Vols. 1 and 2, Washington, D.C.: Government Printing Office, 1900.

U.S. Bureau of Education. *Annual Report of the Commissioner, 1901*. Washington, D.C.: Government Printing Office, 1901.

U.S. Bureau of Education. *Annual Report of the Commissioner, 1902*. Washington, D.C.: Government Printing Office, 1902.

U.S. Bureau of Education. *Annual Report of the Commissioner, 1912*. Washington, D.C.: Government Printing Office, 1912.

U.S. Bureau of Education. *Annual Report of the Commissioner, 1915*. Washington, D.C.: Government Printing Office, 1915.

U.S. Commission on Civil Rights. *Puerto Ricans in the Continental United States: An Uncertain Future*. Washington, D.C.: U.S. Commission on Civil Rights, 1976.

U.S. Department of Commerce. *Economic Study of Puerto Rico*. Washington, D.C.: Government Printing Office, 1979.

U.S. Department of War. *Census of Puerto Rico*. Washington, D.C.: Government Printing Office, 1899.

U.S. Immigration Commission. *Report of the Immigration Commission*. Washington, D.C.: Government Printing Office, 1911.

United States-Puerto Rico Commission. *Report on the Status of Puerto Rico*. Washington, D.C.: Government Printing Office, August 1966.

U.S. Senate. *Education in Porto-Rico*. 56th Congress, 1st Session, Senate Document 363. Washington, D.C.: Government Printing Office, 1900.

Vega, Bernando. *Memoirs of Bernando Vega: A Contribution to the History of the Puerto Rican Community in New York*. Edited by Cesar Andreu Iglesias and translated by Juan Flores. New York: Monthly Review Press, 1984.

Vogt, Lynn; Jordan, Cathie; and Tharp, Roland. "Explaining School Failure, Producing School Successes: Two Cases," *Anthropology and Education Quarterly* 18 (Dec.: 1987): 276–286.

Vygotsky, Lev S. *Thought and Language*. Translated by Eugenia Hanfmann and Gertrude Vakar. Cambridge, Mass.: MIT Press, 1962.

Vygotsky, Lev S. *Mind in Society: The Development of Higher Psychological Processes*. Edited by M. Cole; V. John-Steiner; S. Scribner; and E. Souberman. Cambridge, Mass.: Harvard University Press, 1978.

Wagenheim, Kal, with Jimenez de Wagenheim, Olga. *The Puerto Ricans: A Documentary History*. New York: Anchor Books, 1973. Wagner, Stephen. "The Historical Background of Bilingualism and Biculturalism in the United States." In *The New Bilingualism: An American Dilemma*, edited by M. Ridge. New Brunswick, N. J.: Transaction Books, 1981.

Wallerstein, Nina, and Bernstein, Edward. "Empowerment Education: Freire's Ideas Adapted to Health Education." *Health Education Quarterly* 15 (Winter 1988): 379–394.

Walsh, Catherine E. "The Phenomenon of Educated/Educado: An Example for a Tripartite System of Semantic Memory." *Bilingual Review* 10 (Jan.–April 1983): 33–40.

Walsh, Catherine E. "The Construction of Meaning in a Second Language: The Import of Sociocultural Circumstance." Doctoral dissertation, University of Massachusetts at Amherst, 1984.

Walsh, Catherine E. "Language, Meaning and Voice: Puerto Rican Students' Struggle for a Speaking Consciousness." *Language Arts* 64 (Feb. 1987a): 196–206.

Walsh, Catherine E. "Schooling and the Civic Exclusion of Latinos: Toward a Discourse of Dissonance." *Journal of Education* 169 (Spring 1987b): 115–131.

Walsh, Catherine E. "Literacy as Praxis: A Framework and an Introduction." In *Literacy as Praxis: Culture, Language, and Pedagogy*, edited by C. E. Walsh. Norwood, New Jersey: Ablex, 1990.

Walters, Joel. "Grammar, Meaning, and Socio-cultural Appropriateness in Second Language Acquisition." *Canadian Journal of Psychology* 34 (December 1980): 337–345.

Weedon, Chris. *Feminist Practice and Poststructuralist Theory*. New York: Basil Blackwell, 1987.

Wei, Deborah. "The Asian American Success Myth." *Council for Interracial Books for Children Bulletin* 17, no. 3–4 (1986): 16–17.

Weiler, Kathleen. " 'The Tidy House that is a Tidy House No More': Children, Language, and Class." *Radical America* 18 (March–June 1984): 51–57.

Weinberg, Meyer. *A Chance to Learn: A History of Race and Education in the United States*. New York: Cambridge University Press, 1977.

Wertsch, James V. *Vygotsky and the Social Formation of the Mind*. Cambridge, Mass.: Harvard University Press, 1985.

Wertsch, James V., and Stone, C. Addison. "The Concept of Internalization in Vygotsky's Account of the Genesis of Higher Mental Functions." In *Culture, Communication, and Cognition: Vygotskian Perspectives*, edited by J. V. Wertsch. New York: Cambridge University Press, 1985.

White, E. Frances. "Listening to the Voices of Black Feminism." *Radical America* 18 (March–June 1984): 7–25.

Williams, Geoff. "Language Group Allegiance and Ethnic Interaction." In *Language and Ethnic Relations*, edited by H. Giles, and Saint-Jacques. New York: Pergamon Press, 1979.

Williams, Raymond. *Marxism and Literature*. London: Oxford University Press, 1977.

Willis, Paul. *Learning to Labour*. Westmead, England: Saxon House, 1977.

Wittgenstein, Ludwig. *Philosophical Investigations*. Oxford: Blackwell, 1972.

Wuthnow, Robert; Hunter, James Davison; Bergesen, Albert; and Kurzweil, Edith. *Cultural Analysis: The Work of Peter L. Berger, Mary Douglas, Michel Foucault, and Jürgen Habermas*. New York. Routledge and Kegan Paul, 1984.

Zentella, Ana Celia. "Language Variety Among Puerto Ricans." In *Language in the USA*, edited by C. Ferguson, and S. Brice Heath. New York: Cambridge University Press, 1981.

Zentella, Ana Celia. "The Fate of Spanish in the U.S.: The Puerto Rican Experience." In *The Language of Inequality*, edited by J. Manes, and N. Wolfson. The Hague: Mouton, 1985.

Zentella, Ana Celia. "Challenging Linguistic Myths About the Puerto Rican Community." Talk given at the New England Multifunctional Resource Center Literacy Symposium, Cambridge, Mass., March 27, 1989.

Index

About the Author

Catherine E. Walsh is the coordinator of the New England Multifunctional Resource Center at the University of Massachusetts, Amherst, which provides training and technical assistance to school districts and organizations working with language minority students, parents, and communities. She is also an adjunct associate professor in the university's School of Education. Her edited volume *Literacy as Praxis: Culture, Language, and Pedagogy* was published in 1990.